Concorde

AVIATION SERIES

Concorde

Kev Darling

The Crowood Press

First published in 2004 by
The Crowood Press Ltd
Ramsbury, Marlborough
Wiltshire SN8 2HR

www.crowood.com

© Kev Darling 2004

British Library Cataloguing-in-Publication Data
A catalogue record for this book is available from
the British Library.

ISBN 1 86126 654 5

Photograph previous page: Air France Concorde
Foxtrot Bravo approaches Paris to land. Since its
retirement the aircraft has gone to Germany to join
the Tu-144 at Sinsheim. *BBA Collection*

Typefaces used: Goudy (*text*),
Cheltenham (*headings*).

Typeset and designed by
D & N Publishing
Lambourn Woodlands, Hungerford, Berkshire.

Printed and bound in Great Britain by CPI Group,
Bath.

Acknowledgements

Concorde is one of those aircraft that sparked my interest in aviation, the others being
a black Hawker Sea Hawk and a red and white Gloster Javelin. A trip to the mock-up
at Filton would further increase my interest in Concorde, especially as the first production examples were being constructed in the same building; my one regret is that I mis-
laid the leaflets I received at the time. This desire to know more about the aircraft was
reinforced by seeing the prototype, its followers and its chase planes flying over the
Cotswolds either departing or arriving at Fairford. Concorde and I would miss each other
over the next few years before our becoming reaquainted at Royal International Air Tat-
toos, where I would be allowed aboard the flagship of British Airways.

As the story of Concorde involved the efforts of many, so did the effort required to
put this book together and therefore I must thank my co-conspirators for their inputs.
The first as ever is Peter Russell Smith, who as always allowed me to rampage through
his photograph collection for those interesting shots. My good friend Dennis Jenkins
provided the usual encouragement, plus help in securing images from the NASA collection. John Battersby, Curator of the Bristol Aircraft Collection, assisted with many
photographs, while Capt Peter Duffey provided much useful information. The staff at
the Fleet Air Arm Museum and the Public Record Office, Kew were, as ever, their smil-
ing, helpful selves, as also were their counterparts at BAE Systems and the Heritage Centres. The PR departments at Air France and British Airways were more than helpful,
although I never did get my complimentary ticket! Others who rose to the occasion
included Lee Howard, Phillipe Juret, Bernard Charles, Nick Challoner, plus Justin
Cederholm in New York and Jose M. Palacios from Portugal, who came up with the
impounded photographs and the Pepsi photographs, respectively. Also high on the mention list are Adrian Falconer for the in-depth Concorde walk-around taken at the Concorde Facility, Filton, and last but never least, Henry Matthews for those snippets of
information concerning test pilots.

To all, my sincerest thanks, and it goes without saying that any goofs are mine and
mine alone.

Kev Darling
South Wales, 2003

Contents

A sight that will no longer grace our skies with any regularity is that of Concorde. Here the ill-fated F-WTSC banks away from the camera. Whether any aerobatics were ever performed using a Concorde has never been revealed. However, except for upsetting the passengers, there is no reason why such gyrations could not have been attempted. BBA Collection

CHAPTER ONE

The Supersonic Civilian

Prehistory

The 1960s were described by politicians at the time as giving birth to the 'white heat of technology'. Out of this period came the nuclear power station, the six-lane motorway and the most successful supersonic transport aircraft to date, the BAC/Aérospatiale Concorde. Of the three, the nuclear power station has become a political embarrassment and a potential disaster, the six-lane motorway has become a car magnet and perpetually clogged, while Concorde is still awaiting the verdict of history to confirm whether it was an expensive white elephant or one of the most significant advances in aviation technology since 1945.

The stories of the development of the supersonic transport and Concorde are completely intertwined and would encompass both Britain and France, with significant contributions from the USA and the USSR. It has to be conceded that war has the habit of pushing the bounds of technology both further and faster, not only those then in development, but those that existed only at the theoretical level. In the closing years of the Second World War the piston-engined fighter was at the zenith of aircraft development, not only as a combat machine but in pure aeronautical terms and included the Rolls-Royce Merlin-powered, North American P-51 Mustang, the Griffon-powered Spitfires, the radial-engined Fw 190/Ta 152 series of German fighters and the Hawker Tempest.

However, waiting in the wings were emergent technologies that were being driven by the industrial might and technical muscle of Britain and America for the Allies, while opposing them were the innovative organizations in Nazi Germany supporting the Axis forces. The Third Reich had begun to provide support to the Heinkel aircraft company and in total contravention of the terms of the Treaty of Versailles. Not only were aircraft being developed that were capable of being converted for combat purposes, but, more importantly, in 1937 the

The Me 163 was one of two designs by Messerschmitt that featured swept wings, the other being the Me 262 jet. This earlier, rocket-powered aircraft had wings of moderate sweep; even so, it gave a remarkable performance, albeit with a tendency to crash. BBA Collection

same company had begun work on the jet engine. After much development work and not a few setbacks a workable engine, an axial flow powerplant, made its maiden flight in the specially designed Heinkel He 178 in 1939. The success of this flight would lead to the further development of the axial flow jet engine, albeit by Junkers as the main contractor instead of Heinkel. With this new powerplant looking promising, airframe construction was placed in the hands of Messerschmitt who would create the Me 262, powered by Junkers Jumo engines, and the Me 163 Komet, powered by rocket motors. Although the latter powerplant is not relevant to the development of jet-powered aircraft, both featured one important innovation: the swept wing. The use of swept wings had become an important requirement for the furtherance of high-speed flight since their use on an aircraft delayed the onset of compressibility, which, in turn, delayed

the onset of generated drag and possible unpredictability in flight. A further innovation developed by Messerschmitt was the nose-wheel undercarriage, which had been found necessary to replace the original tail-wheel arrangement now found wanting at both take-off and landing. Even Heinkel had experienced similar problems with its He 178 trials aircraft; in this case the company extended the tail-wheel assembly to compensate.

Across the Channel such innovations were viewed by the establishment with suspicion, if not downright hostility and scorn. In the field of powerplant development Frank Whittle, later and deservedly so Sir Frank, was pursuing the development of the jet engine as well as his career of being a junior RAF officer at Cranwell. Being able to take a sabbatical and the creation of Power Jets Ltd, allowed Whittle to push forward work on the centrifugal jet engine. In contrast to the more complicated axial

The most successful jet fighter available at the war's end was the Me 262. Not only did it combine swept wings and a carefully blended structure, it also used axial-flow turbojets, although the MTBF (mean time between failure) was limited to approximately seven hours. Real Wings Photographs

powerplant, the progress of the centrifugal engine was speeded up by its simplicity. Although Power Jets and Whittle would also experience some interesting problems, one of the better known ones was a bench test-run when the throttle failed to control the engines output; eventually the engine was shut down by the simple expedient of cutting the fuel supply, which prevented further damage to the machine, which was redlining on the attached gauges. In the fullness of time, as with all such projects, dedication and careful redesign meant that the Whittle engine could be test run without too much trepidation on the part of the

operators. To further prove the concept, the Gloster Aircraft Company was contracted to construct an airframe to specification E.28/39 to house a development engine. What emerged to make its first flight at RAF Cranwell was a low-wing monoplane aircraft with a tricycle undercarriage, unlike its German counterpart with its tail-wheel undercarriage and mid-fuselage-mounted wings. After a series of ground taxi runs, this flying test bed made its maiden flight on 15 May 1941. The success of the E.28/39 during its test flight led to the Gloster Meteor fighter which entered service with 616 Squadron in July

1944. In contrast to the German aircraft, the Meteor still revealed its earlier piston antecedents and came complete with fairly straight wings that carried with them the problems of extra drag and associated speed limitations. Although both fighters would enter service with their own air force, no head-to-head combat ever ensued, much to the chagrin of those who relish such things. What subsequently emerged, however, was that the axial flow jet engine had a short service life, being limited to some 7 flying hours before requiring an overhaul, whereas the far simpler centrifugal powerplant pushing the Meteor could stay in the airframe far longer before needing removal.

With the final defeat of Germany, the Allies descended upon its manufacturers and test establishments to remove the spoils of war: teams from the USA, Britain, France and the USSR departed with information on the axial flow jet engine and the principles of swept wings, plus the associated skill of wing–fuselage blending. In Britain under the aegis of, among other bodies, the Brabazon Committee, the theory of transonic and supersonic flight were not only understood but were being actively pursued. The major problem facing both the designers and the aircraft manufacturers was that of the hardware to test the theories and the powerplants to propel the designs. Before any attempt was made to develop any high-speed transport, the decision had already been reached concerning

The Gloster Whittle, built to Specification E. 28/39, was constructed purely to prove that the Whittle centrifugal jet engine was viable. Few real aerodynamic refinements were incorporated. Real Wings Photographs

the type of powerplant needed, and the centrifugal engine was not the answer. Although this type of engine was fairly simple and robust, it was recognized that further development would be fairly limited; thus the temperamental axial flow engine was seen as the best bet for the future.

The Military Imperative

Given the human desire to strive for improvement, the technical deficiencies would eventually be overcome. The Royal Aircraft Establishment at Farnborough became home to a series of wind tunnels that were more than capable of providing the airflow needed to test scale models and full-size sections, while the major engine manufacturers, mainly Rolls-Royce and Armstrong Whitworth, made strenuous efforts to improve the reliability of the jet engine, thereby increasing its mean time between failures rate to an economically sustainable level. To give these efforts substance, experimental specification E.24/43 was issued by the Ministry of Supply. This called for an aircraft capable of achieving 1,000mph, although no inclination towards either civil or military status was implied. The manufacturer eventually chosen to develop this futuristic aircraft was Miles Aircraft, a surprising choice, perhaps, given that their previous experience was geared to the building of light aircraft more orientated towards light sport, touring and training. In later years it was postulated that there was great scepticism that such an aircraft could be built, let alone flown safely, therefore to grant the contract to a company with no experience in this kind of design would lead to failure, whereas with another, bigger company the chances of immediate success were greater. To the consternation of many, Miles Aircraft presented the M.52 design to the Ministry of Supply in 1942 for consideration. Looking much like a bullet with wings, the aircraft featured a flush-fitted cockpit that was not only jettisonable, but was fully pressurized while still attached to the airframe. (This idea would gain further prominence when General Dynamics designed the F-111 fighter bomber with a similar module.) Within the presentation given to the Ministry were ideas for several wing planforms, since this was the primary area that was giving the greatest headache. All were either capable of performing adequately in the subsonic or the

Contrasting with the foregoing photograph is the Gloster Whittle just after reassembly at Cranwell. Soon afterwards, the aircraft made its first flight, and was painted and acquired secondary fins on the tailplanes to improve longitudinal stability. BBA Collection

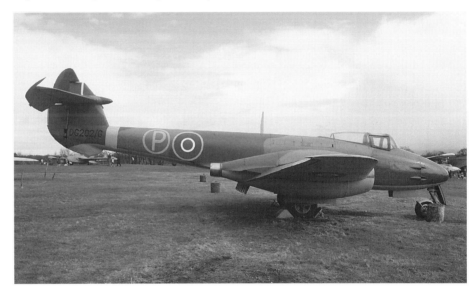

The first jet-powered aircraft to enter RAF service was the Meteor. This is DG202/G, a preproduction version built by Gloster Aircraft. The engines that powered this series of aircraft were centrifugal in type, a blind alley since the axial flow engine was seen as a better prospect. BBA Collection

supersonic speed range, but none satisfied the need for positive control behaviour across the proposed speed envelope. This notwithstanding, Miles began construction of a wooden mock-up with short span, straight wings. Engine development was by the Whittle company, utilizing the W2/700 engine with an afterburner which was later developed into the Rolls-Royce Derwent, although the afterburner was

deleted. Further power was to have been obtained by fitting a specially ducted fan to increase airflow through the jet system.

After Ministry approval, a contract was issued which authorized the release of funds to build a single prototype. All this valiant effort came to naught in February 1946 when the entire project was cancelled. The reasons frequently quoted for this decision include the potential serious risk to any

Miles M.52

Following the cancellation of the M.52, the government instituted a new programme that involved no danger to test pilots and a limited purpose. The Royal Aircraft Establishment was responsible for the development of a suitable rocket motor, and in charge of aircraft design was Barnes Wallis on detachment from Vickers Armstrongs. The drones were $\frac{3}{10}$th scale replicas of the M.52 and designated the Vickers A.1. The flight control system was a two-axis automatic pilot, while external control and data transmission were via radio telemetering equipment; the first test launch took place on 30 May 1947. A Mosquito light bomber took off from St Eval airfield in Cornwall with an A.1 drone complete with its 8ft (2.4m) wings mounted in its belly. It was intended to launch the drone from a height of 30,000ft (9,100m) before heading westwards over the Atlantic. This was not to be; as the Mosquito entered a storm cloud at 20,000ft (6,100m) the pilot lost control during the ensuing turbulence. It would take a 14,000ft (4,300m) drop for the pilot to recover control, by which time the drone had been torn off and had disappeared into the Bristol Channel. A further test flight was undertaken on 8 October off Land's End, using drone A.2. This was followed by two other flights on 9 June and 9 October 1948 using drone A.3. This latter run was successful and a speed of Mach 1.5 was obtained; however, instead of diving into the sea as planned, the drone ignored radio commands and was last observed on radar heading into the Atlantic. During this period the NOTAMS (Notices to Air Mariners) would indicate that an area some 14 miles (22.5km) west of the Bishop Rock lighthouse off the Scilly Isles was off limits. All pilots were warned of the possibility that pilotless drones would be operating within a radius of 11.5 miles (18.5km) from the lighthouse and that there was a danger of drones falling from 40,000ft (12,200m) and diving into the sea. The final chapter of this story came to an end when even these rocket trials were suspended, the reason being the high cost for little apparent return, although once Mach 1 was achieved the lead in this field was handed over to the Americans. All design data were sent to Bell Aircraft in the USA for further development, the result of which was that in 1947 the sound barrier was broken by the Bell XS-1, which was similar in outline to the Miles M.52. As well as airframe data being transferred to America, the Rolls-Royce Derwent engine would later appear as the General Electric Type 1 powerplant.

pilot flying the machine and the possibility that Miles Aircraft, with its production facilities firmly rooted at the light-aviation end of the market, would be unable to sustain a reasonable rate of production, should the M.52 prove successful. In reality, although the pilot safety aspect probably had a bearing on the cancellation, it is more likely that the limited production capability available allied to an impoverished Britain were closer to the point. Although the full size M.52 would be terminated, the general specification was worked on by Vickers Aircraft, who would build a series of rocket-powered, scale models for development in the fields of supersonic flight and air-launched missiles. The launch vehicle for the trial models would be a modified de Havilland Mosquito bomber and the rockets would be successfully flown at speeds up to Mach 1.4 unguided.

By the time Vickers had begun their unguided rocket test programme thoughts on aerofoil design had progressed beyond the earlier idea of short, stubby wings and were concentrating on the swept wing, in all of its varieties from gentle to severe. As the information recovered from Germany had been shared to some degree between the major airframe manufacturers, all would begin to investigate the integrating of such advances in current and future projects. One of the first to do so was de Havilland, who took a modified Vampire fuselage pod and used it to create the DH 108 Swallow, a tailless, swept-wing machine. The first prototype would undertake its maiden flight on 15 May 1948, with Geoffrey de Havilland at the controls, before being transferred to RAE Farnborough for in-depth investigative test flying. A second DH 108, also based on the Vampire, would be rolled out some months later. Unlike its predecessor, this version of the Swallow was intended to breach the sound barrier from the outset. To ensure that this version stood a greater chance of success, the airframe had undergone considerable modification and refinement. The wing leading-edge sweep had been set at 45 degrees and the flight controls had been changed from the earlier, mechanically-assisted type to being fully powered. The wings also featured leading-edge slots to assist with stability, while changes applied to the fuselage included the fitting of a more pointed nose section. After a series of proving flights, the Swallow would be pushed to its limits, successfully setting a world speed record of 616mph (992km/h) on 23 August 1946 with John Derry at the controls. This jubilation would soon turn to tragedy on 27 September when the airframe, being piloted by Geoffrey de Havilland, the son of the company founder, would break up while it was being used to investigate the behaviour of aircraft in the Mach 0.9 to 1 region. Even though the second Swallow had been lost in tragic circumstances, a third machine was built and this would successfully breach the Mach 1 barrier on 9 September 1948, although it would require a dive from 40,000ft (12,200m) to achieve this. Piloted by John Derry, later to lose his life in the DH 110 crash at Farnborough, the entire exercise consumed 10,000ft (3,000m) of altitude before success was achieved. Once the DH 108 series had managed to breach the Mach 1 barrier, their contribution to the development of high-speed flight would be complete since they were inherently unstable. Thus the two survivors would eventually be scrapped as no further use could be found for them.

Although the de Havilland Swallow had paved the way for supersonic flight, the baton would be passed on to two machines being developed for military purposes. One was being designed for the bomber role, while the other was intended to operate as a fighter; both would have a significant bearing on the development of Concorde. The bomber would emerge as the Avro Type 698 Vulcan and the fighter would become known as the English Electric Lightning, both would enter service with the RAF and the annals of British aviation history. From the Avro Vulcan development programme the designers of the future would gain the necessary information on the behaviour of the delta wing at various heights and speeds. Some data would come from the several versions of the Vulcan and the wing planforms they employed; but most was generated by a unique series of development and trials machines that were designated Type 707. The first of these machines would be lost in a fatal crash due to a malfunction of the airbrake circuit. Although this accident was at first seen as a setback, it did give the Avro design team a chance to review the kind of airframe required for this research and thus the subsequent Type 707s were more orientated towards high-speed flight, even though there were differences in performance and behaviour. While the Avro machines were intended to support the Vulcan programme, most would be flown by the RAE for research purposes. Both Avro and the RAE would quickly come to the conclusion that the pure delta wing was unstable in flight and therefore two separate routes were pursued to remedy this deficiency. The first required that the bomber's wing be cranked and drooped forward of the front spar, while the flight controls would require that their power operating units be

The DH 108 Swallow was based on the Vampire fighter bomber fuselage and was intended to prove that swept wings were viable. This aircraft is TG283/G, the first proof-of-concept vehicle. The next airframe was further modified and exceeded the speed of sound. BBA Collection

BELOW: The Lightning's contribution to the Concorde project included proving that supersonic speeds could be reached by using reheated or augmented engines. BBA Collection

slaved to pitch and yaw dampers. The fitting of both of these enhancements would immediately improve the bomber's stability, even though it would always retain a tendency to traverse a mild arc in a level plane of flight.

On the other hand, the Lightning, although having separate wings and tailplanes, described a delta shape in planform. This, however, was not the Lightning's main claim to fame as far as Concorde is concerned, since the fighter contributed to the development of the engine power necessary to drive an airframe at speeds up to Mach 2.

The first beneficiaries of these technological advances would be the military, but the civilian market also saw some benefits from all them. The planning of civilian transports had begun in 1943, two years before war's

ABOVE: **The contributions of the Vulcan included the use of elevons for roll and pitch control and of mixing boxes and feel units to assist in controlling the aircraft.** BBA Collection

LEFT: **The Avro Type 707C was originally developed to support the Vulcan programme; however, its delta wing gave pointers towards the development of the Concorde wing.** BBA Collection

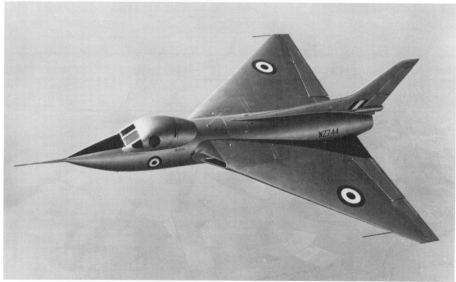

end, but in the immediate post-war period the only available aircraft that could be used to establish routes to generate income were converted military transports such as the Avro York and the Douglas DC-3 and DC-4. This hiatus gave the aircraft industry time to concentrate on creating a new generation of civilian airliners. However, some of their earlier efforts, such as the Brabazon, would never go beyond the initial prototype. The only jet-powered aircraft to emerge from the Brabazon Committee's deliberations would be the de Havilland Comet. The first production version of this landmark aircraft

would be subject to a series of accidents that would eventually lead to its grounding and eventual withdrawal. Although the Comet Mk.4 was a far better aircraft, the loss of development lead to the Boeing and Douglas aircraft companies meant that sales were limited. The next generation of airliner to be built was exemplified by the Vickers VC 10. Although a speedy and elegant aircraft, the VC 10 would not achieve great sales in comparison to its American rivals and would in reality be the final airliner created in Britain until the appearance of Concorde.

The French Join In

Although British aircraft manufacturers had gained a certain advantage from the secrets removed from Germany, the French had not been privy to so many of them. However, engineers in France gained more physical embodiments of them to work from; thus access to jet engines was obtained from airfields around the country, as were examples of swept-wing aircraft. These benefits were passed on to the French aircraft manufacturers for further development work. Before the French industry could deliver designs of its own, the *Armee de l'Air* would have to rely on aircraft purchased from overseas. Many would come from de Havilland in Britain and were powered by its Nene engine. Having entered the jet age, French manufacturers then began to work on several designs at the behest of government, a major financial investor at the time. Numerous paths of development were pursued, some led to a dead end while the remainder would culminate in the Dassault series of delta-winged fighters and bombers. While Dassault were leading the development of military airframes towards the supersonic era, the company most involved with developing aircraft for the civilian airline market was Sud Aviation. Underpinning the efforts of both these organizations was the engine manufacturers SNECMA. From the efforts of Sud Aviation emerged the Caravelle airliner, which bore a marked resemblance to the Comet in many respects, even down to the similar flight deck and pilots' panels.

While Britain and France were actively developing military and civilian jet-powered aircraft for their air forces and airlines

they were also investigating the application of advanced flight aerodynamic and engine developments to match. Some of the resulting aircraft were rightly described as weird and wonderful, but they did give some insights into the behaviour of aircraft at differing heights, speeds and angles of attack. In Britain the first approach towards a high-speed, delta, jet-powered airliner resulted in the Avro Type 720 Atlantic, developed from the Vulcan, while a further advance based around the supersonic Type 730 was also on the drawing board. In its initial guise the latter was originally a supersonic bomber constructed of stainless steel and powered by eight engines, while the former married the Vulcan's delta wings to a more conventional fuselage, albeit still minus a tailplane. Although neither design would progress far beyond the confines of the wind tunnel, their very existence would prompt RAE Farnborough to begin to develop a supersonic transport (SST). To control and steer the research in the correct direction and to reduce the potential financial waste, the Morgan Committee was formed on 25 February 1954, under the chairmanship

of Morien Morgan (later Sir Morien), the deputy director of the RAE. Within months of its formation this steering group delivered its first report, which concluded that a supersonic airliner with fifteen passengers and crew aboard for commercial flights between London and New York was entirely feasible.

Farnborough and the RAE wind tunnels would be where much of the original design work would be concentrated. Formal proposals into research and development were formally set out at a meeting held at the Ministry of Supply on 1 October 1956. Present at this gathering at Shell-Mex House in London and chaired by Sir Cyril Musgrave of the Ministry were representatives of the major manufacturers, the Ministry of Transport and Civil Aviation plus delegates from the two major airlines, British European Airways (BEA) and the British Overseas Airways Company (BOAC). The result of this meeting was the creation of the Supersonic Transport Aircraft Committee (STAC), which would also be chaired by Morgan. Joining him as part of STAC would be personnel drawn from Avro, Armstrong

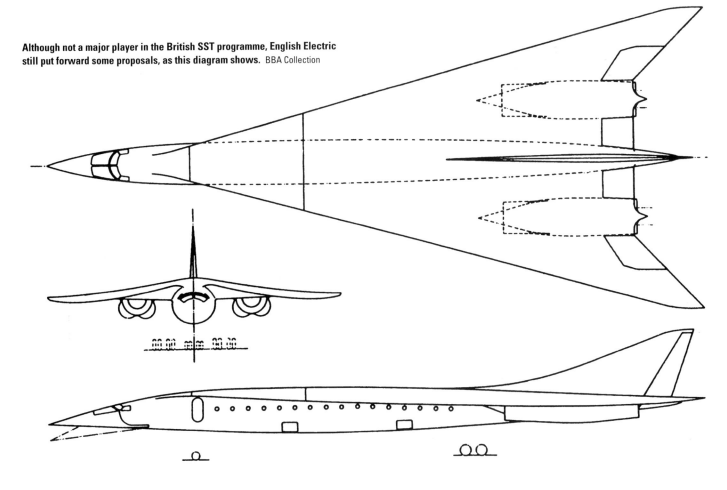

Although not a major player in the British SST programme, English Electric still put forward some proposals, as this diagram shows. BBA Collection

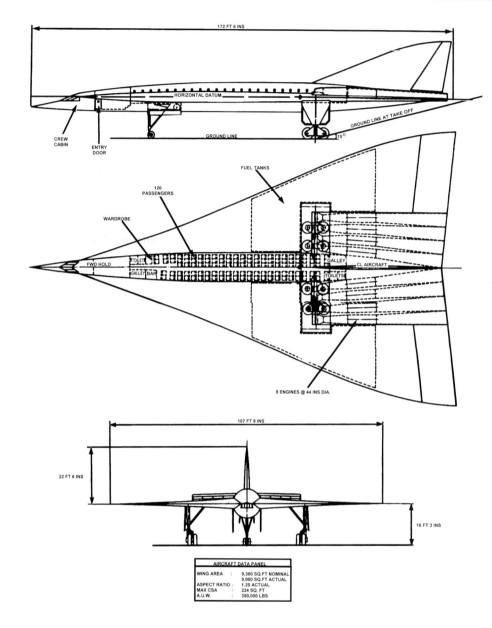

172 FT 6 INS

HORIZONTAL DATUM

GROUND LINE AT TAKE OFF

CREW CABIN

ENTRY DOOR

GROUND LINE

15°

FUEL TANKS

120 PASSENGERS

WARDROBE

FWD HOLD

TOILET

GALLEY BAR

GALLEY

CL AIRCRAFT

TOILETS

8 ENGINES @ 44 INS DIA.

107 FT 9 INS

22 FT 6 INS

16 FT 3 INS

AIRCRAFT DATA PANEL

WING AREA	:	9,300 SQ.FT NOMINAL
		9,000 SQ.FT ACTUAL
ASPECT RATIO	:	1.25 ACTUAL
MAX CSA	:	224 SQ. FT
A.U.W.	:	350,000 LBS

The Handley Page HP 109 design, planned as a large transatlantic transport, had eight engines in a central block. BBA Collection

Whitworth, Bristol, de Havilland, Handley Page, Short Bros and Vickers Aircraft. Joining the airframe manufacturers were delegates from the powerplant constructors: Armstrong Siddeley, Bristol Aero Engines, de Havilland Engine division and Rolls-Royce. Further industry participation would be added at a later date when Fairey and English Electric were also invited to contribute to the programme in November 1957. The first consultative meeting of STAC would be held on 5 November 1956 at St Giles Court, London. This initial briefing confirmed the findings of the

scientists from the RAE that an aircraft could be built that was capable of travelling between 800 and 1,200mph (1,300 and 1,900km/h); however, this was the easy part as it was quickly realized that research needed to be concentrated more on some areas in which Britain was weakest. To speed this up, the participating companies agreed to co-operate with RAE as neither group had the resources to proceed alone. These combined resources would bring together all the workshops, wind tunnels, computing systems as well as the technical facilities, project offices and drawing offices. To fund all

these efforts the Ministry of Supply would issue contracts to individual organizations for research. To push the research effort forward was a technical subcommittee backed up by seven specialist working groups; the subcommittee met for the first time on 30 November 1956 where the RAE briefed the technical staff from the participating companies on the problems to be concentrated upon. The working groups would concentrate upon project and assessment studies, operations, cruising aerodynamics, low-speed aerodynamics, structures, powerplants and engine installation.

Once the work had started, further interested bodies were invited to send representatives to join the subcommittee and thus people from the Air Registration Board, the Aircraft Research Association and the National Physical Laboratory plus some from the College of Aeronautics at Cranfield would soon add their expertise. After two years of meetings, trials and intensive investigations and the writing of some 400 research papers, a final report was ready for delivery to the Controller Aircraft, Air Chief Marshal Sir Claude Pelly, at the Ministry of Supply on 9 March 1959. To get this far the main committee had met seven times, the technical subcommittee at least twelve times and the working groups innumerable times, while the RAE staged meetings at Farnborough at vital points during the process. This document confirmed the feasibility of the SST concept and provided strong pointers towards its design and development. The report would emphasize one recommendation most strongly: the requirement for two separate aircraft designs. The first would concentrate upon a long-range design which would need to travel further and faster and the other specification would centre around an airframe catering for medium ranges. The shorter-range aircraft was intended to have a range of 1,300 miles (2,100km) and a top speed of Mach 1.3 and the longer-range machine was estimated to have a range of 3,000 miles (4,800km) and a top speed of Mach 2. This was seen as the maximum feasible speed possible using conventional construction methods and materials. This proviso meant that the use of exotic materials in airframe construction was not required to combat the higher temperatures generated above Mach 2; it also meant that manufacturing and development costs could be kept within reasonable levels. The STAC report also stated that, if the design work were not progressed from this point, then the British aircraft industry would effectively abrogate any industrial lead gained from the research thus far. None of this report was based on the fanciful, as the reasons given for a recommendation to proceed noted. Thus the efficiency of the turbojet engine and its behaviour in high speed flight were already ascertained, as was the ability of the aircraft manufacturers to build the airframe from conventional materials so long as the maximum expected speed did not stray too far above Mach 2. A further point concerned the design of the airframe itself, where much work had already been completed, taking as its basis the ideal supersonic delta and modifying it for low-speed operation. This conclusion had been the result of a two-pronged approach: the first based upon the pure delta shape and the second looking at the creation of a wing that featured a shock-free aerofoil, to which was added subsonic leading and trailing edges, all of which formed an aerodynamic compromise aimed at producing a wing capable of performing adequately throughout the required speed range. As both wings appeared to offer the solution to different parts of the speed range, it was decided that the final product would be a judicious blend of both.

The STAC Report

The STAC report also highlighted other development areas that were either under active consideration or giving rise for concern. These included the dispersion of heat created by kinetic energy, although no revisions to the method of construction would be needed. Beyond the heating problem and how it would affect the structure, another of the working groups had also raised concerns about possible problems with control-surface flutter, structural oscillations, vibration effects on the structure and the behaviour of the airframe under the effects of aero-elasticity. These points, the committee concluded, would require extensive research into the required strength and stiffness of candidate materials, plus the performance of substructures and complete assemblies under a full range of heating and loading effects throughout the intended speed envelope.

Unlike the airframe that carries it, the powerplants were identified as needing little in the way of extra research. However, the working groups and the STAC conceded that the British industry lacked the required in-depth knowledge to cater for

the extra cooling needed for engines operating at high speeds. With the technology available at the time it was deduced that the chosen engine would experience its optimum efficiency at Mach 2 to 2.5, although it was recognized that kinetic heating and low-speed handling might compromise this. Allied to this was the more pressing concern of the noise on the ground that would be generated by a powerplant engineered for this kind of performance; thus investigations would be needed into how to reduce this without compromising performance, otherwise the whole project would be put in jeopardy. Consideration was given to the use of special engines, specific throttle-handling techniques and the use of engine-silencing devices.

First consideration was given to the use of a turbofan bypass engine which would operate efficiently up to Mach 1.2 and with which the ground noise component would be reduced. But for operations above this speed the engine and the nozzles would require modification, otherwise the noise problem would recur. Fortunately, a solution appeared to be at hand in the form of a mixing duct which provided noise attenuation and the ejected air which would also supply a small extra thrust. The design of these mixing ducts was viewed as critical, otherwise there could be weight or drag penalties. To combat this it was recognized that great skill would be needed in the design and integration of both the engines and the airframe. It was also recognized that the complete propulsive system needed to be fitted in such a way that the engines' performance was not compromised. Having dealt with the type of engine and noise suppression required for the emergent SST, attention was turned to the types of intake needed to feed the powerplants. Up to a speed of Mach 1.2 fixed intakes were deemed acceptable; however, beyond that point it was realized that variable geometry intakes would be required since they offered distinct advantages over the control of the incoming air mass when compared with fixed intakes.

Beyond the basic technical requirements each relevant working group also provided the committee with information concerning the airworthiness and operational aspects of SST operations. By this time it was recognized that the increased complexity of modern airliners required extensive flight testing to ensure the long-term airworthiness of the aircraft. Added to this

were the extra requirements brought on by supersonic flight, which, it was noted, would increase the amount of test flying needed to clear the design for commercial usage. It was also proposed that the test requirements and schedules should be developed alongside the aircraft design stage in order to cater for any possible failures in the early stages of the flight-test period. It was also noted that such an approach would reduce the number of test flying hours required.

The STAC was one of the first to see that such an airliner needed to have its support equipment designed and tested together with the airframe. Also requiring development were air-traffic control services, ground handling, navigation, plus take-off and landing aids. Away from the scientific and technical fields the committee began to speculate about the potential sales of such an SST. In 1959 the committee suggested, that by 1970, potential sales could be between 150 and 500 airframes. What did confuse it to some extent were the mathematics concerning the operating costs of an SST even under cruising conditions, although these were not unusual during the introductory period of a new airliner. The only answer STAC could provide was that the careful integration of all the efforts by the working groups would result in lower costs eventually, which, in turn, would lead to a parity of operating costs with competing subsonic aircraft. In an attempt to provide some sort of initial operating and first purchase costs the committee turned to that stalwart formula of the British aircraft industry: the pound sterling per pound weight value, which gave a return of one-third greater for an SST in comparison with its subsonic equivalent.

The committee was convinced that the British industry was advanced enough to design and build an economically viable SST for sale around the world and that a reasonable stab could be made with regards to the costs of operating such an aircraft. It was recognized by the STAC that the development, design and manufacture of a British SST would have to be of the highest order since its greatest rival, the USA, had greater resources in all areas of manufacture and marketing and would be quick to seize upon any perceived deficiencies.

With the decision made to use conventional alloys for constructing the airframe, the committee turned its attention to determining the aerodynamics required for a supersonic transport. Ideas on the drawing board at several manufacturers were studied

When Armstrong Whitworth produced its SST design, the company were trying to combine the benefits from both fore and aft swept wings. Note the area ruling applied to the fuselage, hence the coke bottle effect. BBA Collection

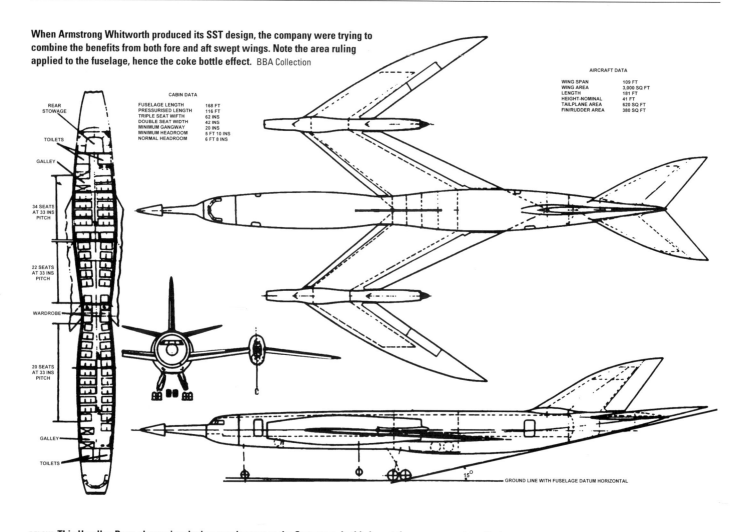

CABIN DATA

FUSELAGE LENGTH	168 FT
PRESSURISED LENGTH	116 FT
TRIPLE SEAT WIFTH	62 INS
DOUBLE SEAT WIDTH	42 INS
MINIMUM GANGWAY	20 INS
MINIMUM HEADROOM	5 FT 10 INS
NORMAL HEADROOM	6 FT 8 INS

AIRCRAFT DATA

WING SPAN	109 FT
WING AREA	3,000 SQ FT
LENGTH	181 FT
HEIGHT-NOMINAL	41 FT
TAILPLANE AREA	620 SQ FT
FIN/RUDDER AREA	380 SQ FT

REAR STOWAGE

TOILETS

GALLEY

34 SEATS AT 33 INS PITCH

22 SEATS AT 33 INS PITCH

WARDROBE

20 SEATS AT 33 INS PITCH

GALLEY

TOILETS

15°   GROUND LINE WITH FUSELAGE DATUM HORIZONTAL

BELOW: This Handley Page slew-wing design was known as the Sycamore. In this layout the passengers travelled in the wing while the pod housed the crew. The idea was abandoned. BBA Collection

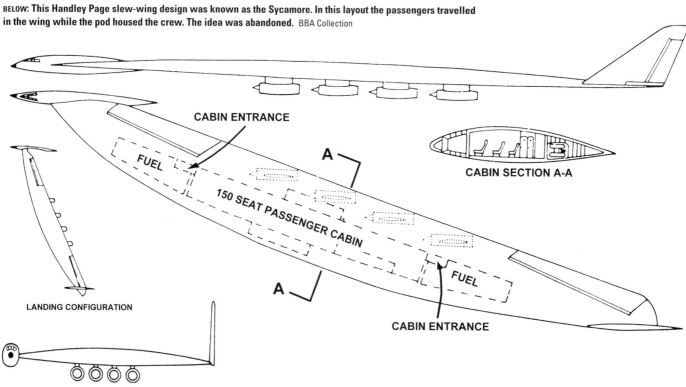

CABIN ENTRANCE

FUEL

A

150 SEAT PASSENGER CABIN

A

FUEL

CABIN ENTRANCE

LANDING CONFIGURATION

CABIN SECTION A-A

to judge their possible use; however, all were rejected as being inefficient. Even though applying brute-force engine power would have had the desired effect the operating costs would have been unacceptable. Analysis of all the available data would eventually reveal that a slender delta-wing planform would be the ideal shape for an SST flying at a high sustained speed and swept wings were viewed as the best for subsonic handling. To blend the best of both some unusual designs were proposed. From the drawing boards of Armstrong Whitworth came an airframe based around an M-shaped wing and Handley Page developed an airliner that was based around a slew-wing layout, a totally impracticable concept that remained on the drawing board. With the unusual and the impracticable out of the way, the design teams returned to the delta-wing layout, although their first task would be to overcome the handling problems inherent in it. The primary concern that needed to be tackled was the tendency for a delta wing to transfer its centre of lift aftwards as the speed increased; to compensate for this it was proposed that any aircraft designed for this role must include fuel transfer tanks that would enable the centre of gravity and hence the centre of lift to be altered to compensate.

One avenue that was followed for a while before it was abandoned was that of creating an airliner that was virtually a pure flying wing, this being based on an earlier proposal put forward by Avro for the Type 698 Vulcan bomber. In a similar manner to Roy Chadwick at Avro, the Morgan Committee would eventually discard this idea as impractical since the flight control technology did not then exist to make this idea workable. Also militating against such a design were the potential structural difficulties brought to the fore by trying to integrate a sufficiently large passenger compartment and flight deck into the layout, while problems with high drag, skin friction and all the penalties of excess heat would have needed to be solved.

Eventually all these design configurations and investigations would be compressed into one concise report that the STAC would present to the Ministry in March 1956. Contained within it were details and diagrams that covered three different configurations that were deemed worthy of further investigation and development. The one proposal that was strongly recommended was a supersonic transport designed to convey 150 passengers over a single-stage length of 3,000 miles (4,800km), this made the aircraft capable of flying the Atlantic non-stop. The proposed cruising speed was Mach 1.8, which was entirely feasible and would give a crossing time of approximately 3hr. Travelling at these speeds would ensure that the heat generated by kinetic energy would be kept under control but still allow for the use of conventional alloys and steels in its construction. The committee also recommended that investigations be undertaken in developing the design to reach Mach 3, although a combined programme in concert with the military was seen as the best course in order to reduce development and production costs. The third and final proposed SST design was a smaller version of the first proposal, although this had a passenger capacity of 100 passengers and a single-stage range of 1,300 miles (2,100km). This last aircraft was seen as ideal for routes across Europe and domestic routes across the USA. The report from the STAC, backed by the Ministry of Transport and Civilian Aviation, was also exceptionally optimistic regarding sales since at least 200 were projected as being sold by 1970. Another area in which there was great optimism was that of development costs, those indicated by STAC being that no more than £95 million would be needed for the building of six prototypes and the required type certification.

The three designs proposed were general in nature, it would be up to individual manufacturers to develop their own proposals. Those companies that put forward definite proposals included Avro, English Electric and Handley Page, who based their designs around the delta-wing shape; but it would

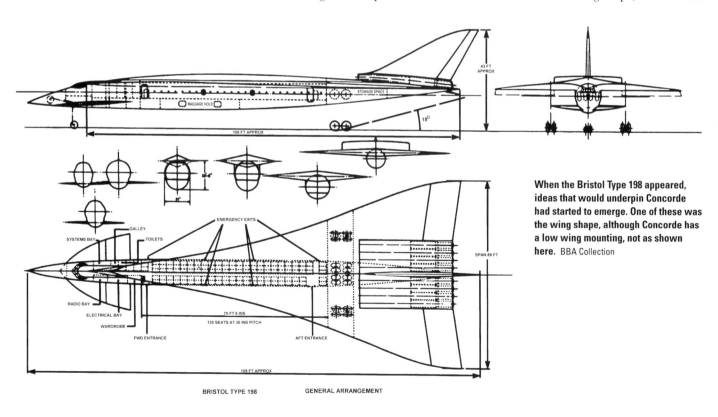

When the Bristol Type 198 appeared, ideas that would underpin Concorde had started to emerge. One of these was the wing shape, although Concorde has a low wing mounting, not as shown here. BBA Collection

BRISTOL TYPE 198   GENERAL ARRANGEMENT

be the Bristol Aircraft Company and its Type 198, first revealed in October 1958, that would capture the attention of STAC and the two Ministries. In its first iteration the Type 198 was seen as an eight-engined, slender delta-winged aircraft, this being a shoulder-mounted, ogee-shaped wing with canards. Further development of the proposal would see the number of engines reduced to six and the deletion of the canards. To assist Bristol Aircraft, the Ministry of Supply would award the company a contract in order that comparative studies could be undertaken on different structures. One would look at the structure of an airframe capable of Mach 1 and built of light alloys and another would consider the layout of an aircraft built with steel and titanium for use in Mach 3 operations. As would be expected, the latter was quickly ruled out as being too expensive to manufacture and operate, plus the penalty of an extended development period.

As a follow up to the impressive Bristol design, the Ministry of Supply would issue a joint contract to both Bristol and Avro to develop an SST jointly that would combine the ideas evolved through the former's Type 198 and the latter's Type 735. What would emerge at the end of this process was a completely redesigned aircraft. Deleted was the earlier mid-mounted wing, which was replaced by a low-mounted, delta wing above which was a long, slender fuselage. Power came from six Rolls-Royce Olympus engines in clutches of three in two nacelles under the wings. Regarded as an optimum design, the Ministry issued another contract in October 1960 to allow both companies to continue further development. However, this was a period of government-sponsored consolidation within the British industry and so Avro would eventually be left out of the second part of the SST design process as this company was taken into the Hawker Siddeley Aircraft Group, and Bristol Aircraft merged with English Electric and Vickers to form the British Aircraft Corporation (BAC). Although Avro was thus effectively excluded, the blueprint that emerged from BAC in August 1961 was largely based on the Type 198 issued in October the previous year. As before, the powerplants were proposed as the Rolls-Royce Olympus rated at 26,700lb each, these driving an airframe that weighed in at 385,000lb (175,000kg) with a proposed range of 3,260 miles (5,200km). Accommodation was set at 136 passengers with the seats being pitched at 33in

(84cm). By the end of 1961 there was concern about the economies of scale linked to the size of the aircraft, the use of six engines and the complexity of the intakes needed to supply mass airflow to the engine compressors. A further look at the design by BAC would see the emergence of the Type 223 powered by four Olympus 592/3 engines coupled to a gross weight of 260,000lb (118,200kg) and capacity for 110 passengers. Retained from the original specification was the capability to fly the London–New York route as a single stage. The reduction in size of the BAC SST meant that the Type 223 design was the preferred option; thus the larger Type 198 was eventually abandoned.

While the Ministries and manufacturers were wrestling with the technology required to create a supersonic transport the STAC raised concerns about the creation of sonic booms and, more importantly, their effects on people below the flight path. Although no serious in-depth research concerning the public's view on these was carried out, the committee deduced that the best way to understand public tolerance would be to

explore it and react to the complaints generated, although it was quickly conceded that acceleration to supersonic speeds should be delayed until the aircraft was over the sea.

In France the government and the aircraft manufacturers it sponsored were also investigating the possibilities of a supersonic airliner during 1957. Behind the sudden flurry of interest in it was the main French airline, Air France. Initial approaches had been made by the company with a specification that required a mid-range-capable SST for use within Europe. As a result the specification was extremely modest, requiring, as it did, a range of some 1,900 miles (3,000km) with a passenger loading of between sixty and seventy. The reason given by Air France for such a modest specification was that the airline wanted a follow-on from the extremely successful subsonic Caravelle which was in widespread use. The negative side of this approach was that Air France wanted a supersonic airliner that could be operated at subsonic costing, an unrealistic proposal from the outset as events would subsequently prove.

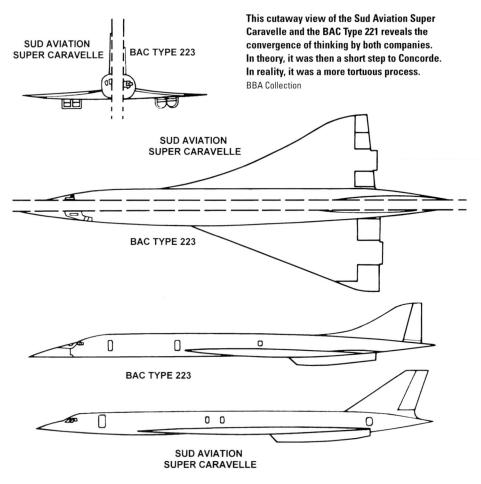

This cutaway view of the Sud Aviation Super Caravelle and the BAC Type 221 reveals the convergence of thinking by both companies. In theory, it was then a short step to Concorde. In reality, it was a more tortuous process.
BBA Collection

SUD AVIATION SUPER CARAVELLE   BAC TYPE 223

SUD AVIATION SUPER CARAVELLE

BAC TYPE 223

BAC TYPE 223

SUD AVIATION SUPER CARAVELLE

By the time the tender for proposals was ready for sending to manufacturers the French aviation industry had been reduced to just three major players, these being Nord Aviation, Sud Aviation and Avions Marcel Dassault. All would begin their own design approaches in 1958–59, although by 1960 there would be only one design being pursued assiduously. This would be a combined effort between Sud Aviation and Avions Marcel Dassault who would fuse their similar efforts together into one proposal. The other manufacturer, Nord Aviation, would eventually decide to withdraw from this particular development process. Although the resultant French submission was not as advanced as that of BAC there was enough of a resemblance to suggest that a joint Anglo-French approach might be the course to follow. It was at this point that the politicians from both countries would begin their involvement which would result in a merger of ideas that would eventually lead to Concorde.

The Technological Challenge

Having assessed the potential and the politics of designing a supersonic transport, attention now turned to the mathematics and physics associated with such a design. To simplify the behaviour of supersonic flight it can be regarded as varying with the square root of the air temperature, which in its turn decreases with height, although relationship is limited to the lower atmosphere, the tropopause, and the region above that, the troposphere. Above that is the stratosphere in which temperature and thus speed are constant. To add figures to this statement, the International Standard Atmosphere was defined thus: at sea level the speed of sound is approximately 760mph (1,200km/h). For the corresponding 50,000 to 60,000ft (15,200–18,300m) band where an SST flies, to be both economic and speedy has an ISA rating around the 660mph (1,060km/h) mark. The scale indicating the speed of sound was devised by Ernst Mach, an Austrian scientist who investigated the behaviour of objects passing through the air. Research on the effects of sonic booms eventually revealed that a high-speed object passing through air produces a distinctive bow wave which forms a cone; the boom comes from the shock cone intersecting with the ground and thus the change in air pressure causes the well-

known sonic boom, the most conspicuous aspect of compressibility. At subsonic speeds the air can act as a non-compressible fluid, but at supersonic speeds changes occur in the shape of the wave in front of the object travelling at speed. Under Mach 1 the waves begin to bunch together, but at the point of transition to Mach 1 the wavefront becomes a completely flat shock wall. As the speed increases above Mach 1 the cone begins to form and will remain in place until the object reduces speed. Getting an aircraft up to supersonic speed requires that the lift:drag ratio be as efficient as possible; therefore that of a subsonic airliner has a ratio of 16:1 which reduces sharply as Mach 1 is approached. However, an SST with its slender, pointed fuselage and delta wings has a lift:drag ratio of 8:1, which gradually decreases above Mach 2 before evening out.

When the scientists and engineers turned their attention to the type of engine required to give sustained supersonic performance it was apparent that only two types would be available to power an SST: the turbojet, which literally turns fuel into propulsive energy and becomes more efficient as speed increases, or the emergent turbofan, which is firmly anchored in the subsonic regime and becomes less efficient as Mach 1 approaches.

As the proposed SST was intended to fly at between 50,000 and 60,000ft, there were other factors to take into consideration besides those that normally affect subsonic aircraft. Changes in temperature, pressure and wind direction and the gas dynamics of the air, which behaves like a compressible fluid at this height and speed, all affect an SST's performance. Against these variables the technical teams found that there was one bonus: the behaviour of the preferred turbojet engine, which becomes more efficient as altitude increases. Behaviour inside the cabin was also taken into consideration since there were other variables to be taken into account, such as changes in cabin pressurization at different altitudes and temperatures, and, surprisingly enough, variations in external temperature that could affect the behaviour of the air-conditioning system. Fortunately, wind variations at such height and speed normally fail to affect an SST, although there have been some problems with high altitude jet streams kicking the autopilot out of lock.

As with all such aircraft that travel at supersonic speeds, an SST is subject to the temperature built up by its passage through

the air. Known as kinetic heating, the airframe experiences the heat generated by skin friction, this being proportional to the square of the aircraft's velocity. The shape of an aircraft governs the dispersal of the heat generated; however, some of this is eventually offset by radiation cooling and internal conduction. But after a period in flight the dispersion pattern for the heat range settles down to an average of 90°C overall, although the tip of the nose is subject to a maximum of 127°. To combat the varying heat ranges generated by speed and altitude, the surface skin of the aircraft expends and contracts; the passengers in their air-conditioned cabin would notice none of this since the conditioning remains constant. These heat differentials cause thermal stresses within the structure that need compensation in the design process to reduce the causes of potential fatigue failure.

Because an SST design would be limited in the quantity of fuel it could carry owing to its weight and size, it was down to the designers to ensure that the airframe exhibited the greatest aerodynamic efficiency possible, powered by an engine with the best cruise efficiency where the lowest possible specific fuel consumption was matched to the best possible thrust output. Another factor that guided the design was the requirement to keep the basic weight as low as possible, otherwise the total weight of the aircraft would grow beyond a prohibitive level, especially as 50 per cent of the fuel is consumed in the subsonic part of the flight.

To create an SST that complied with all these requirements was a complex business, especially as above Mach 1 the aircraft is subject to a phenomenon known as wave drag. This is the hidden penalty that controls the size of an aircraft's fuselage. In the subsonic regime, expansion in the cross-section of the fuselage brings little increase in wave drag; but above the limit of the sound barrier the opposite applies and thus a slender fuselage is the only option available for high-speed flight. In contrast, the design of a supersonic wing is fraught with contrasting complications. In theory the best wing for supersonic flight is one as slender as possible, yet this brings its own penalties in that there is an increase in induced drag caused by the generation of lift. To counteract this requires that the wing shape should be modified to achieve the greatest lift:drag ratio as possible. Having tweaked the wing for the best performance at supersonic speeds it would require further changes to perform efficiently under low-speed handling conditions.

Once all of these factors had been taken into consideration the designers were able to settle down to the task of creating the Anglo-French Concorde. The STAC would, however, have further input into the design process as it was proposed that, instead of using size, range, take-off/landing performance to define the aircraft, they suggested that to relate size to payload instead of all-up weight might make the concept more saleable to potential customers. Even so, the design was never going to exceed a maximum capacity of 200 passengers since the available data suggested that a larger airframe would be uneconomic to operate. Careful consideration would also have to be given to the manufacture of each part of the airframe as any marked discrepancy in this area would increase operating costs, especially in airframes being operated over longer distances and at speeds between Mach 1.2 and 1.8. This proviso was also aimed at the engine manufacturers since failure to control all aspects of the design could put the airlines against any SST. These possible deficiencies were greatly lessened if the required range were reduced, and thus the committee concluded that the proposed SST should be built in two versions: the shorter-ranged vehicle would be regarded as the lead in to the longer-ranged, definitive aircraft. In this manner, it was concluded, any defects in design and performance could be rectified in the machine built later.

Although the committee had, in concert with the relevant working groups, discussed the behaviour of the jet engines on previous occasions, they were still particularly concerned about the nuisance noise generated by this type of powerplant and, of course, the potentially destructive behaviour of the sonic boom. In dealing with the first requirement, the committee were reaching for the impossible in requiring that the acceptable generated noise should be kept to the same level as, or just below that of contemporary piston-engined airliners because jet engine noise is more pervasive. Thus a limit of 103dB was seen as the highest acceptable. After starting and taxiing, the next part of the sequence was the take-off. Yet again noise was the prime factor; here the committee asked that the engine manufacturers take into consideration the design of powerplant, the velocity of the exhaust, total engine output and the climb performance of the aircraft. Given the

nature of the aircraft involved, it was reasoned that its engines would have a higher specific thrust and jet velocity during take-off, hence an increased noise quotient would be inevitable. Allied to this was the shape of the SST's wing, which is very inefficient at low speeds and therefore more power would be needed to climb clear of the runway. To compensate for these potential noise problems, the committee concluded that an increased angle of climb and a shortened period of full power application would be sufficient to negate any problems. Having achieved flight, the STAC recommended that the engines be throttled back within the designed safety margins as soon as possible to maintain a low noise output. As the engines intended for the SST would be fitted with thrust augmenters, complete with variable nozzles, the reduced thrust output would be compensated for by the air mass flow remaining consistent, and thus jet velocity and noise would be reduced.

Engines and their number for driving a Mach 2 airliner weighing in at 350,000 to 500,000lb (159,000–227,000kg) would also exercise the collective minds of STAC. Should smaller, low-thrust powerplants be developed to satisfy the SST requirement? Or would a new design of engine be better? As the expected power requirement was in the 150,000 to 200,000lb thrust range, a number of engines, between eight and twelve, was proposed, each with a thrust rating of 20,000lb or more.

On the subject of sonic boom the committee reiterated that the public would be the final arbiter of what was acceptable; however, as a starting point, they would recommend that supersonic flight be kept above 35,000ft (10,700m) as this was deemed acceptable. It would also be recommended that, in the case of transatlantic departures, supersonic speed be restrained until the aircraft was over the sea; conversely, supersonic speeds would be prohibited over land. As part of the proposed development of the SST in the future it was suggested that a form of automatic engine control be developed; this was seen as a good selling point to prospective airlines.

As well as a form of automatic control for the engines, the committee also discussed the possibility of an automatic, aerodynamic, balancing system. But this idea would be placed on hold as its development was seen as a long-winded process, especially as the requirement for the manual reversion of the flying controls was built into the specification. This latter need would be made more

difficult due to the changing centre of pressure that would occur as the aircraft travelled across the Atlantic; yet if such a system could be devised it would allow for a reduction of the size of the power units, although the SST would need the already envisaged powered flight controls and an artificial feel system.

It seems strange to relate that, at the outset of the STAC investigation, the aerodynamics working group were unsure whether a feel system of any kind would be needed. This attitude quickly changed when the experience of those already engaged in developing Mach 2 fighters and a particular delta-wing bomber were brought in. However, it was realized, that since this was a civilian application, not only would a feel system be needed, but duplication for safety reasons would be essential. Thus an extensive programme of development, including the use of specially designed testbeds, would be required. Further systems development covering an automatic blind-landing capability was also seen as a necessity, although whether this would be by direct vision, television or some form of periscope had not been determined. All these innovations were warmly welcomed by the participating airlines, although they would express some reservations concerning their application since any deterioration in controllability in manual mode was seen as unacceptable.

As the British SST design was set to incorporate many radical changes, the committee concluded that initial R&D contracts could be ready for issue in January 1960, with a completion date sometime in 1962. The target date for airline entry was put at 1971–72. This date was set for the long-range aircraft while the shorter-ranged machine was set for service entry some three years earlier. Costs were a thorny point in the STAC report as accurate figures were impossible to predict; but they did present some figures which would entail the expending of £51 million, to include the prototype and the development programme up to Certificate of Airworthiness standard, which would entail the use of up to five production machines. These figures covered only the Mach 1.2 part of the programme because the development of the Mach 1.8 aircraft would lift the final cost to approximately £91 million. This then was the British Supersonic Transport in all its paper glory; much had already been learned, more would need to be learned before the aircraft known as the Concorde became a reality.

CHAPTER TWO

Design and Development

John Bull and Marianne Become Engaged

With all the technical, scientific, theoretical and operational meetings, discussions and papers completed, it was time for the politicians to enter the arena. It had been realized early on that the design, development and production of a supersonic transport using only the resources available to an almost destitute Britain would put a great strain on the economy, therefore approaches were made by representatives of the British government to their counterparts in France, Germany and the USA. These were given a mixed reception; Germany declined any offer to become involved for the reason that they could see no use for such an aircraft under their current civilian aviation requirements; the other nation to decline the invitation was the USA which had intimated plans to undertake development of their own SST based upon the experience gained from the unique XB-70 Valkyrie, Mach 3, six-engined bomber. The only country to accept the invitation was France since they too were still impoverished after the war and had already begun to investigate their own version of an SST, a Sud Aviation design powered by four Rolls-Royce RB167-1 engines. To this end Peter Thorneycroft (Minister of Aviation) made approaches to his French counterpart Robert Buron (Minister of Public Works and Transport) in April 1960. As these talks had come to an amicable conclusion it was proposed that a meeting be held between design teams from the favoured British and French manufacturers. The British team from Bristol Aircraft was led by Dr Archibald Russell; his counterpart from Sud Aviation was Pierre Satre. As these initial discussions proved that there was common ground, it was proposed that there should be further ones, although both the manufacturers would continue to develop their own design in the meantime.

During the Paris Air Show of 1961 a further spur towards collaboration appeared on the Sud Aviation trade stand when the company displayed a scale model of their own Super Caravelle SST. Since the similarities between the Sud Aviation model and the proposed Bristol Type 223 design were fairly obvious, an official meeting between representatives from both companies was quickly convened in Paris on 8 June. By this time Bristol Aircraft had been absorbed by BAC as part of a shake up of the British industry, while the French representatives were still part of Sud Aviation. A reciprocal meeting between the two groups would take place at Weybridge, once home of Vickers Aircraft, on 10 July, where the first serious discussions concerning the adoption of a common design and the pooling of resources were undertaken. While the airframe manufacturers were taking their first, tentative steps towards collaboration, the engine manufacturers were also engaged in negotiations concerning the development of a common engine and supplementary items. The two selected primary contractors were originally Bristol Engines at Filton, later to become part of Rolls-Royce, and the French conglomerate SNECMA (Société Nationale d'etude et de Construction de Moteurs d'Aviation), who signed a preliminary declaration of co-operation in November 1961.

With the manufacturers seemingly coming to a consensus, it was time for the politicians to finalize their aspects of the project. Present at this meeting in Paris on 7 December 1961 were Peter Thorneycroft and Robert Buron. The outcome was a joint formal request to both groups of manufacturers to co-operate fully in the design and development of an Anglo-French supersonic transport, its systems and engines. Although the politicians and the official entourages were presenting a united front to the world, the airframe manufacturers were still at odds over the exact nature of the airliner required. BAC was still pushing for an aircraft capable of flying the Atlantic in a single stage, on the grounds of manufacturing and operating-cost viability, while Sud Aviation would continue to persist with the vision of a shorter-range design. Given these two obviously disparate views, it was not surprising that many of these meetings ended in arguments as both parties continued to assert their own requirements.

Since this situation could not be allowed to continue, the politicians would exert pressure on both groups of manufacturers to come to a consensus. This would result in a full-blown project review held in Paris on 17 January 1962, where the airframe manufacturers decided to continue the development of both designs, albeit with as much commonality as possible. Fortunately, the blueprints presented by both groups were similar in outline, both being powered by Olympus 593 engines; the major difference was the quantity of fuel in each version and the number of tanks required to house it. It was also recognized that there might be differences in the radio and navigational requirements for each version; however, the aircraft's fundamental systems were the same for both versions. As well as using similar, standard materials for construction, it was intended that both versions would include a high proportion of common parts and components. To further increase commonality, the production tools and assembly jigs were identical. Given that the structure for both versions was the same it was decided to follow a similar R&D programme, which would encompass static strength, aero elasticity and fatigue life calculations. The initial design drawings, countersigned by Dr William Strang and Lucien Servanty, revealed a common layout dimensionally, the only differences being in fuel capacities which were 12,500 and 17,400gal, respectively (57,000 and 79,000ltr) and maximum take-off weights calculated as 209,400 and 253,500lb, respectively (95,000 and 115,000kg) for each version. At this point the SST design was shown with both a fixed and a variable geometry nose, although the maximum set angle of attack was 13 degrees, which would result in the fixed nose being dropped. Agreement had been reached, however, on the materials to be used in construction. Most of the structure was to be built using aluminium alloy to BR58 (British Standard) or its French equivalent A-U2GN, while the remainder would use high-tensile steels in high-stress areas and titanium in areas of high temperature.

A further meeting held on 17 January 1962 between the two manufacturing groups led by Dr Russell and Dr Strang of BAC and Pierre Satre and Lucien Servanty of Sud Aviation resulted in a declaration of intent which allowed for the continued development and refinement of both designs so that a final decision concerning the configuration and the details regarding the workshares, supposedly equally, could be hammered out. The declaration read:

> It is feasible to have a common basic aircraft in two versions one of which would comply with the needs expressed by the French government and approved by Sud Aviation and Air France for medium range operations while the other would comply with the requirements requested by the British Ministry of Aviation and approved by BAC for use on the London– New York transatlantic route.

On 26 March a further meeting was held in London between Thorneycroft and Buron at which it was agreed that the preliminary designs were close enough to act as a basis for an Anglo-French SST with the whole being carried out on a 50–50 basis. After these negotiations the first major milestone in the Concorde programme was passed. This was the announcement of the 'Anglo-French Supersonic Aircraft Agreement' which was presented to the world's press on 25 October. This historic document was countersigned by representatives of the two governments in London on 29 November. Encapsulated within it were points covering the equal sharing of all development and design costs, including the pursuit of potential sales on a worldwide basis. However, nine days earlier it had been touch and go at a Cabinet meeting held to decide the future of the entire project. Present at this meeting were the Prime Minister, Harold MacMillan, and his son-in-law, Julian Amery (who had replaced Thorneycroft as the Minister of Aviation) and members of the Treasury. An intense discussion revolving around development costs and potential sales were finally resolved and would allow Concorde to continue. It would also affirm the commitment to progress both versions in parallel. Also within this document were fuller technical proposals for the SST, which included a passenger cabin capable of carrying 100 at a maximum speed of Mach 2.2.

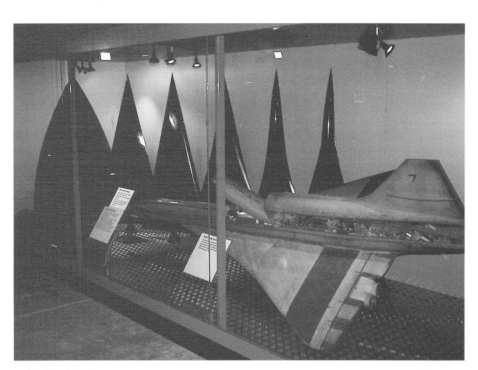

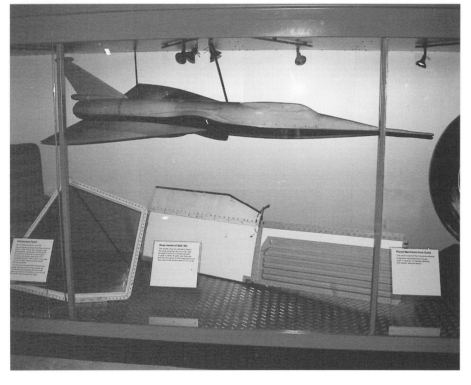

TOP: With a backdrop of aerodynamic test shapes is this unpowered, drop-test model of Concorde preserved at the Fleet Air Arm Museum, Yeovilton. BBA Collection

LEFT: Before the Fairey FD.2 was rebuilt as the BAC 221, this drop model was manufactured to test its behaviour in flight. BBA Collection

Joint Oversight

Overseeing the whole project was a standing committee drawn from both countries. This would include a chairman/managing director, a vice chairman/deputy managing director, a French technical director, a British deputy technical director, a British director of production, finance and contracts, who would have a French deputy director, a British and a French sales director and a director representing Sud Aviation and one from BAC doing the same job. To instil a degree of fairness the two top posts alternated between the British and the French members, who would change posts every two years. Working in concert with the oversight committee was a civil servant contingent from each country whose purpose was to supervise the project and liaise between the technical and finance directors. The role of the oversight committee was to keep both governments informed of progress and to make proposals for economy and efficiency, arrange for joint airworthiness and operational regulations and give appropriate advice if required to the manufacturing groups. Even with this agreement in place there would still be some friction between the manufacturers that would end only when a design was chosen. One of the first decisions made by the new organization was the name of the aircraft, Concorde. Even this was not without controversy as BAC had decided not to spell the name with a terminal 'e' while the government had steadfastly promoted it; the manufacturers finally gave in during December 1967 as much of the extant paperwork reveals. This minor bureaucratic spat aside, the management of the project itself was under stress due to the size of the several management organizations that had evolved in support.

As both countries had created a team of considerable size, the decision-making process was being slowed down considerably and this in turn had begun to push up the development costs, which had originally stood at £95 million but had begun to creep inexorably towards the £1 billion mark. What saved the situation were the belief, dedication and management skills of Sir George Edwards, the BAC chairman. His opposite number, the chairman of the Airframe Committee, Andre Puget, would also exert maximum influence on his side of the Channel to hold the programme together. A further spanner in the works came in 1964 when a Labour government assumed power. One of its earliest acts was to try to cancel all outstanding aviation contracts in both the civil and the military field. A memorandum to the Prime Minister, dated for 24 June, cast doubt on the project's viability as costs at that date had already reached £275 million, enough to build two Channel tunnels. The paper also stated that to get the aircraft into service with BOAC at an early date could have far-reaching effects on the only British subsonic airliner already in production, the VC-10. The proposed course was to drop Concorde and proceed with the Channel tunnel while passing the SST baton to the USA, which had expressed a wish to continue to develop its supersonic transport at a more leisurely pace. The apparent pay-off was that the VC-10 would have an easier passage into the American market. The next paragraph then turned the previous statement on its head as the French part of the agreement came into play. Although not blatantly stating that the cost of pulling out was being used as a lever to keep the United Kingdom involved, the government decided that a policy of no enthusiasm was the answer, so that a get-out clause

could be created for an easy escape, thus allowing Britain to spend no more than a further £30 to £50 million. Fortunately for history, there was a 'no break' clause in the November 1962 agreement which carried heavy financial penalties should either side decide to back out. Having run into this brick wall, the government was forced to continue the project, although it used everything in its power to cause as many delays as possible and cancelled other projects instead.

Changes had also occurred in the design process as both of the airframe manufacturers were now working on a single project, for 100 passengers at a maximum speed of Mach 2.2. This airframe still retained the medium-stage capability of 2,400 miles (3,840km) for Air France as well as the longer range capability preferred by BOAC. This gave maximum all-up weights of 220,500lb (100,230kg) for the medium version while the longer-ranged aircraft would have a maximum of 262,500lb (119,300kg). Other changes applicable to the shorter-ranged SST included airbrakes to reduce the landing run and a ventral air stair to allow for a more flexible usage pattern on smaller airfields with fewer facilities.

For the following two years development on both versions of the Anglo-French SST would continue, although, as expected, not without rancour. The main sticking point remained as before: the British team still hated the idea of the extras required to produce the medium-range Super Caravelle since they regarded it as economically unviable, while the French disliked the longer-range aircraft being pushed by BAC since they could see no need for the extra range capability. Eventually BAC and Sud Aviation came to an agreement as common sense and a realization of the economies of scale prevailed and the British version was

Anglo-French Concorde Management Committees

Airframe Management Committee		Engine Management Committee	
Gen Andre Puget	Chairman/Managing Director alternates with:	Sir Arnold Hall	Chairman/Managing Director alternates with:
Sir George Edwards	Vice-Chairman/Deputy Managing Director	H.A. Desbrueres	Vice-Chairman/Deputy Managing Director
Pierre Satre	Technical Director	Dr E.J. Warlow-Davies	Technical Director
Dr A.E. Russell	Deputy Technical Director	M. Garnier	Deputy Technical Director
J.F. Harper	Director of Production, Finance, Contracts	R. Abel	Director of Production
Louis Giusta	Deputy Director of Production, etc.	W.F. Saxon	Deputy Director of Production
A.H.C. Greenwood	Sales Director	J. Bloch	Sales Director
W.J. Jakimiuk	Sales Director	W.H. Rees	Sales Director
G.E. Knight	Director		
B.C. Vallieres	Director		

adopted for continued development. The end of this uncertainty meant that the decision was made to virtually redesign the whole aircraft in 1964. The most obvious alteration was an extension to the fuselage by 14ft (4.3m), which would grow by another 6.5ft (2m) during the following twelve months. This change to the fuselage allowed the number of passengers to be increased to 140. A further reworking affected the wings whose gross area was increased by 15 per cent, the final result was an increase in gross weight to 367,000lb (166,800kg). To drive this bigger Concorde Rolls-Royce offered an improved version of the Olympus 593 which gave a final maximum thrust of 40,000lb (178kN) per engine.

It was at this point in the development process that research aircraft began to make their presence felt. One of the most expensive to build and operate was the Bristol Type 188 which was constructed mainly from stainless steel and powered by a pair of Rolls-Royce Gyron engines. The main purpose of this aircraft was to probe the behaviour of an airframe flying at speeds exceeding Mach 2. In this part of the flight envelope the main area of study was the effect of sustained kinetic heating on an aircraft. The first of these unique airframes, XF923, made its maiden flight on 14 April 1961, being followed by a second Type 188, XF926, on 29 April 1963. To study the behaviour of the wing during various phases of flight it was decided to allow Bristol Aircraft to rebuild the Fairey FD 2. Originally this delta-winged test aircraft had been used solely in research on this wing planform before being diverted to this new task. The rebuilding of the airframe meant that a completely new wing was fitted, of a slender ogee shape. To ensure longitudinal stability the fuselage was lengthened, the new airframe being

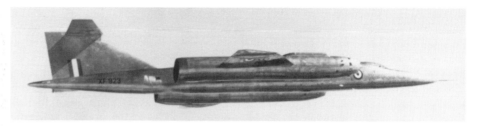

The Bristol Type 188 was constructed mainly of stainless steel for research into high-speed flight. The aircraft was not a success since it was expensive to build and operate due to its high fuel consumption. BBA Collection

Before the appearance of the Fairey FD.2 research aircraft, the company built the delta-winged FD.1 for much the same purpose. However, VX350 was not the success envisaged since it suffered from excessive drag and instability. BBA Collection

ABOVE: Undertaking a slow flypast for the camera is the BAC.221, rebuilt from a Fairey FD.2. Not only were the wings modified to an ogee planform, but a droop nose was incorporated and shown in action. BBA Collection

Another Concorde feature that was trialled on the BAC.221 was the extended undercarriage that the airliner would need to allow for intake clearance. BBA Collection

RIGHT: **To explore the behaviour of the delta wing at low speeds, Handley Page was contracted to build the strange-looking HP.115 research aircraft.** C.P. Russell Smith Collection

BELOW: **One of the first experimental tailless aircraft built to test the delta wing was the Boulton Paul BP.111A seen here at Cranfield. It had a pure delta wing with elevons at the trailing edge. The seemingly overlarge fin was required for better stability along the longitudinal axis.** C.P. Russell Smith Collection

BOTTOM: **Seen touching down at Farnborough is the Handley Page HP.115. Since it was required only for low-speed handling trials the undercarriage units were fixed.** BBA Collection

redesignated as the Type 221. It would make its maiden flight on 1 May 1964. In its new guise the BAC 221 was used to provide valuable data on high-speed handling on behalf of the Concorde programme. To cater for the low-speed handling data requirements, the Handley Page HP115 was specially constructed. This too sported a delta wing, although with a straight leading edge, and made its maiden flight on 17 August 1961. For the next four years the HP 115 made numerous, occasionally unstable, flights in support of the programme before retirement to the Fleet Air Arm Museum at Yeovilton.

The French SST development team were also drawing on the test results gained from a number of unique test airframes. To investigate pure high-speed flight the Sud-Ouest 9050 Trident II research aircraft had been constructed, its propulsion being delivered by a pair of wingtip-mounted rocket engines. Delta-wing research had been carried out with the Sud-Est SE212 Durandal and the Nord 1502 Griffon, which would eventually lead to the Mirage series of fighters and the Mirage IV strategic bomber. As the French industry had the greater experience in delta-wing flight, it came as no surprise to find that Sud Aviation would assume the design and construction lead for the front section of this major component plus the elevons. In the event, Sud Aviation eventually gained the greater share (60 per cent) of the airframe design and construction work. In contrast, the British benefitted from an increase in the workshare in engine development as Rolls-Royce were chosen as the primary contractor to develop the Olympus 593 for Concorde. Responsibility for the design, development and manufacture of the relevant major components was assumed by the relevant division of the four primary contractors, and all would in turn be overseen by the joint-manned oversight committee. In Britain most of the airframe work was concentrated at the old Vickers plant at Weybridge, where the rear fuselage, fin and rudder sections were designed and manufactured. The forward fuselage became the responsibility of the BAC, ex-Bristol Aircraft, plant at Filton, while the centre fuselage section was manufactured in France, even though it was designed at Filton. Beyond the four primary manufacturers was Marshalls of Cambridge, now Marshalls Aerospace, whose responsibility was the unique droop nose. The design and manufacture of these assemblies were concentrated at their bases in Hurn and Cambridge.

Estimates of Design Costs

	Mach 1.2 Aircraft (£ million)		Mach 1.8 Aircraft (£ million)	
	Existing engines	New engines	Existing engines	New engines
'A' prototype development				
Airframe development and flight costs	17	17	22	22
Engine development and supply of engine costs	6	24	20	26
Total	23	41	42	48
'B' further development to costs of A				
4 development aircraft	12	12	15	15
10,000hr flight tests	16	16	21	21
20,000hr flight tests	24	25	32	32
C = A+B				
10,000hr	51	69	78	84
20,000hr	59	78	89	95

Planned Concorde Costs (£ million)

Year	Airframe	Engines	Total
1962	8.4	3.6	12
1963	8.7	8	16.7
1964	11.6	6.9	18.5
1965	26.4	11.6	38
1966	22.1	5.8	27.9
1967	14.5	3.3	17.8
1968	6.9	0.7	17.6
1969	–3.3	0	–3.3
Totals	95.3	39.9	145.2

The Nord Griffon II was one of the first delta-wing aircraft built in France. Used entirely for experimental purposes, it would make its claim for fame when Andre Turcat passed Mach 2 piloting it in 1959. BBA Collection

BAC also took on much of the responsibility for the strategy concerning the essential systems. Included in this remit were the electrical, fuel (in collaboration with Rolls-Royce), oxygen provision for both passengers and crew, fire protection, air conditioning, de-icing, engine instrumentation and control systems. Also within the British remit were the development of thermal and sound insulation plus calculations on the thermal characteristics of the cabin. The French, led by Sud

Aviation, assumed responsibility for the aircraft hydraulics, flying-control power units, automatic pilot and stabilization systems. Some of the avionics including the radio and aerials and navigation systems (including the pitot static system) were also be handled by French companies, as were power generation and air-conditioning control, plus the complete design and computation of the air-conditioning system. The critical area of engine nacelle design was given to Britain; this included the aerodynamic design and testing of the specification and performance of the nacelles, which also included the intake assemblies and ramps plus the nozzles.

Overall responsibility for the remaining aerodynamic work was under control of the French; calculation of aero elasticity and strength in a three-dimensional aerodynamic loading framework would determine the behaviour of the aircraft at critical speed points and was the responsibility of the British, while general airframe calculations were undertaken by the French. Centre of gravity and weight estimation were the responsibility of each country's own design team and calculation of the centre of gravity for each aircraft version was the responsibility of the French manufacturers, who were also charged with providing the 'manufacturer's empty weight' figures, and a combined team would calculate the forward weight and centre of gravity estimates plus the projected 'operator's empty weight'. All these figures covered in-flight ranges for both versions.

To ensure continuity, each manufacturer would normally design and build each sub-assembly and install the relevant wiring and subsystems into each where applicable. Any modifications were discussed under the aegis of the joint committee, who assisted in gaining approval and ensured that the work-share process would stay in balance at 40 per cent for Britain and 60 for France. The responsibility for the powerplant was under the guidance of Bristol Engines whose areas of responsibility included the basic engine. This baseline item included the compressor, combuster system, turbine, primary fuel-control system, nozzle-area control system and the majority of engine-mounted accessories and drives such as the combined drive unit. SNECMA gained responsibility for the reheat fuel-control system, the reheat unit, the convergent-divergent nozzle and a jet pipe equipped with a noise suppresser and a thrust-reverser control system. To speed

The SNCASE, later Sud Aviation, SE-212 Durandal was another French delta-wing trials aircraft that would exert some influence on the Concorde programme.
BBA Collection

The Gerfaut II was yet another delta-winged aircraft in which Andre Turcat set another record in 1957. Although the original concept behind the aircraft was to act as a fighter prototype, it remained as a trials aircraft until the end of its life.
BBA Collection

The SNCASE 9000 Trident was a mixed powerplant aircraft featuring a jet engine in the fuselage and rocket engines mounted on the wingtips. Turcat used it to push the French quest for speed even further. BBA Collection

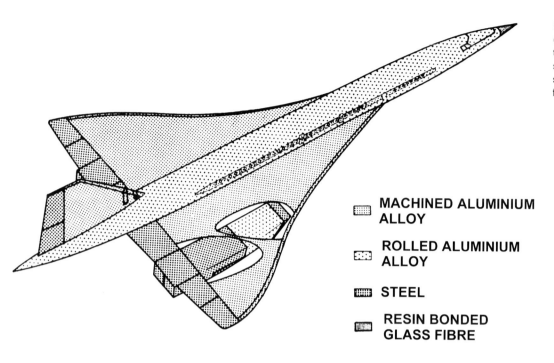

Concorde was mainly constructed from aluminium, as this diagram reveals. Other construction materials used included steel, titanium and resin-formed fairings. BBA Collection

▨ MACHINED ALUMINIUM ALLOY

▨ ROLLED ALUMINIUM ALLOY

▨ STEEL

▨ RESIN BONDED GLASS FIBRE

Photographed alongside the French prototype Concorde F-WTSS is the second Dassault Mirage IV. Both would benefit from earlier development programmes. BBA Collection

BELOW: This diagram breaks down the production allotments for the manufacturing partners. Although production aircraft were reputedly built in jigs with little variation, investigations after the Paris crash showed that each airframe was virtually handbuilt, therefore all differ. Sections 2.2.1 and 2.1 are extra fuselage sections for pressure testing. BBA Collection

▨ BRITISH   ▨ FRENCH

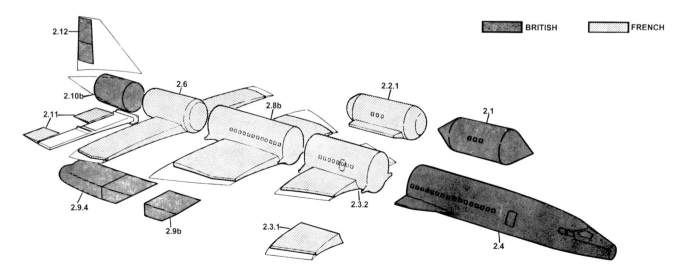

PRODUCTION MANUFACTURE BREAKDOWN – MAJOR ITEMS

COMPONENT		DESIGN	MANUFACTURE
07	Air Intakes	BAC	BAC – Preston
08	Engine Bay	BAC	BAC – Filton
09	Droop Nose	BAC	BAC – Hurn
10	Nose Fuselage	BAC	BAC – Weybridge
11	Forward Fuselage	BAC	BAC – Weybridge
12	Intermediate Fuselage	BAC	A-S – Marignane
24	Rear Fuselage	BAC	BAC – Weybridge
26	Fin	BAC	BAC – Weybridge
27	Rudder	BAC	BAC – Weybridge
13	Forward Wing	Aerospatiale	A-S – Bouguenais
14	Centre Wing	Aerospatiale	A-S – Marignane
15	Centre Wing	Aerospatiale	A-S – Bouguenais
16	Centre Wing	Aerospatiale	A-S – Toulouse
18	Centre Wing	Aerospatiale	A-S – Toulouse
20	Centre Wing	Aerospatiale	A-S – St Nazaire
21	Outer Wing	Aerospatiale	A-S – Bourges
23	Elevons	Aerospatiale	A-S – Bouguenais
51	Main Landing Gear		Hispano/Messier
51	Nose Landing Gear		Hispano/Messier
06	TRA Nozzles		SNECMA
	Engines		Rolls-Royce (1971) Ltd.

SYSTEMS RESPONSIBILITIES

BRITISH AIRCRAFT CORPORATION	AEROSPATIALE
Electrics	Hydraulics
Oxygen	Flying Controls
Fuel	Navigation
Engine instrumentation	Radio
Engine controls	Air conditioning supply
Fire	
Air conditioning distribution	
De-icing	

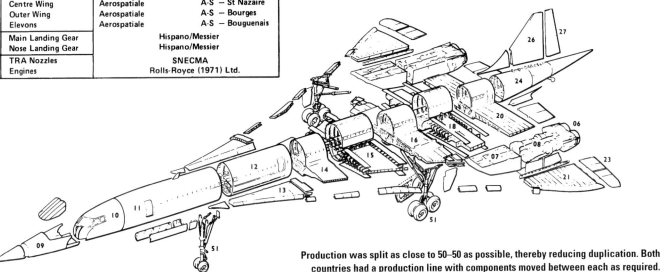

Production was split as close to 50–50 as possible, thereby reducing duplication. Both countries had a production line with components moved between each as required. The items shown here are the sections destined for fatigue testing. BBA Collection

the process up, optimal use was made of all available test facilities, including the government-owned laboratories in both countries. At the beginning of the initial manufacture process SNECMA manufactured and tested certain parts of the test engines. As the process continued, the work share meant that Rolls-Royce (Bristol) carried out 66 per cent of the development work while SNECMA would carry out the remainder. Production was divided at 60 per cent for the British company and 40 for the French.

The Manufacturers Get Together

In a similar manner to the oversight committee, the manufacturers also formed a committee to oversee the day-to-day engineering requirements. Heading this organization was Lucien Servanty who had been designated as director of engineering by Pierre Satre from the oversight committee,

while his deputy was Dr Strang and a third appointee was Etienne Escola as the assistant director of engineering. Their remit was to make maximum usage of each company's management structure by which means it was hoped any problems could be resolved quickly. To provide support for the engineering directorate R.S. Brown was appointed as the production manager, his deputy being Alfred Asselot and an assistant was also appointed, George Gedge from Britain. Their responsibilities were defined thus: Asselot would take charge of production issues in France and was empowered to accept engineering requirements on behalf of Sud Aviation and Gedge would fulfil a similar role in Britain. Each of these members of the production committee was ably supported by representatives from both BAC and Sud Aviation. To ensure that there was no discrepancy between the British and the French organization it was arranged for all the drawings and documents to be duplicated between the manufacturers, this would act as a fail-safe

system and confirm structural integrity and ensure that each team was made aware of changes when they occurred.

Rolls-Royce covered the responsibility for developing the basic Olympus 593 engine; however, beyond this SNECMA had the oversight of developing the engine thrust augmenter assemblies and their interfaces and BAC at Filton were charged with the design of the complete engine bay assemblies, plus the intakes and associated ramps. In France there were four Sud Aviation factories assigned to airframe design and construction and in Bourges Dassault took on the responsibility for the manufacture of the outer wing panels. Other manufacturers in Europe were also involved in creating assemblies for Concorde; thus Hispano Suiza, once famous for its cannon, received the contract for the manufacture of the main undercarriage legs while the nose undercarriage leg was designed and manufactured by Messier. Other, smaller concerns in France also gained lucrative contracts for the manufacture of flight

Photographed at an SBAC Farnborough show, this Concorde model defined the end of the research programme and the start of the manufacturing programme. BBA Collection

controls, navigation system components, hydraulic valves and jacks, communications components and parts of the air-conditioning system. In Britain the remainder of the system items were manufactured by such companies as Normalair Garrett and Dunlop. All assemblies and sub-assemblies were then fed into a production line, one per country; however, such was the planning already in place that there was no duplication of production in either country.

Given the way in which each aircraft industry approached certain aspects of design, development and manufacture it is hardly surprising that there were incompatibilities between the parts of the organization. One of the major differences was in the system of measurements since France used the metric system and Britain used imperial measurements. After a series of meetings conversion tables were eventually drawn up that satisfied both parties, and, having settled this difference, construction of the first prototypes could begin. First metal for the Anglo-French SST prototypes was cut in April 1965 in both Britain and France.

With manufacture well under way, the construction of the major sub-assemblies proceeded rapidly, which allowed the first section to be delivered to CEAT in Toulouse in October. After the first combined wing/centre fuselage section had been placed in

the construction jigs, the remainder of the airframe sections were delivered on schedule, so that by March 1966 the first prototype was complete enough to allow static and thermal testing to be undertaken. In April final construction and fitting out of prototype Concorde 001 began at Toulouse, and at Filton the final assembly of Concorde prototype 002 began in August. Even though the SST had progressed far beyond a paper exercise certain areas had already

been identified for closer investigation. These included the electrics, which were undergoing rapid modification, at least thirty changes being proposed in January 1966. The intakes were delayed until May–June 1967 instead of February, these having been modified by altering the intake honeycomb structure which required further testing. The changes to the intake lips also resulted in alterations to the engine nacelle assemblies, which, in turn, also required fresh testing. Even if the airframe had been almost ready a further hold up involving the on-board escape hatch mechanism and its blast shield had not been cleared. A similar situation also arose concerning the pilots' personal safety equipment which urgently needed testing and clearing for flying. Yet another problem regarding the crew related to their seats which were found to be uncomfortable and needed a drastic redesign, not only for the prototype trials but also for the production aircraft.

Running in parallel with the airframe was development of the powerplant; thus in November 1965 a bench-test engine, an Olympus 593B (Big) engine, began test running at Filton. By June 1966 a development Olympus 593 powerplant, complete with variable geometry exhaust assembly, undertook its first bench-test runs at Melun-Villaroche in France. With the successful completion of the initial ground runs, the whole assembly was transferred to the National Gas Turbine Establishment at Pyestock in England where it was subjected to extensive testing in the high-altitude testing facility. After extensive testing of the

Avro Vulcan B.1, XA903, never entered service with the RAF, being used for trials throughout its working life. This front-on view shows the bomber with a Concorde part nacelle complete with Olympus engine under the bomb-bay. BBA Collection

ABOVE: **Having completed the initial flight trials for the Olympus engine, Vulcan test bed XA903 was modified to carry a water spray rig in place of the bomb aimer's blister on the nose to simulate foul weather.** BBA Collection

RIGHT: **Heavily modified Canberra WV787 was used by the RAE and the A&AEE for icing trials. The rig at the rear of the fuselage was used to spray water at the prototypes; depending on the altitude, spray came out either as water or ice.** BBA Collection

engine, plus its augmenter assembly, it was returned to the Saclay testing facility in France. Here during April 1967 it underwent further high-altitude simulation trials which covered all aspects of engine behaviour. As the ground testing was proceeding fairly smoothly, it was time for airborne trials to begin. The aircraft chosen for these was that Farnborough stalwart the Vulcan B.1 XA903. This veteran was fitted with a half nacelle complete with powerplant and auxiliary systems in the bomb-bay.

Additional equipment mounted in this space included an independent fuel system which would feed the test engine only. The reason for this was that an accurate, complete record of fuel consumption was needed to evaluate the performance of the powerplant under all aspects of the flight envelope. Another modification to XA903 was the complete deletion of the bomb-aimer's blister under the nose. Mounted in its place was a water spray rig which allowed rainstorms to be simulated. Icing

simulation was not carried out with this, instead an especially modified Canberra bomber, WV787, flew in front of the Vulcan, discharging its icy cargo from a spray rig mounted under the rear fuselage.

To reinforce the fact that Concorde was regarded as a prestigious project in both Britain and France, an extensive fatigue-testing programme was instituted from the outset. To this end a complete nose and forward fuselage section, some 70ft (21m) in length, was delivered for testing. Another

With a protective cover over the pitot head, and neither engines nor PFCUs fitted, Concorde 002 is rolled out at Filton. J.A. Todd Collection via Lee Howard

part Concorde airframe was also constructed at Filton during late 1966, although its purpose was more cosmetic in nature. It consisted of a cabin and flightdeck mock-up which became available for inspection from February 1967. It would soon have positive results as sixteen airlines would express an interest in the purchase of up to sixty-seven aircraft.

Behold, the Prototypes

The prototype Concordes, 001 and 002, were regarded from the outset as trials and evaluation airframes only and thus further changes were undertaken as new and different requirements came to the fore. In May 1966 a revised fuselage was unveiled for the preproduction Concorde airframes. In this version the fuselage had been extended by a further 8.5ft (2.6m) and other modifications included a redesigned one-piece visor and a fuselage step which replaced the earlier two-piece assembly and periscope to give improved visibility.

To fit this extension in, much of the extra length was accommodated forward of the wing, while the remainder was gained by moving the aft pressure bulkhead further to the rear. These changes would allow the passenger compartment to carry 128. Other changes allowed for the inclusion of an extra passenger door close to the leading edge of the wing and the cabin windows were reduced in size slightly to comply with American Federal Aviation Authority regulations. The first appearance of this updated Concorde was at Filton on 17 December 1971 when the British-built Concorde 02 was rolled out to public view. It was during 1971 that the first Royal approaches were made by the Commandant of the Royal Flight on behalf of Prince Phillip, who had expressed an interest in flying in one of the prototypes. This request was viewed with some trepidation by the government, who were about to undertake a review of the project that year and were worried that a good interview from the Prince might make any attempt

to cancel it very difficult. In the end, however, the government acquiesced.

On 11 December 1967 the first French-built Concorde prototype 001, F-WTSS, was shown to an audience of the press, dignitaries and staff from the manufacturers just before the start of its flight trials. The British-built prototype, Concorde 002 G-BSST, appeared in public during September 1968, although it had already undertaken extensive taxi trials at Filton before then. Once both prototypes had made their bow they began intensive trials involving the engines, brakes and flight controls. To gain the most from these, both Concordes were taxied up and down the runways at their own airfields, thus Filton and Toulouse reverberated to the Olympus engines while the flight test crews proved the validity of the aircraft systems. Both machines would pass these trials successfully, which would allow the French prototype to be cleared for its maiden flight at the end of February 1969. Proudly wearing the registration F-WTSS, the French initials for supersonic transport, Concorde 001 taxied out to the end of the Toulouse runway on the afternoon of 2 March. The crew for this historic flight was Andre Turcat as chief test pilot, the others being Jacques Guignard (co-pilot), Henri Perrier (flight engineer) and Michael Retif (flight test engineer). Taking their positions alongside the prototype were an especially modified Gloster Meteor NF.11 from CEV-Bretigny for use as an observation aircraft and a Morane Saulnier Paris, which was to be used as the photographic chase plane to record for posterity and evaluation the stages of the flight. Once cleared for take-off, the throttles were advanced to full normal power before being pushed through the gate to allow the thrust augmenters to kick in to full reheat power. After all the gauges had been checked and cleared the brakes were released and the Concorde began to roll down the runway. At 15:38 local time the nose-wheel left the ground and Concorde 001 climbed smoothly into the sky. For this first flight the undercarriage was left in the down and locked position. Even with this restriction this maiden flight, all 29min of it, proceeded smoothly before the aircraft turned and lined up for a perfect landing. On touchdown the tail brake parachute was deployed to slow it down and reduce the loading on the brakes.

Five weeks later, on 9 April, the British prototype Concorde 002, with the registration G-BSST (to some the right way

Andre Turcat

Famed for being the Sud Aviation test pilot for the first Concorde flight, Andre Turcat was born in Marseilles on 23 October 1921, the son of a noted vehicle manufacturer. He undertook the latter part of his education at the École Polytechnique from where he graduated in 1942. Three years later the young Turcat enlisted in the post-war French Air Force, earning his navigator's wing by June 1947 and his pilot's wings the following month. His time with the Armée de l'Aire was spent flying Douglas DC-3 Dakota aircraft as part of the Touraine and Anjou operations groups. Much of his flying was undertaken in Indochina during the war there. In December 1950 Turcat was seconded to the Flight Test Centre, this being followed by his assuming command of the Test Navigator School. Turcat finished his time with the French Air Force in late 1953, then joined the aircraft manufacturer SFECMAS, later to be absorbed by Nord Aviation. With both companies he was the Assistant Director of Flight Testing, being promoted to Chief Test Pilot not long afterwards. One of his first duties was to test fly the NORD 1402 Gerfaut I on 15 January 1954, in which he became the first European pilot to exceed the sound barrier in level flight on 3 August. This aircraft would later be modified to the Gerfaut 1B and be flown by Turcat supersonically in level flight on 11 February 1955.

Following on from the Gerfaut, he test-piloted the Griffon I on 16 February 1957 from Melun-Villaroche. This version of the Griffon was superseded by the Mk.II, which Turcat piloted supersonically using the built-in ramjet on 17 May. A further test flight of the Griffon Mk.II on 27 October 1958 was made at Mach 2.05, with a combination of the jet engine and ramjet. Andre Turcat set a world closed circuit record on 25 February 1959 for a maximum speed of 1,020mph (1,640km/h). This was followed by a ceremony on 11 December when he was awarded the International Harmon Trophy by Vice-President Nixon for service to aviation.

In 1962 Turcat joined Sud Aviation where he took part in the development flying of an autopilot system, using a Learjet and a Caravelle as testbeds. On 27 September 1962 Turcat, in company with co-pilot Max Fischl, made an automatic landing using the Caravelle testbed; this was followed by three further landings in zero visibility on 5 March 1963.

On 1 September 1964 he was named as Sud Aviation's Flight Test Director, being heavily involved from this time onwards with the development of Concorde, also known as the *Transporte Super Sonique* (TSS). Turcat was in command when the first prototype Concorde 001 made its maiden flight on 2 March 1969 in the presence of over 400 from the media, invited VIPs and an audience of millions. He was also in command on 30 June 1973 when an especially equipped Concorde outfitted for astronomical purposes carried seven scientists, following an eclipse of the sun for 74min over Mauritania.

Turcat retired in March 1976, although his involvement with Concorde was not completely over since in 1987 he was instrumental in a successful attempt to preserve the first Concorde 001 prototype from the scrap heap.

The French Concorde prototype F-WTSS, departing Le Bourget on a test flight.
C.P. Russell Smith Collection

This unusual angle of Concorde F-WTSS reveals clearly the subtle curves that define the ogee wing. The box-like objects on the outer wing are covers for the outboard PFCUs. BBA Collection

round!), made its maiden flight, although in this instance it was not without incident as the No.4 engine initially failed to light up correctly. After an engine restart the aircraft finally left the runway at Filton at 14:24 local time. The crew for this flight was Brian Trubshaw as chief test pilot, John Cochrane (co-pilot) and Brian Watts (flight engineer). Also on board acting in the role of observers were M.R. Addeley, J.C. Alland and P.A. Holding. As with the French prototype flight, the British prototype would

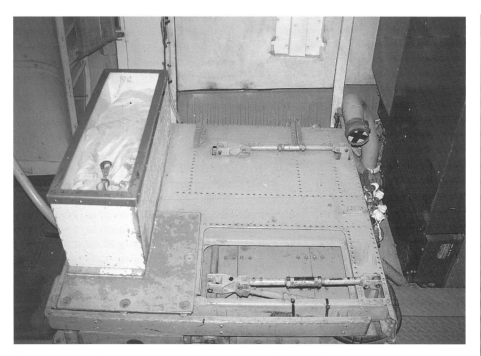

The internal face of the forward escape hatch in the prototype Concorde. Attached to the door is a rope ladder to assist in escape in an emergency. BBA Collection

Touchdown for the British Concorde prototype at Fairford after its maiden flight. The subtle blending of the wing and the prominent tail bumper is clearly shown. BBA Collection

Brian Trubshaw

Born on 29 January 1924, Ernest Brian Trubshaw was educated at Winchester before joining the RAF in 1942. His pilot training was undertaken in the USA where he trained on Boeing Stearman biplanes. After conversion training, Trubshaw joined Bomber Command in 1944 where he flew Stirlings and Lancasters. After a tour with the Command, he transfered to Transport Command. His flying skills were rated as exceptional, which led to his being transferred to the King's Flight in 1946.

After that, Trubshaw began teaching at the Empire Flying School and the RAF Flying College from 1949 to 1950. He was almost sent to Malaya as one of only two RAF pilots who also had helicopter experience. However, this move was cancelled and he was given permission to leave the RAF to become a test pilot for Vickers-Armstrongs, where he remained for 30 years, becoming chief test pilot in 1960 and Director of Test Flying from 1966. Trubshaw worked on the development of the Valiant V-bomber, the Vanguard civilian transport, the VC-10 and the BAC-111, all of which he test-flew. His coolness in saving Britain's prototype VC-10 from disaster on an early test flight won him the Derry and Richards Memorial Medal for 'outstanding test flying contributing to the advance of aviation' in 1965: structural failure had been threatened when an elevator section broke loose and the aircraft shook 'as though the tail was shaking the dog'. Due to the excessive vibration caused by the elevator failure, Trubshaw could not read the instruments, but broadcast the aircraft's behaviour back to base in case he could not return the aircraft to Weybridge; he then managed to land with only half the elevator control functioning. He later described this manoeuvre as 'one of my trickier moments'. Three years earlier Trubshaw had been awarded the same medal for his work in the early 1950s on the Valiant jet bomber, on which he tested the delivery system for Britain's first nuclear bomb, the 10,000lb (4,500kg) *Blue Danube*. In 1985, on the eve of his retirement, he revealed that, while flying a Valiant V-bomber, he had been compelled to drop a concrete replica of the weapon into the Thames estuary to save the aircraft from crashing.

Concorde was the aircraft that would propel Brian Trubshaw into the public eye when he first flew it in April 1969 from Filton to the test base at RAF Fairford. After the Concorde development programme he moved to become the divisional director and general manager of the Filton works of British Aerospace from 1980 to 1986. From 1986 to 1993 he was a member of the board of the Civil Aviation Authority and worked as an aviation consultant. He was awarded the OBE in 1964, the CBE in 1970 and the French Aeronautical Medal in 1976.

On 25 March 2001 Trubshaw died peacefully in his sleep at his home near Tetbury, Gloucestershire. Commenting upon the Concorde crash, he would say, 'I have never heard so much bloody rubbish in my life, Concorde is the safest aircraft I have flown.' Let that be his epitaph.

also make its maiden flight with its undercarriage down and locked. Only one other minor problem would plague this flight: a malfunction on both radio altimeters on the approach, although the landing was completed without further incident. As with

001, the British Concorde would use a tail brake parachute to slow the aircraft down.

Even though both prototype flight tests were the more reportable events for the aviation press, they were the culmination of many months of actual and theoretical trials. Design calculations, extensive computer analyses, wind-tunnel testing and simulator flying would provide the data needed to create Concorde. At least the pilots were spared the ordeal of learning to steer the aircraft by using a strange, modified road vehicle that had been employed during the de Havilland Comet programme. The final stage of these trials was the comprehensive series of flight tests that would eventually clear the aircraft for general usage. Even this stage was subject to the usual round of international wrangling. However, after many meetings an in-depth flight test schedule was hammered out which was acceptable to both BAC and Sud Aviation and their respective aviation authorities. This

RIGHT: **Concorde G-BSST generates the usual pollution as it lifts off from RAF Fairford. To allow for improved airflow and cooling the intake auxiliary doors are fully extended.** BBA Collection

BELOW: **An excited gathering of press, guests and officials watch as Concorde prototype G-BSST lands at Fairford at the completion of its maiden flight.** BBA Collection

schedule was divided into three distinct sections, although there were overlaps. The first would cover flight development and was followed by certification and endurance flying. The first phase was essentially aimed at developing the aircraft's complete flight envelope to ensure that Concorde would perform as predicted. Any problems identified during this sequence of flights would have to be rectified by modification before the whole regime was undergone once more during the certification process.

Flight Tests

The final agreement on the flight-test schedule was completed in January 1969 and covered some 1,935hr for development flying, 795 were allocated for certification flying and a further 1,500 were allocated for route proving and endurance flying. To cover these 4,230 flight-test hours it was established that seven aircraft were needed to complete the programme in a reasonable time. To cover this workload would require the use of both prototypes, the two preproduction aircraft and three of the early production aircraft. The plan was that supersonic flight would be achieved by mid 1969, with the Mach 2 point being slated for passing in early 1970. If all proceeded

LEFT: This dramatic nose-on shot of Concorde reveals the location of the nose chines and the complex shape of the wing. At the extreme nose end is a pitot head with a full range of sensors fitted. BBA Collection

BELOW: One of the safety precautions fitted to Concorde G-BSST was a tail chute to assist in braking. By the time the production aircraft were built this feature had been deleted. BBA Collection

With its nose partly lowered and the visor fully retracted, the British Concorde prototype lands at Fairford. Prominent on the fin are the fairings for the rudder PFCUs. BBA Collection

The primary escort for Concorde at the start and the end of its flights was this Canberra, on detachment from the Farnborough Aero Flight. BBA Collection

On the ground at Fairford are three prototype and preproduction Concorde airframes: on the left is 001, on the right is 002, in the centre is Concorde 01. BBA Collection

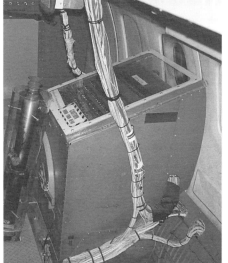

ABOVE: **Attached to a tug and surrounded by escorting vehicles, British Concorde prototype G-BSST is towed out for another test flight. Because it had been standing for a time, the flight control hydraulic pressures had dissipated allowing the surfaces to droop.** BBA Collection

ABOVE: **To allow for external airframe checks of the prototype Concorde a periscope was fitted. Note the cable looms around this installation.** BBA Collection

RIGHT: **On board Concorde 002 are Brian Trubshaw (chief British test pilot) on the right and Andre Turcat on the left. Note the Canberra chase aircraft in the background.** J.A. Todd Collection via Lee Howard

without incident, airline services were scheduled to being by the end of 1973. The reality would see supersonic speed being achieved by Concorde 001 on 1 October 1969 and Mach 2 achieved by the same aircraft on 4 November 1970. Unfortunately, the most vital area, that of airline sales, would have to endure delays as political and environmental issues came to the fore. The former were due to the British government, which had become openly hostile to the Concorde programme, while the latter was due to an American environmentalist and his supporters who began a vociferous campaign to stop Concorde flights into the USA and to New York in particular. Even now no one is precisely sure why this came about, especially as assurances had been given concerning noise and pollution outputs, although the aircraft industry was seen as the prime suspect. These enforced delays would mean that Concorde would not enter revenue-earning service until 1976, three years later than planned.

Although the British government was indulging in its usual interference, the execution of the flight-test schedule carried on apace even though Sud Aviation had been absorbed by Aerospatiale, along with Nord and SEREB, in January 1970. In France the flight-test schedule was under the jurisdiction of the test pilot Andre Turcat and in Britain Brian Trubshaw fulfilled the same role. Communication between the two and their staffs would ensure that there was no duplication of effort, and so the French team concentrated on developing the flight envelope and the British focused on the performance of Concorde, but even so there were areas where there were inevitable overlaps.

Not long after the Concorde flight-test programme had begun a few problems were identified. These concerned the variable geometry intakes and the slight flutter of the control surfaces. Many of these surfaced during the initial flights of prototype 01, F-WTSS; this aircraft and the British prototype started to give cause for concern since they were to different build standards than the following preproduction and production aircraft. Although the intakes and control surfaces were troublesome there had been good news since the drag coefficient of Concorde had been overestimated and thus the aircraft was able to travel faster with a reduced kinetic heat signature. Handling was also better than predicted, being

smoother throughout the entire speed range, while its behaviour after a simulated engine failure was also better than expected. Curing the flutter of the elevons was seen as paramount and therefore the gear ratio, initially set at 1:1 in pitch, was altered to 0:2 for the preproduction machines and again to 0.7:1 for production-build aircraft since 0:2 was seen as rather conservative, a result that had

been borne out by further flight testing. Another modification that was introduced into the flight control system was a stick shaker that became operative should the aircraft start to approach the stall. This addition had been seen as a necessary requirement since Concorde had a high sink rate and it was possible for the crew to overreact to correct this behaviour, which, in turn, could

The prototype Concorde was well equipped with communications equipment, as the contents of this rack reveal. Some were purely for contact use, other equipment was used for telemetry purposes. BBA Collection

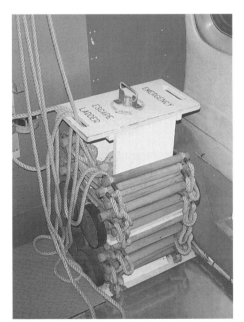

For such a hi-tech aircraft, some of the escape measures look decidedly primitive as this rope ladder by the escape hatch shows. BBA Collection

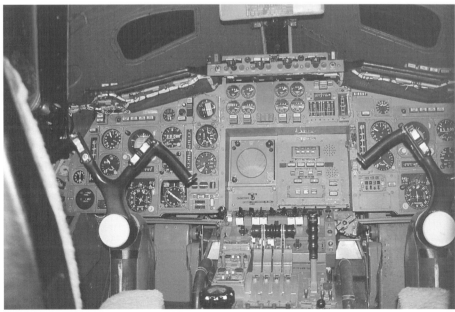

Unlike the production Concorde fleet, the pilot's panel on prototype G-BSST was comparatively bare since the number of engine gauges was kept to a minimum. The view is dominated by the moving map display. BBA Collection

ABOVE: Concorde prototype G-BSST is seen here with everything retracted including the visor. The numerous, differently coloured patches underneath the aircraft are clearly visible. BBA Collection

LEFT: Located in this rack are many of the black boxes containing navigational equipment. In the production airframes all these were replaced by three INS systems. BBA Collection

induce a stall. The stick shaker would come into play if an angle of attack of 17 degrees were reached, while at the 20 degree point the stick shaker would increase its output. Since this was quite violent it was impossible for the crew to ignore and therefore the only way to reduce the output required the crew to take action. To assist the crew in further handling Concorde, an auto-stabilization package was developed that was also integrated into the autopilot system.

With the elevon flutter trials under way, it was time to integrate the behaviour of the intakes and the flight-test schedule under several flight conditions. Running them side by side was seen as essential since incorrect interaction between the airframe and the nacelles could give rise to safety and economic issues. To induce flutter in the elevons three types of inducer were fitted: the first was an electrically driven stick exciter, while later a mechanical system was installed. A final exciter used with Concorde was the interestingly named 'bonkers'. These were small explosive charges that could be set off in sequence to induce a sudden deflection of the control surface; in this flight-test programme they were used during the transonic flight regime. All the activity generated during these flights was recorded on electromagnetic tape for later analysis on the ground.

During September 1970 a further series of test flights began. These concentrated on the effects of the sonic boom shock-wave on people and buildings and required fifty flights to be undertaken. These were flown along a route that later got the nick-

name of 'Boom Alley'. Using Concorde 002, each sortie departed Fairford before turning east; after this the aircraft turned north, accelerating all the time until the required speed was reached. At the northern tip of Scotland Concorde then turned southwards to pass down the west coast of

Britain at supersonic speed. Once abreast of Fairford, speed was reduced and the aircraft turned towards the airfield for landing. In all, these flights revealed that the general over-pressure levels were far lower than had been expected, although a few complaints about noise were received.

Brian Trubshaw photographed outside one of the prototype Concordes. BBA Collection

BOTTOM: **Photographed on the flight deck of the prototype Concorde are Brian Trubshaw (left) and Roy Radford (right).** BBA Collection

Up to this point in the flight-test programme neither of the prototypes had managed to break through the Mach 2 barrier. The first attempt to do so was undertaken on 4 November 1970 when Trubshaw aboard Concorde 002 pushed the throttles as far forward as they would go. Even as the SST accelerated, the speed run had to be aborted as a fire-warning light came on for No.2 engine, although this was be traced to a hot air gas leak. In contrast, the French prototype, airborne on a similar mission, would manage to pass through the barrier, with Turcat as pilot. The British team finally claimed success with their aircraft on 12 November.

By January 1971 the Concorde programme had achieved 100 supersonic test flights, although not without a few incidents. On 27 January Concorde 001 was airborne, undertaking deliberate power-plant surge testing in the Mach 2 region of the flight envelope. During a recycle of the reheat/augmenter system, the engine overspeed switch on No.3 engine malfunctioned, causing the Olympus to overspeed and surge. Since this was one of a pair, the next-door engine (No.4) also began to surge. Such were the forces induced by this reaction that the front ramp drive coupling failed, this being followed by the ramp tearing free, with parts entering the engine compressor faces and causing damage to both. Once the situation regarding the starboard engines had been stabilized, Concorde was turned towards Fairford, where a gentle landing was carried out. Inspection of the right-hand engine group and nacelle revealed that No.3 engine had suffered extensive damage, although the strength of the engine and the design of the nacelle assembly explosion blankets had ensured that the aircraft itself had suffered only minor damage.

As the aircraft was needed to continue the test programme, the engines and ramp control systems were quickly replaced while repairs were carried out to the airframe and nacelle; this would allow 001 to undertake its first intercontinental flight to Dakar in West Africa at the end of May

as part of the hot and high trials sequence. A successful completion of this segment would lead to a demonstration tour to South America in September. In contrast with the fortunes of 001, prototype 002 departed from Fairford in June 1972 for an extensive sales tour of the Middle and Far East plus a side trip to Australia. Support services were provided by the Royal Air Force since they had the only aircraft large enough to cover the logistics requirement. On both demonstration tours presentations were made to the interested parties from the airlines, who were treated to speeds of Mach 2 on a regular basis.

Although both Concorde prototypes had contributed extensively to the initial stages of the SST development programme, they were not representative of the preproduction nor production aircraft. In the light of this, it was decided to retire both aircraft from operational test flying. The first to shut down its engines for the last time was

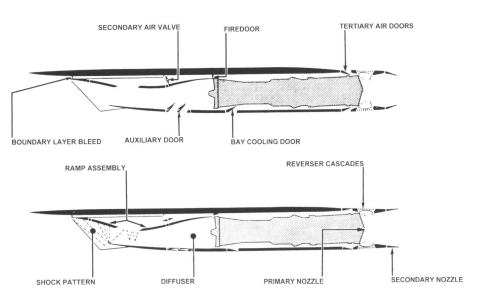

Diagram showing the two primary operating modes of the Olympus engine as fitted to Concorde. The upper illustrates the aircraft in low-speed flight, while the lower is the configuration for supersonic cruise. In both cases the ramps control the entry of air to the engines. BBA Collection

One of the extra escape routes in the prototype Concorde was this hatch at the rear of the cabin. This feature would have been incorporated in production machines as an air-stair, had the French medium-range design gone ahead. BBA Collection

With anti-FOD air intake guards in place, Concorde 002 has its wheels and tyres inspected. The leg fairing is fixed to the leg and thus moves with it. This view also shows the torque links between the main casting and the bogie.
J.A. Todd Collection via Lee Howard

DATA COMPARISON: PROTOTYPE AND PRODUCTION AIRCRAFT

PROTOTYPE

PRODUCTION

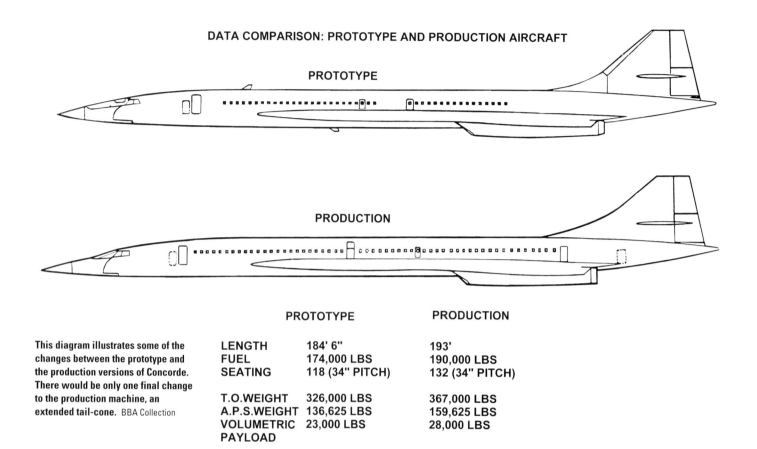

	PROTOTYPE	PRODUCTION
LENGTH	184' 6"	193'
FUEL	174,000 LBS	190,000 LBS
SEATING	118 (34" PITCH)	132 (34" PITCH)
T.O.WEIGHT	326,000 LBS	367,000 LBS
A.P.S.WEIGHT	136,625 LBS	159,625 LBS
VOLUMETRIC PAYLOAD	23,000 LBS	28,000 LBS

This diagram illustrates some of the changes between the prototype and the production versions of Concorde. There would be only one final change to the production machine, an extended tail-cone. BBA Collection

prototype 001, which was flown from Toulouse to the Musée de l'Air at Le Bourget by Turcat on 19 October 1973. During its short but significant career, the Concorde had flown just in excess of 812hr in 397 test flights. Within this sequence 254hr had been spent at Mach 1 or over. The second aircraft, prototype 002, was retired to the Fleet Air Arm Museum at Yeovilton, where it is displayed alongside the BAC 221, WG744. Throughout its career 002 had achieved 836 test flight hours, during which 438 sorties were flown of which 173 were spent in the supersonic regime. During its short career Concorde 002 suffered only one real scare in trials flying. This occurred in August 1974 when a fault developed with the left main undercarriage supports which had become detached from the main structure. Fortunately for both crew and aircraft, the undercarriage emergency blow-down system worked as advertised and thus the crew were able to execute a safe but difficult landing. Post-flight investigation of the mounting failure would lead to modifications being made to the undercarriage mountings on both prototypes and they were incorporated from the outset in the preproduction and production machines.

Enter the Preproduction Models

After the retirement of both prototypes the greater part of the types' trials work was shouldered by the preproduction Concordes 01 and 02. Their first task was to investigate a reported thrust drag discrepancy which had been noted on the prototypes and had recurred on both preproduction machines. Careful redesign by both the airframe and engine manufacturers eventually resolved this deficiency. The first airframe to have these changes applied was Concorde 02 which made its maiden flight on 10 January 1973, piloted by Brian Trubshaw and crew. The main changes to the airframe were applied to the wing, where the camber and the leading edge droop were altered, and the fuselage was lengthened by 11ft (3.4m) by the fitting of an extended tail-cone. Rolls-Royce and SNECMA had also made some changes to the Olympus reheat/thrust augmentation system, mainly concentrated on the secondary nozzle. At the end of the first sequence of test flights further modifications were necessary since the behaviour of the wings flexing in flight needed to be recalculated because the earlier improvements had

not completely removed the thrust drag discrepancy. Curing this problem required that the wingtip be redesigned, which, in turn, improved the behaviour of the wing. While the structural changes were being made, the opportunity to upgrade the engine management system was taken and the nacelles were further strengthened to protect the airframe from damage should there be a powerplant failure. These modifications were incorporated into the production Concordes from the outset, which would, in turn, allow for an extension of the type's performance limitations. The primary change was an increase in the permissible take-off weight from 400,000 to 408,000lb (182,000–185,500kg) and the available fuel was increased by 3,300lb (1,500kg). Performance would also be improved as the subsonic cruise figure was increased from 0.93 to 0.95, which reduced total fuel consumption by 1.3 per cent.

While BAC were concentrating on the development and construction of the Concorde airframe, their engine partners, Rolls-Royce, were applying themselves to bringing the Olympus engine up to speed. Originally developed by Bristol Engines at Filton, the Olympus made its first flight in a Canberra bomber testbed during 1952. In its original form the engine was rated at 11,000lb (49kN) dry thrust, although a series of steps saw the final unreheated version, the Mk.30101 ECU fitted in the Vulcan B.2 bomber, running at an output of 20,000lb (89kN). It was the development potential of this robust engine for use in the TSR2 strike aircraft that led to its selection for Concorde. The TSR2 engine, the Olympus Mk.22R was rated at 30,610lb (136kN) dry thrust and 33,000lb (147kN) reheated. Although this outstanding aircraft was cancelled through alleged extensive cost overruns and governmental decision, the principle of the reheated Olympus engine had been successfully established. Given this success, it was no surprise that the company chose this engine for Concorde. Bristol, later Rolls-Royce, initially constructed some Olympus 22R and 301 powerplants for use in full-scale development tests, these being followed by the Olympus 593 engines. Once the 593 had undertaken its full development programme, both companies were required to supply engines, jet pipes, convergent-divergent nozzles plus all the required spares and tools.

At the beginning of the Concorde programme the powerplant project leader, Bristol Engines, were joined by the French manufacturer SNECMA. This company was given the responsibility for the design and development of the thrust augmentation or reheat system and the variable nozzle system. While SNECMA were concentrating on the extras, Bristol Engines were concentrating on redesigning the Olympus engines to withstand higher operating temperatures and an increased thrust output. The major change was to the compressor stage, where a stage was removed from the high pressure fan while another was added to the low

pressure stage. This would allow the pressure ratio to remain at 12:1 but increase the mass air flow into the engine. Other modifications were made to the powerplant cooling layout, which were needed to compensate for the increased operating temperature. All these modifications resulted in the appearance of the Olympus 593D, which was intended as the development standard engine. Only two of these powerplants were constructed for ground testing, the first would have a thrust output rated at 28,100lb (125kN) while the second engine

was rated with a slightly higher thrust output. When Concorde underwent its airframe redesign a similar exercise was undertaken by Bristol Engines which resulted in the appearance of the Olympus 593B, dimensionally slightly larger all round. This increase in size led to an extra gain in dry thrust output which was increased to 32,000lb (142kN), and thrust augmentation output with limited reheat was increased to 35,000lb (156kN). Initial design contracts were granted in 1962 and called for the provision of engines for the

The crew seats in the development Concordes were part of the airframe, unlike those in the Tu-144 which were ejectable. Note the mic-tel and oxygen connectors clearly visible on the engineer's seat.
Helio Coelho

BELOW: The aborted BAC TSR.2 provided one important element to the Concorde programme: the reheated Olympus engine.
BBA Collection

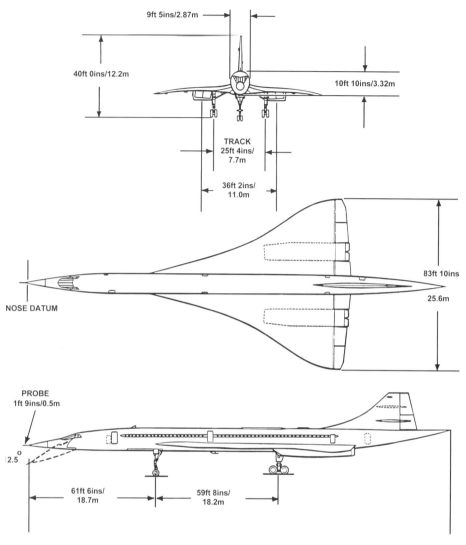

9ft 5ins/2.87m

40ft 0ins/12.2m

10ft 10ins./3.32m

TRACK
25ft 4ins/
7.7m

36ft 2ins/
11.0m

83ft 10ins

25.6m

NOSE DATUM

PROBE
1ft 9ins/0.5m

2.5°

61ft 6ins/
18.7m

59ft 8ins/
18.2m

In common with most aircraft, Concorde had a general arrangement diagram issued that displayed its main dimensions. In this case both imperial and metric measurements were used, illustrating a then current difference between Britain and France. BBA Collection

BOTTOM: This artist's impression shows Concorde in BOAC livery, a finish it would never wear since BA was the operator when it finally went into service. BBA Collection

first prototype in January 1966, with flight clearance tests being completed in June. Type testing of the engine was to take 150hr and be completed by June 1967 and flight certification trials were scheduled for completion by December 1969. The costs of engine development were based on the requirement for the design and development phase which included the Olympus 22R and 301 engines, twenty Olympus 593 engines for testing and flight trials usage, plus thirty-six Olympus 593 engines intended to be retrofitted to the prototypes, the preproduction aircraft and the first two production standard machines. The cost estimates also included spares, overhauls, estimated at every 4,000 flight hours, and tooling to produce the Olympus 593 series. However, in a gesture of parsimony, the estimates did not include any funding for the building of much-needed test facilities.

To ensure that the Olympus engine was safe for operations under all flight conditions, it was extensively tested. The aircraft chosen to act as the airborne testbed was the heavily modified Vulcan B.1, XA903. The first flight of the Concorde Olympus engine was undertaken on 9 September 1966, with clearance for Mach 1.6 being obtained in a preproduction Concorde in 1968. When the first Concorde prototype flew it was powered by series Dash 3B powerplants rated at 34,370lb (153kN) each. When the preproduction Concorde began test flying, the powerplant fitted was the Dash 4 engine, which had a rated thrust output of 35,080lb (156kN). When the production aircraft began to appear each was powered by the Olympus 593 Mk.610-14-28, each being rated at 31,350lb (140kN), plus the availability of reheat which lifted the final output to 38,050lb (169kN). Given that the small Concorde fleet spent much of its time flying at supersonic speeds it is estimated that the total of such hours flown comfortably exceeds the supersonic experience of all the world's air forces.

CHAPTER THREE

Skin and Bones

Concorde, from a technical point of view, was a subtle blend of cutting-edge technology and tried and tested technology. As the aircraft progressed through the development process, the British- and the French-built machines were close to identical; only in the passenger cabin and additions to the on-board systems would there be any recognizable, cosmetic differences. The design engineers were faced with many new challenges, not the least of which was creating an advanced supersonic transport that was complex in the extreme. The problem, of course, with complexity is that it in turn

drives costs up, which gave the design team something else to cope with. Beyond the complexity of the proposed systems the designers were also faced with another problem of supersonic flight: the low payload in relation to the overall weight of the aircraft. In the case of Concorde only 6 per cent would be available for any kind of payload, a stark contrast to the proportion in a subsonic, wide-body aircraft which hovers around the 20 per cent point. This meant that any growth in the weight of the airframe would eat into the available payload. However, careful management of the

programme would mean that any growth in weight was kept in ratio with available payload and engine power.

Testing the Airframe

From a structural point of view the Concorde airframe is fairly conventional. The chosen material used was an aluminium alloy, referred to in its 1967 patent application as Hiduminium RR58. This particular alloy had the ability to compensate for overageing and alloy creep, both of which

Coming close to completion and on its undercarriage, Concorde preproduction airframe 002 was photographed at Filton. Note the numerous access panels in the upper wing; these proved useful when it was necessary to modify the production airframes after the Paris crash. J.A. Todd Collection via Lee Howard

may cause weakening at the atomic level and possible failure of the structure. Extensive testing of this alloy showed that RR58 had high resistance to stress creep, thermal cycles and fatigue loading, from both normal flying and thermal loading. The cost of developing this alloy for use in Concorde eventually cost about £2 million, a far cheaper option than the £200 million that was estimated for a titanium structure. The in-depth trials on the alloy revealed that it should have a thermal lifetime of some 20,000hr. Fatigue loading tests were essential in proving the structural strength and safety of Concorde and therefore major sections of it were subjected to extensive failsafe tests. The loading applied to each section pushed each assembly to its limits, even as far as causing cracks and determining how much residual strength remained. The undercarriage also underwent rigorous testing that included static, drop and fatigue tests. The culmination of all these sub-assembly fatigue trials was the testing of two complete airframes for certification purposes. The full-scale static loading test was carried out at the Centre d'Essais Aéronautique de Toulouse (CEAT) on the third airframe, while the full-scale fatigue trial was undertaken at RAE Farnborough on the sixth one. The airframe at Toulouse was assembled between May 1968 and March 1969 and covered a two-part static test programme, the first covered the nominal take-off weight of 385,000lb (175,000kg) while the second stanza increased the all-up weight to 400,000lb (182,000kg). It should be noted that the airframe used in these trials was the third preproduction airframe, but all the tests were applicable to a production machine. Fuselage-pressurization differential trials placed the cabin structure under twice the normal expected load, these being followed by cold soak trials to simulate the most severe conditions of flight. During these trials the aircraft would simulate take-off, landing, steady under power climb outs and low supersonic

speeds, all of which placed their own stress loads on parts of the airframe. Possibly one of the most potentially destructive trials was the limit load; this was the greatest possible load ever experienced by an airframe in its life and Concorde needed to pass this without the airframe showing any signs of deformation. Having survived this test, certain parts of the aircraft were subjected to a test deemed the ultimate load trial. Under these conditions the stress factor was increased to 1.5 times the previous limit load. This was the only trial where deformation and cracks were allowed, although total failure of the airframe was not allowed.

Once the bending, stretching and cold trials had been completed, the test airframe was subjected to tests of its behaviour under hot conditions. To create these, the airframe was blanketed by heat from infra-red heaters, while the structure was put under various stress loads by means of 60-ton hydraulic jacks. As before, the full range of a flight was simulated as closely as possible from take-off to landing and included the behaviour of the structure as the aircraft slowed down. During all these tests any failures were repaired in the sub-assemblies before being applied to the main trials specimen. Once the airframe modifications had been proved, they were applied to the drawings destined for the production machines. The trial period at CEAT in Toulouse lasted from August 1969 to June 1973, after which time Concorde was certified for flight.

At RAE Farnborough they were faced with creating a sequence of tests to simulate the fatigue stresses generated by everyday flight. Once test specimen four had been assembled, a series of trials was begun to establish the temperature profiles that would be experienced by Concorde during flight. It was soon discovered that the temperature range would dip soon after take-off, this being followed by a rise to a steady plateau. Once Concorde dropped out of the intended cruise speed, the skin temperature would descend below zero before rising again. Internally, the airframe structure would follow a similar pattern, although the temperature changes were smoother. To simulate this at a faster rate than the actual airborne fleet would experience, Farnborough subjected the test specimen to temperatures outside the expected range. When each of these simulated flights was undertaken the cruise phase was shortened while the climb and the landing phase were subject to increased heating and cooling, as appropriate. Given these radical extremes,

each simulated flight was classified as two supersonic flights. The test specimen was housed in a specially constructed rig at the RAE facility at Ball Hill, home of the Structures Department, that totally encompassed the airframe. This monstrous creation could not only put the test airframe under mechanical stress, but was also capable of fully simulating all the possible temperatures that Concorde might experience.

Although Concorde was a technical marvel, the Farnborough test rig was also a great technological achievement, not only as hardware, but in developing software to control the whole ensemble. The rig was large enough to cope with the Concorde airframe, which weighed 80 tons (82 tonnes) plus a simulated fuel load of 40 tons (41 tonnes), leaving only the wingtips and the tip of the tailplane exposed. As these portions were slim in section it was thought that they were too thin to be significantly affected by thermal fatigue. The remainder of the aircraft was surrounded by heating ducts and supported by numerous hydraulic jacks used for load simulation. To create the required temperature ranges two plant houses were constructed, these fed their output into the ducting. Heating the air was managed via heat exchangers that drew their charge from superheated, pressurized water maintained at 180°C. The same matrices were used to provide the initial cooling part of the process, although in this instance chilled water was used. To drive the temperature down below zero liquid ammonia was the preferred medium. The fuel was simulated by a simulant oil, which was preferred for safety reasons to the real thing. The reason for this simulation was that in the real Concorde the fuel load was needed as a heat sink, therefore to leave this component out would have produced inaccurate fatigue data. To control this mass of machinery bespoke software needed to be developed for the computer complex. This computer system was also responsible for managing and monitoring the test conditions, plus recording and analysing the data generated during each test run. These thousands of individual inputs covered temperature, stress, strain and deflection.

The British trials began at Farnborough in August 1973 and covered the heat and mechanical fatigue tests. During the first years of operation the rig and airframe simulated approximately 17,500 flights, although each would be only some 2.5hr in

The torture machine designed to simulate hours of flying on a static test airframe. As well as the usual selection of hydraulic jacks to simulate loading in flight, the rig used high-pressure air for more accurate simulation. The rig was also capable of simulating extremes of temperature. BBA Collection

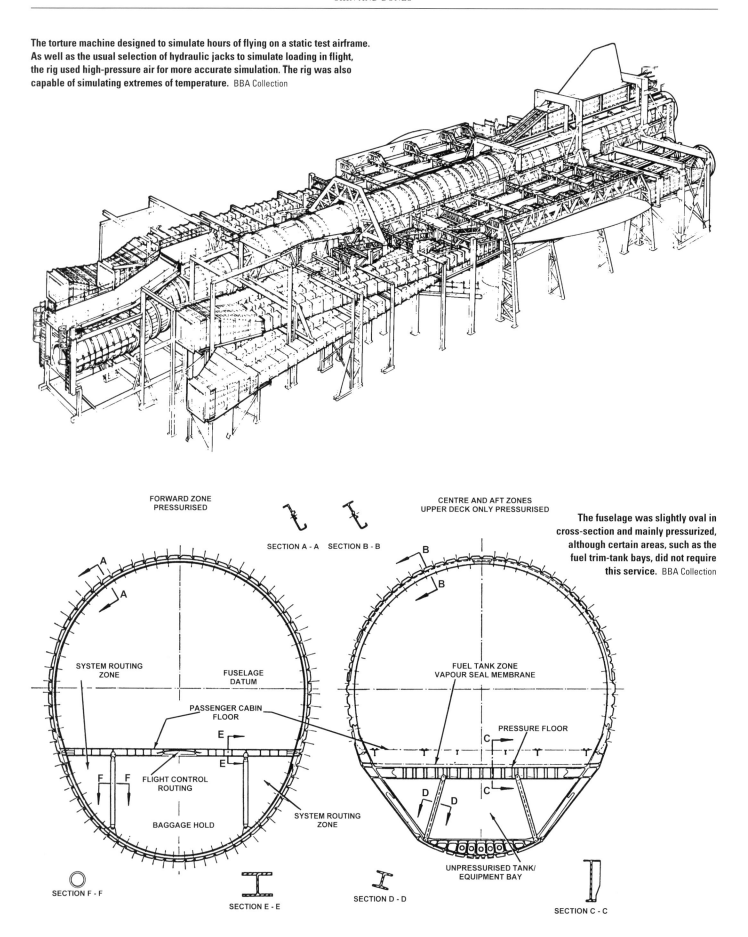

FORWARD ZONE
PRESSURISED

SECTION A - A   SECTION B - B

CENTRE AND AFT ZONES
UPPER DECK ONLY PRESSURISED

The fuselage was slightly oval in cross-section and mainly pressurized, although certain areas, such as the fuel trim-tank bays, did not require this service. BBA Collection

A
A

SYSTEM ROUTING
ZONE

FUSELAGE
DATUM

PASSENGER CABIN
FLOOR

E

E

F   F   FLIGHT CONTROL
ROUTING

BAGGAGE HOLD

SYSTEM ROUTING
ZONE

SECTION F - F

SECTION E - E

B

B

FUEL TANK ZONE
VAPOUR SEAL MEMBRANE

PRESSURE FLOOR

C

C

D   D

UNPRESSURISED TANK/
EQUIPMENT BAY

SECTION D - D

SECTION C - C

duration, but even so a total of 44,000hr were accumulated. A hiatus of nearly a year followed while the rig underwent a much needed overhaul and the airframe was thoroughly inspected. It was during this inspection that cracks were discovered in the lower booms of the wing spars and therefore a programme of inspections and modifications was put into place to monitor the situation continually for those aircraft already in service. Although the cracking in the spars gave some slight cause for concern, the rig had come close to proving in the 6 years of its operation that the required designed fatigue life of 45,000hr covering 24,000 flights was more than achievable. As safety was always a major consideration in the SST programme, it had been intended to run both test rigs to double the expected life of the service machines at a factor of 3:1. This last figure had been chosen as the ideal to cover any possible variations in Concorde's usage. However, the utilization of the operational Concorde fleet was, in reality, much lower than expected; in early 1981 the fleet leader had made only 2,200 flights. Since running the fatigue rigs was

expensive, it was proposed that both be shut down by 1984. The decision was finally approved in 1981, the accrued savings annually being estimated at £63 million. From 1981 until the end, testing was concentrated on those sections of the airframe that were considered to have been under-tested during the original regimen. Even these trials eventually ended in 1983 at which point some 21,000 flight cycles had been performed, representing nearly 6,700 real flights that included significant supersonic time. Once the RAE part of the programme ended, the responsibility for testing and support for in-service Concordes devolved in April 1984 to British Airways and Air France.

The pressurized fuselage, originally circular but changed to an oval section for the production machines, consisted of fabricated, machined, alloy frames pitched at a distance of 21.5in (54.6cm), these being held in position by extruded alloy stringers and load-bearing longerons, all of which were clad in an stressed alloy skin, much of it chemically machined. At each end of the pressure cabin was a pressure bulkhead out-

side of which were the unpressurized nose and tail-cone assemblies. Although it seemed to be one complete assembly, the fuselage was actually manufactured in five distinct sections, these consisting of the nose and the forward, the intermediate, the centre and the rear group. Inset into these sections was a single row of windows that ran down each side of the passenger cabin. Each window assembly was multilayered and comprised a load-bearing panel married to a thermal insulation panel. In turn, each window was mounted into a frame individually machined from an aluminium ingot. To allow for fuselage expansion and contraction, the window, in its frame, was not rigidly fixed to the airframe but could move in response to the thermal loads placed upon the structure. Not only did this deal with the thermal loading, it also reduced the possibility of structural failure due to localized stress-overloading of the fuselage. A similar idea on a grander scale was applied to the cabin floor which floated on load bearers and would allow the fuselage to act as a separate entity in periods when thermal stresses were placed on the fuselage.

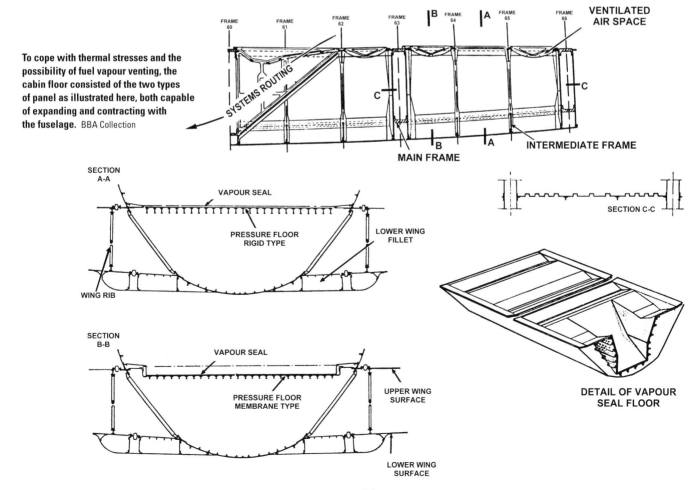

To cope with thermal stresses and the possibility of fuel vapour venting, the cabin floor consisted of the two types of panel as illustrated here, both capable of expanding and contracting with the fuselage. BBA Collection

The Wing

Bolted under the fuselage was the cantilever wing which was ogee in planform and based on a slender delta with slight anhedral and varied camber on the leading edge. Structurally the wing was a multi-spar assembly with many interspar ribs for structural strength. Internally the wing was skinned with stretched aluminium alloy panels

OPPOSITE: **Mounted in its jig, a Concorde frame is being prepared for assembly. Note the use of English and French on the jig frame.**
Bristol Aero Collection

RIGHT: **The assemblies at Filton in this photograph would soon be rolled out as the first prototype.**
Bristol Aero Collection

BELOW: **The structure of the Concorde wing was more complicated than that needed for a subsonic aircraft and gave the aircraft great strength.** BBA Collection

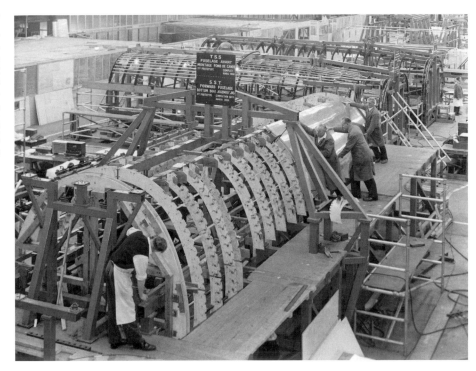

RIB 23 BETWEEN SPAR POINTS 63-66

63   66   A

PIN JOINTED STRUTS

MACHINED EXTRUSION

SECTION A-A

RIB 14 BETWEEN SPAR POINTS 60-63

60   B   63

CLEAT CLIPS   GUSSET PLATES

SECTION B-B

RIB 8 BETWEEN SPAR POINTS 69-72

69   C   72

MACHINED WEB

SECTION C-C

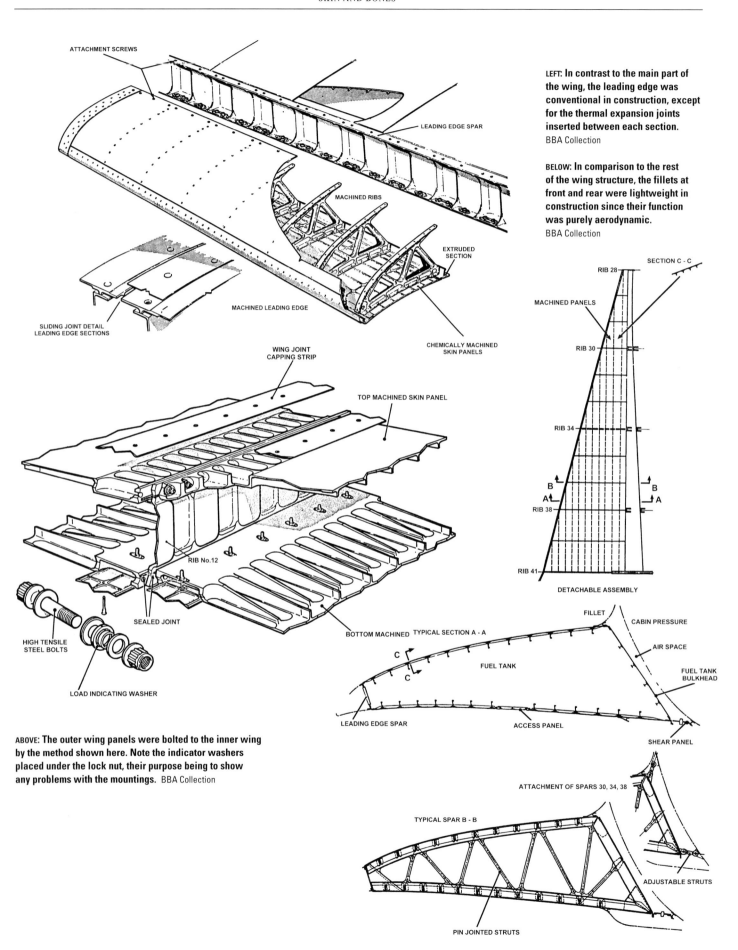

ATTACHMENT SCREWS

LEADING EDGE SPAR

MACHINED RIBS

EXTRUDED SECTION

MACHINED LEADING EDGE

SLIDING JOINT DETAIL
LEADING EDGE SECTIONS

CHEMICALLY MACHINED
SKIN PANELS

LEFT: In contrast to the main part of
the wing, the leading edge was
conventional in construction, except
for the thermal expansion joints
inserted between each section.
BBA Collection

BELOW: In comparison to the rest
of the wing structure, the fillets at
front and rear were lightweight in
construction since their function
was purely aerodynamic.
BBA Collection

WING JOINT
CAPPING STRIP

TOP MACHINED SKIN PANEL

RIB No.12

SEALED JOINT

HIGH TENSILE
STEEL BOLTS

LOAD INDICATING WASHER

BOTTOM MACHINED

ABOVE: The outer wing panels were bolted to the inner wing
by the method shown here. Note the indicator washers
placed under the lock nut, their purpose being to show
any problems with the mountings. BBA Collection

SECTION C - C

RIB 28

MACHINED PANELS

RIB 30

RIB 34

B

A

RIB 38

RIB 41

DETACHABLE ASSEMBLY

FILLET

CABIN PRESSURE

AIR SPACE

TYPICAL SECTION A - A

FUEL TANK

FUEL TANK
BULKHEAD

C

LEADING EDGE SPAR

ACCESS PANEL

SHEAR PANEL

ATTACHMENT OF SPARS 30, 34, 38

TYPICAL SPAR B - B

ADJUSTABLE STRUTS

PIN JOINTED STRUTS

manufactured from single alloy billets. The wing spars were continuous across the fuselage, the whole wing being regarded as one assembly that reached from one engine nacelle to the other. The forward wing sections were built as separate entities attached to each side of the fuselage. At the trailing edge of each mainplane were three separate elevon sections which were primarily manufactured from steel and mounted on the airframe with bearings through which were fitted close-tolerance mounting bolts. To gain access to the parts of the airframe for maintenance purposes, Concorde was liberally designed with removable panels. Many of these were chemically-manufactured, stressed items with a series of alloy strengtheners to spread the load and maintain the shape of the panel. Externally, the whole airframe was clad in chemically-machined skins with cut-outs for the access panels, each being reinforced with alloy landings. Above the fuselage were the fin and rudder sections which consisted of similar multi-spar assemblies and, in the case of the fin, acted as a torsion box to give greater strength to the whole. Mounted on the forward face of the fin were the dorsal fin and leading edge panels, while the trailing edge provided mountings for the rudder-powered flying control units (PFCUs) and the control surfaces themselves. The rudder was a two-part light alloy structure whose primary structural member was a single spar to which was attached the strengthening and shaping ribs, all covered by alloy skinning.

The Nose

Unique features of the Concorde design are the retractable visor and the drooping nose developed to give greater visibility during the landing and take-off phases. The droop nose consists of a single structure hinged at its lower edge and raised and lowered by hydraulic jacks. The subcontractor for this assembly was Marshalls of Cambridge, who originally began work on the jigs to construct a circular-shaped structure only to find that they had to redo the whole job for a more oval-shaped nose-cone. Protecting the main windshield assembly was a retractable visor whose purpose was to divert kinetic heat away from the inner screens and provide a more aerodynamic shape to the nose. In the prototype aircraft the visor area of visibility was quite limited, however, the production aircraft were built with visors with panels greater in area, thus improving the available area of vision. In the fully-up position, the nose and visor gave Concorde an extremely clean aerodynamic shape. To maintain both components in this position the hydraulic jacks moved both items simultaneously to the correct position where mechanical locks engaged to spread the load and hold them in place. In the down position the nose and visor were held in place through hydraulic pressure and counterbalance springs.

Nacelles, Engines and Intakes

At first glance the engine nacelles might look as if they were integral to the airframe; they were, in fact, manufactured as separate assemblies. Contained within each box-like structure was a pair of Rolls-Royce Olympus 593 engines. Each nacelle was built from two sub-assemblies, one consisting of the engine bays and the other the air-intake structures. To the rear of the engine bays was an extension that housed the secondary variable nozzles, these being mainly constructed from steel and alu-

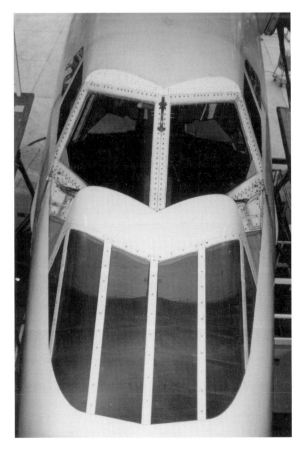

ABOVE: **This view of the nose-cone in the fully raised position shows the location of the pitot probe (when this was taken the airframe completely lacked all paint work).** Adrian Falconer

LEFT: **Ensconced in the Filton nose dock, this Concorde has its visor retracted. Note the difference between the visor and the main flight-deck windscreens. This was due to the gold film heating elements embedded in individual screens.** Adrian Falconer

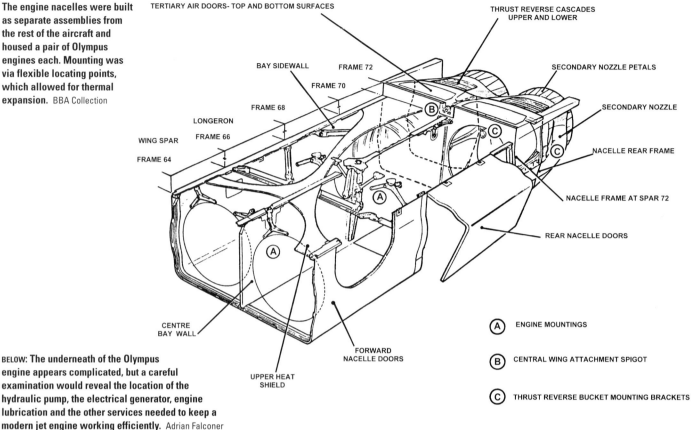

The engine nacelles were built as separate assemblies from the rest of the aircraft and housed a pair of Olympus engines each. Mounting was via flexible locating points, which allowed for thermal expansion. BBA Collection

TERTIARY AIR DOORS- TOP AND BOTTOM SURFACES

THRUST REVERSE CASCADES
UPPER AND LOWER

BAY SIDEWALL

FRAME 72

FRAME 70

SECONDARY NOZZLE PETALS

FRAME 68

SECONDARY NOZZLE

LONGERON

FRAME 66

WING SPAR

FRAME 64

NACELLE REAR FRAME

NACELLE FRAME AT SPAR 72

REAR NACELLE DOORS

CENTRE
BAY WALL

FORWARD
NACELLE DOORS

UPPER HEAT
SHIELD

(A) ENGINE MOUNTINGS

(B) CENTRAL WING ATTACHMENT SPIGOT

(C) THRUST REVERSE BUCKET MOUNTING BRACKETS

BELOW: The underneath of the Olympus engine appears complicated, but a careful examination would reveal the location of the hydraulic pump, the electrical generator, engine lubrication and the other services needed to keep a modern jet engine working efficiently. Adrian Falconer

minium. In contrast, the intake assemblies were mainly of aluminium construction, although the leading edges were of stainless steel to protect them from erosion and heat damage. The nacelle box itself was mainly of steel honeycomb construction,

this including the integral engine-bay dividing wall. At the rear of the nacelle much of the structure was of steel sheet for greater strength. The mounting of this combined intake, nacelle and exhaust assembly was achieved by using mounting pins with

flexible joints and deformable seals located between the nacelle and the underwing skin to maintain airflow integrity.

The version of the Olympus turbojet installed on Concorde was a twin-spool engine where the low- and the high-pressure compressors are driven by separate turbines. Controlling the engine to give its best performance was the responsibility of three separate processes. The first concerned the intake ramps which were automatically adjusted to provide the greatest air mass to the compressor face. In the subsonic part of the flight envelope the ramps are in the fully open position, although as speed increases the ramps progressively close. The throttle lever was the second engine control, which exerted great influence on the management of the powerplant. Its task was to govern the rate of fuel flow into the combusters. This, in turn, limited the speed, also known as N2, of the high pressure turbine driving the high-pressure compressor. The other parameter, sometimes known as N1, governed the rotation speed of the low pressure turbine and hence the low pressure compressor by varying the primary convergent-divergent nozzle. This, in turn, matched the N2 figure and the flight conditions, hence N1 was the primary sensed parameter that

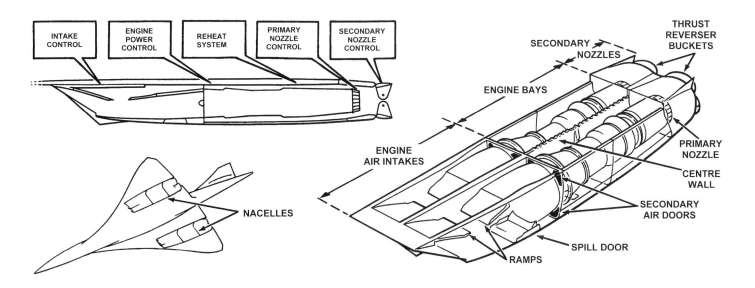

ABOVE: The engine nacelles were divided into zones, as shown here. This not only helped during maintenance but assisted in the containment and suppression of fire. BBA Collection

RIGHT: The rear end-on view of some of the business part of Concorde. The inboard elevon has its access cover missing and the engine-bay doors are open for inspection.
Adrian Falconer

BELOW: The position of the intake ramp was dependent on the speed of the aircraft as set against any external data inputs, although there was a limit system to protect the engine from incorrect system commands. BBA Collection

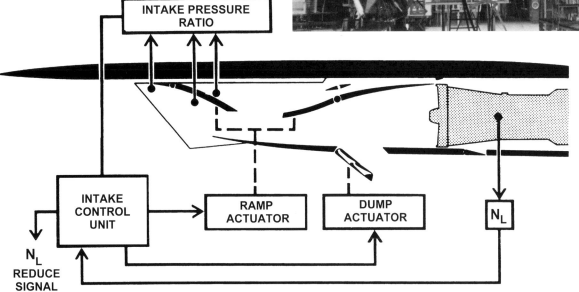

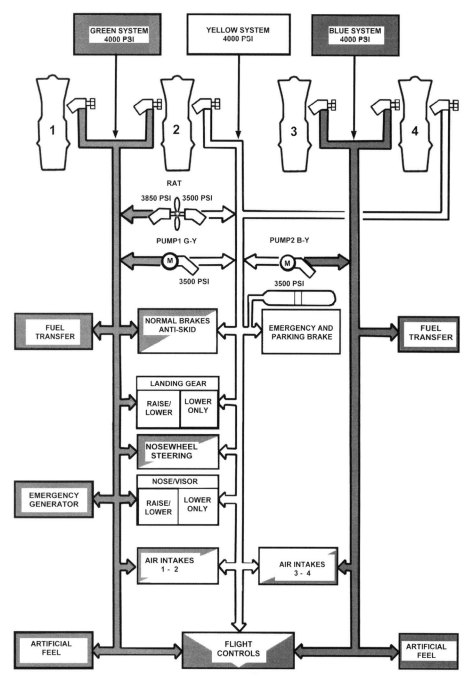

This diagram illustrates Concorde's hydraulic system, showing items operated by each colour, their points of interaction and the location of the ram air turbine (RAT), available for use in an emergency. BBA Collection

The Concorde engine-control system was designed to operate in a wide variety of temperatures, therefore the control surfaces were driven by hydraulics while the actual function of the system was computer-driven. The bonus with this kind of control was that any changes required to the parameters of the flight-control system could be quickly engineered in software and flight-tested almost immediately. In fact, the normal sequence would be to define the requirements, rework the software overnight and refly the changes next day. A similar analogue system was used to control the engines, although at least one sequence of test flights was undertaken using an experimental digital-control system; however, this was not accepted for general use even though there were few reported problems with it. From the pilot's point of view, the engine-control system was highly automated and therefore he used a mode selector to define engine behaviour, and to give a degree of flexibility the engines had separate switches. Selectable modes included: take-off, climb, transonic acceleration and cruise. This degree of automation meant that, theoretically, the pilot could place the throttle fully forward, press the start button and let the powerplant move through the complete sequence to ground idle revs, then accelerate to take-off power. In reality, moving Concorde required an output just above idle to taxi the aircraft to the runway. At this point a retardation to idle power was needed to comply with noise abatement regulations. Since these need to be followed rigorously, the use of the engine modes was negated; however, once airborne the interlinks to the sophisticated autopilot came into play. The settings of the Mach and altitude locks meant that the throttle responded to commands from the autopilot, as did the intake ramps. Since these systems were fully automated, the normal role for the flight engineer was that of monitoring; however, should a fault occur the engineer had the facility to assume manual control.

From the point of view of flight and engine management Concorde was a well-rounded product. It was in regard to the payload where there was always some concern since the aircraft's ability as a transatlantic transport was marginal at best. To illustrate this point, 1,000lb (455kg) of payload consumed 1per cent of the fuel load; this meant that shaving the structure down to its bare minimum would give only a potential diversion fuel load of between 5 and 10 per cent. This concern to create a fuel safety margin

ensured that the intake ramp was at the right position to allow the correct mass of air to enter the engine.

Having matched the engines and intakes, other systems came into play when thrust augmentation or reheat was selected, since the convergent-divergent nozzle had to match the operating parameters of the

engine at the time of selection. These nozzles had different operating modes, they were slightly convergent at take-off, while in supersonic cruise mode they are described as convergent-divergent to give the best rate of expansion efficiency, and the final mode saw the thrust reverser buckets fully closed to provide thrust reversal on landing.

meant that development costs were driven up since no compromise on safety could be allowed. Furthermore, should the safety margin drop to below the 5 per cent level, Concorde would cease to be a safe transatlantic aircraft. During the development process both the prototype and the pre-production machines were subject to many aerodynamic, tolerance and clearance checks which would eventually lead to the Olympus 593 being seen as the most thermodynamically efficient engine ever developed in its class.

To get Concorde to this stage required the development of numerous test rigs, many associated with engine/intake interaction, which was of primary importance. Initially, wind-tunnel testing at various speeds was used to determine the air pressure and velocity flow patterns. Having determined the theoretical layout of the engine/intake interface in the small scale, the next stage was to develop a full-scale mock-up that was

also subjected to similar trials. Once these had been completed an actual intake and engine were tested under simulated ground conditions. To give the same series of tests under airborne conditions the test facility at the National Gas Turbine Establishment at Pyestock was used. Having successfully completed this test series an engine installed in a part nacelle was tested under Vulcan B.1 XA903.

Having proved that the Olympus engine was capable of generating the power required, the whole assembly was then redesigned to allow for ground maintenance since in its original form the powerplant needed to be removed to change a defective component. Also incorporated into the Olympus engine were modifications that allowed for internal inspections while it was still installed in the aircraft. Another development was the application of the magnetic plug system, designed to collect minute particles of ferrous metals which

would indicate a potential bearing failure. Early in the development programme one of the main identified problems was that of the drive shafts' breaking. As the Olympus was a high-speed engine operating in a high-speed environment, such a failure would be disastrous as the turbine and compressor sections would run out of control. As always the solution was fairly simple. Initial investigations on a test-bench engine revealed that there was a temperature difference between the hot top of the engine and the cooler, lower section. This imbalance in heat distribution was the primary cause of driveshaft breakage which was cured by including a slow rotation capability in the engine relight sequence.

The materials used in the Concorde engines would also require expensive development work as new or modified alloys needed to be tried to handle the heat generated. Unlike the standard civil aircraft whose intake temperature hovers around

When a Concorde underwent a major overhaul it was thoroughly stripped in this purpose-built access dock.
Adrian Falconer

Doors

To gain access to Concorde there were six doors, three per side, which allowed the crew, passengers and airline services to enter. Two were designated as passenger doors and the other four as service doors. Other access doors in the lower fuselage gave entry to the upper and the lower baggage and freight hold and allowed ground maintenance personnel to gain access to the aircraft's services. The passenger doors were of the plug type and located on the left-hand side of the fuselage at the front and the mid-point of the cabin and opened outwards. As would be expected, both doors could be opened from the inside and the outside, although they were isolated from inadvertent opening when airborne. The four designated cabin access doors were operated and controlled in a similar manner and all six could be used for emergency egress should the need arise.

Flight Deck and Flight Control

Between the front pressure bulkhead and the forward intermediate bulkhead was the flight deck with accommodation for three crew and an observer, although the prototype had provision for a navigator. The three regular crew for a Concorde were the captain, co-pilot and flight engineer, all provided with individual oxygen and communications equipment. The crew and passengers aboard Concorde used oxygen for emergency breathing, although the crew could select theirs when required, while in the passenger cabin it was either controlled by a detected change in cabin pressure or by the crew's selecting it for deployment. Facing the two pilots were the main instrument panels which contained the usual instruments and switches and a central, shared panel held the engine-monitoring instruments. The roof panel, located above the glare shield, contained the autopilot, VOR/ILS frequency selector and the flight-director autothrottle mode selector. Also on this panel were controls and switches for the external lighting, navigation and landing, de-icing, de-misting, PFCU inverters, autostabilizers, auto trim, artificial feel and engine shut down. Because room in the cockpit was limited, this overhead panel had to be installed in stepped groups, with a final, flat panel to the rear. Accessible to all crew members, this panel had the throttle system switches, high-pressure control

In the process of being fitted out, this engineer's panel shows its complicated layout, with instruments and switches grouped according to role. Bristol Aero Collection

50°C, that of Concorde is nearly three times higher, and even the so-called cooling air for the turbine is proportionally hotter. Having developed the required metallurgy it was the turn of specialist lubricant manufacturers to apply their skills; not only did the oils and greases need to consistently perform under normal operating temperatures, they also had to retain their capabilities and viscosity for the next time.

Nacelle design was also unusual in that the four were different in layout. This was due to the fact that the intakes were toed-in slightly, and that in front of each intake

the wing profile was different. This, in turn, meant that the airflow entry path into each intake was different and therefore a central intake control system was developed that allowed each intake ramp to respond to the requirements of each engine, thus ensuring a smooth flow of balanced air to each powerplant. At the other end of the engine was the convergent-divergent nozzle. This too brought its own problems; however, careful design would ensure that the intake, engine and nozzle would operate efficiently throughout the whole flight envelope.

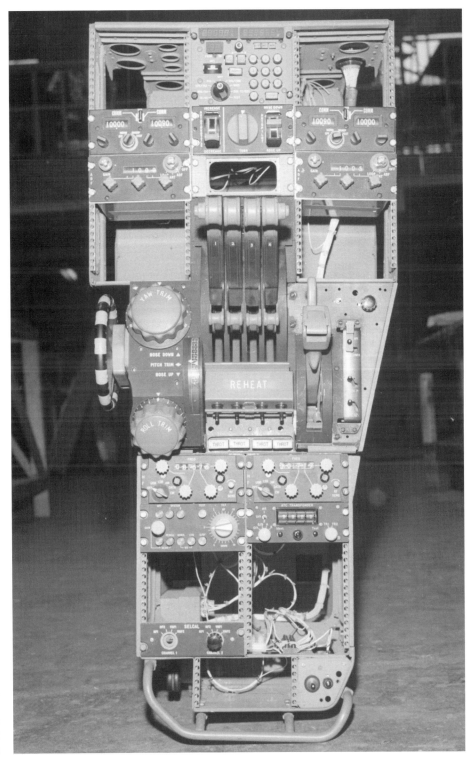

valves, ignition switches, flying control hydraulic system change-over switches and anti-icing controls. On each side outboard of the pilots were consoles on which were mounted the controls for the nose-wheel steering, weather radar, flight-deck and control-panel lighting. Located between the pilots' seats was a console that was home to the throttle levers, thrust reversers and the ganged reheat/thrust augmentation switches, together with the controls for the visor and droop nose and their own stand-by selectors, the normal and the emergency brake lever plus the emergency undercarriage lowering lever; finally, communications, navigation and INS programming panels were also located there.

The flight engineer was seated behind the first officer/co-pilot and had his own selection of panels. Laid out on these, which were sectioned in block form to delineate their different functions, were the aircraft systems' switches and dials. The duties of the flight engineer included management of the fuel flow and balance system plus the hydraulic system and the on-board electrical system which required monitoring of its output and routing.

When it came to designing the flight-control system, the team would draw upon the experience gained from the Vulcan bomber where elevons were used for pitch and roll control. The rudder sections were conventional in nature and controlled yawing and trimming. All the flight-control surfaces were driven by separate PFCUs, each being controlled by an electrohydraulic servo-valve. Due to the location of the engine nacelle boxes, the elevons were split into two groups per wing. The two outboard groups consisted of elevons 1, 2, 5 and 6, which worked in unison, as did the two remaining control surfaces 3 and 4. All six control surfaces had mechanical stops which ensured that they could not be driven past their set deflection range limit without causing major damage to the airframe. Also protecting the aircraft from flight-control reversal during high-speed flight, the outer elevons were locked into the neutral or zero deflection position, which eliminated this potentially disastrous problem. The trimming of Concorde's elevons was also

borrowed from the Vulcan. All the wing surfaces could be trimmed to balance the aircraft; only pitch control was made available in manual, auto-trim and auto-pilot modes since the delta-wing shape has a tendency to rise if not kept under positive control. To assist the pilots in flying Concorde, it was

fitted with an auto-stabilization system whose primary purpose was to maintain the natural stability of the aircraft in the face of any turbulence and to maintain positive control should the aircraft tend to depart from its set flight path after engine failure. Feeding the auto-stabilization system with

ABOVE: **This view of the Concorde fin shows the location of the rudder PFCU and the complicated job for finishers when they painted this area.**
Adrian Falconer

ABOVE: **This view of the Concorde fin shows the location of the rudder PFCU and the complicated job for finishers when they painted this area.**
Adrian Falconer

LEFT: **Seen in close-up is one of the elevon PFCUs. Although it looks complicated, it is essentially a hydraulic, solenoid-controlled jack.**
Adrian Falconer

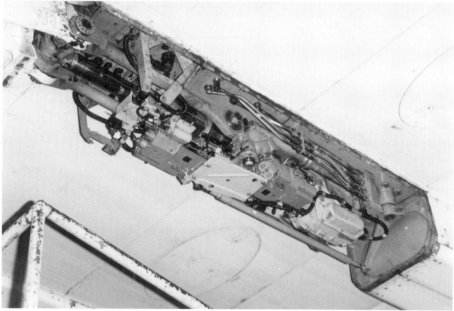

much of its operating data was the air data computer which interpreted signals from motion sensors detecting changes in direction and movement in the pitch, yaw and roll planes. Artificial feel was provided on all three axes, the units being based around a spring the tension of which increased as did speed. As this happens, the range of movement available to the pilots was limited and thus the possibility of airframe over-stress was greatly reduced.

Aiding the flight-control systems was the stall warning system, which received data from the pitch channel of the auto-stabilization/air data computer. The first visible indication given to the pilots that Concorde might be approaching the stall was activation of the stick shaker system. If the aircraft continued to raise its nose, the artificial feel system jacks physically shook the control runs, which, in turn, moved the control yokes. Should these positive inputs still fail to alert the pilots, a second anti-stall system kicked in. Known as the super stabilization system, this came into its own should the angle of attack exceed 13.5 degrees, its physical manifestation being to input a positive down deflection to the elevons. A final stall warning complete with warning lights and klaxons activated when the angle of attack exceeded 19 degrees.

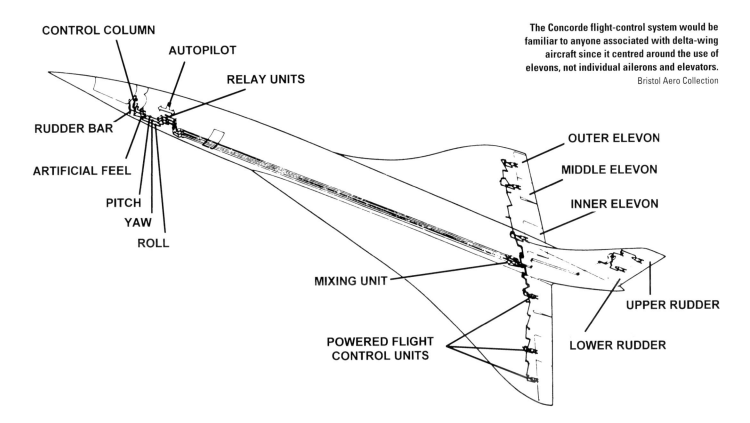

CONTROL COLUMN

AUTOPILOT

RELAY UNITS

RUDDER BAR

ARTIFICIAL FEEL

PITCH

YAW

ROLL

MIXING UNIT

POWERED FLIGHT
CONTROL UNITS

OUTER ELEVON

MIDDLE ELEVON

INNER ELEVON

UPPER RUDDER

LOWER RUDDER

The Concorde flight-control system would be familiar to anyone associated with delta-wing aircraft since it centred around the use of elevons, not individual ailerons and elevators.
Bristol Aero Collection

The control of Concorde was handled by the auto flight-control system, which monitored the behaviour of the aircraft and also supplied the autopilot and autoland functions, the latter being rated as Cat. III capable. Interlinked to these two systems were the autothrottle, warning and landing system indicator displays. In common with most autothrottle systems, this unit controlled the behaviour of the engines throughout the whole flight envelope when it was activated. An available secondary function ensured that the engines were protected from over-speeding when the autopilot was engaged in maximal cruise mode. Further protection for the throttle–engine combination was provided by disconnect switches fitted to throttle levers 1 and 4 there being a final override, the manual disconnect clutches.

When Concorde was flying in autopilot mode its input was via two signal channels that integrated both the autopilot and flight director system feeds. In a similar manner to most autopilot systems, that fitted to Concorde operated in the roll, pitch and yaw axes. When engaged, the autopilot operated a sequence of jacks which, in turn, impinged on mechanical linkages that overrode the pilots' control. In cruise mode, both flight directors were engaged, although only one autopilot channel was engaged, both

became engaged for safety and back-up reasons during landing. If at any time the pilots were required to disengage the autopilot, there were disconnect buttons mounted on each flight-control yoke. Further functions available via the auto flight-control system included a full range of status lights to indicate to the pilots the state of the autopilot and the autothrottle during cruise mode. Extra monitoring functions came to the fore when automatic approach and landing modes were selected. Warning functions were also available should the altitude dialled into the AFCS drift too far from the selected settings. The AFCS also provided monitoring functions of all the other systems inputting data to this system; should there be any change in the status of these functions, further warning lights were illuminated, these being supplemented by attention-getting warning horns.

Concorde's navigation system was dependent upon both internal and external data inputs, one being generated internally by the aircraft while others came from nearby ground stations. To master and process this data, a pair of air data computers, one per side of the droop nose section, were employed. Each computer had a built-in servo monitor system that checked each channel's parameters for altitude, air speed, Mach number, outside air temperature,

vertical speed and aircraft incidence, and warned if any were operating outside set reference points. Concorde was navigated through three independent inertial navigation systems (INSs) that provided navigation, heading and altitude information. The standard practice was for two of the INS platforms to control the aircraft while the third acted as overall monitor and would switch in if one of the primary platforms started to malfunction. Linked into the INS platforms were the VOR and the ADF, receiving their inputs via duplicated radio signals, which indicated their distance to the nearest DME beacon and the closest ILS localizer and glide-slope indicators. Vertical indicator displays were driven by commands from three distinct sources: the VOR, the ILS and the INS.

To ensure the safety of Concorde at lower altitudes was the purpose of a pair of radio altimeters, set to operate between zero and 2,500ft (760m) and capable of cross-checking each other for errors. One of the newer systems to be fitted to Concorde was a ground-proximity warning system, capable of providing audible and visual warnings should the aircraft descend below a predetermined, safe height other than on approach and landing. Concorde was also equipped with a nose-mounted, all-weather radar with a limited ground-mapping facility displaying its results on screens in the cockpit. Communications systems fitted to Concorde included a multi-channel VHF radio, matched by an HF system. SELCAL, an air traffic control transponder plus a cockpit voice recorder, were also integrated. Concorde had its own internal communications system consisting of a cabin interphone/PA system linking the flight deck, passenger cabin, galley, ground services and passenger services together.

More on the Engines

Each Rolls-Royce Olympus 593 engine came complete with a reheat or thrust augmenter unit at the rear. The powerplants were housed in pairs in box-like nacelles, each engine being separated from its neighbour by a central firewall which was stressed to absorb the forces generated by a disintegrating engine. To the front of the nacelle assemblies were the variable geometry intakes, which had hydraulically driven ramps to assist in controlling the amount of air presented to the compressor faces, while any excess was vented by air spill doors. To the rear of the nacelles were the variable area nozzle structures over which were mounted clam-shell shields for the thrust reversers. Aiding the performance and the behaviour of the intakes at high Mach numbers were perforations in the lower surfaces of the intakes which also bled any excess of air away and created a stable boundary layer.

To get Concorde clear of the ground and push it through the Mach 2 barrier, the reheat thrust augmenters fixed to the rear of each engine were used. Once Concorde was safely airborne, the reheat units were deselected in the mandatory noise abatement zone. Once over the sea, the reheat gang switch was selected again. This increased the engine thrust by burning extra fuel, the flow of which was monitored by an electronic control unit. When reheat/thrust augmentation was not engaged, fuel flow was controlled by the full authority digital engine control unit.

To start the engines on the ground, an external, low-pressure start trolley could be used for each engine individually or the engine cross-feed valves could be opened, which allowed one engine to start the remaining three. In the unlikely event of an engine surge or flame-out, Concorde had an auto restart system, backed up by a manual relight system. Control of the variable secondary nozzle was the role of the nozzle angle scheduling unit (NASU). At speeds above Mach 1.1 these nozzles were fully open; however, should the speed drop below this point, the NASU starts to reduce the size of opening, in accordance with signal inputs generated by the engine scheduling unit. To assist Concorde in braking after landing, each engine was fitted with thrust reverser buckets that could be linked to compression switches mounted

ABOVE: Ground running of the engines was undertaken using this specially constructed test house at Filton, fitted with noise suppressors and pollution-prevention equipment. Adrian Falconer

LEFT: The Olympus engine installation, with its many pipes and cables, seemed complicated, although the diagram shows it was entirely logical and gave access to engineers undertaking repairs or changing the magnetic plugs used as part of the engine monitoring and wear-detection system. Bristol Aero Collection

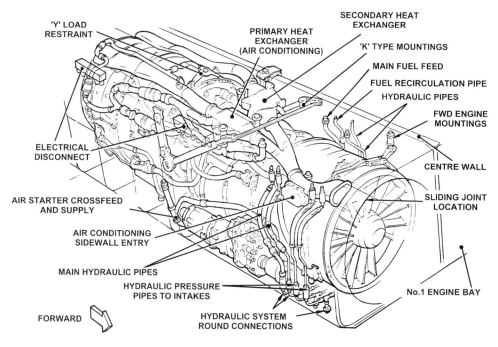

on the main undercarriage legs that ensured automatic deployment on touchdown. Inadvertent operation of the reversers was prevented by a protection control unit; however, there was the facility for the thrust reversers fitted to the outboard engines to be operated in flight, although they would only engage when the powerplants were set in the reverse thrust idle speed band.

In contrast to the fuel system employed by other airliners, that on Concorde was unique in its application. Not only did it supply the four engines, its other task, just as important, was that of balancing the airframe throughout the full envelope of flight. The fuel system in Concorde consisted of thirteen tanks which could contain a maximum usable load of 26,330gal (119,790ltr). The tanks were in three distinct groups: one dealt with engine fuel feed, another was optimized for the main fuel transfer function, and the last was concerned with the fuel trimming in the aircraft. Supplying fuel direct to the engines was the role of the integral fuel pumps, handled by a fuel flow controller. The fuel in the trimming system was used to maintain the centre of gravity (c.g.) throughout the aircraft's full speed range. To ensure that its defined limits were not exceeded, the cockpit c.g. indicators could be set by the crew to define the trim limits.

Although each engine in a powerplant group had its own dedicated collector tank, there was the facility to cross-feed fuel to and from an engine or group of engines should it prove necessary. The filling of the collector tanks was accomplished using tanks 5, 6, 7 and 8 and a sequencer that ensured that the c.g. was not altered too radically. As its name suggests, the trim transfer system was used to move fuel between tanks within a group to the optimum required for take-off, landing, subsonic and supersonic flight. The main controls for the fuel system were located on the engineer's control panel, the system being advanced enough so that an automatic transfer sequence could be set up. The controls for the trim system for both pilots were limited to an override which allowed either to carry out an emergency fuel forward transfer should the need arise. Although all the tanks in this group were equipped with pumps to transfer fuel to the correct location, the rearmost tank was fitted with four pumps for the express purpose of emergency forward transfer. All the tanks installed on Concorde were fitted with a venting system in order to lessen the explosive fumes that remained after the fuel was used, while a

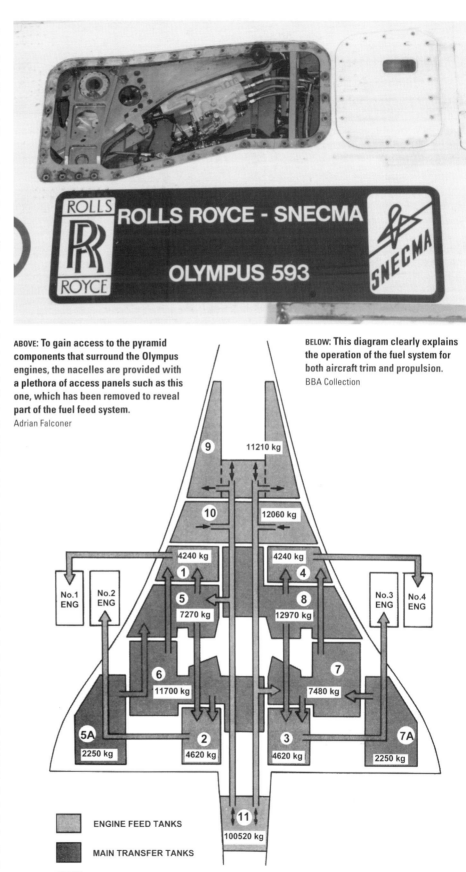

ABOVE: To gain access to the pyramid components that surround the Olympus engines, the nacelles are provided with a plethora of access panels such as this one, which has been removed to reveal part of the fuel feed system.
Adrian Falconer

BELOW: This diagram clearly explains the operation of the fuel system for both aircraft trim and propulsion.
BBA Collection

ENGINE FEED TANKS

MAIN TRANSFER TANKS

TRIM TRANSFER TANKS

NOMINAL TOTAL FUEL 95,430 kg
SPECIFIC GRAVITY = 0.8

tank pressurization system came into operation at high altitude, which assisted the pumps in moving fuel and stopped it from boiling off. In the event of an emergency, fuel could be dumped through a vent pipe at the rear of the airframe, the required venting pressure being supplied by the pumps fitted to each collector group. Putting fuel into the aircraft was done through a pair of pressure refuelling coupling points in the wing lower fairings forward of the main undercarriage bays. These in turn were connected to the trim transfer gallery, the whole being fuelled under pressure. To give a measure of control during the refuelling operation, the refuel panel allowed for a complete sequence refuel of the whole system or for partial refuelling of individual tanks to give an overall calculated percentage. Depending on the degree of control needed, the refuel operator could either set the refuel panel to carry out the replenishment automatically or, for finer control, manual selection was available.

Air Conditioning and Pressurization

Beyond his responsibilities for the engine and fuel systems, the flight engineer also controlled the air conditioning and cabin pressurization systems. The former consisted of four independent groups, each of which was supplied from the relevant engine's high-pressure compressor and fed into the air conditioning system via a bleed valve comprising a shut-off valve and a pressure-reducing valve. Downstream the airflow fed into four cross-bleed valves that allowed cross-feeding throughout the system. These were fitted with an external tapping that allowed for the connection of external cooling trolleys. To maintain a suitable temperature throughout the cabin, the air tapped from the compressors passed through heat exchanger matrices before being mixed with another, colder air supply delivered by the cold-air unit. Further cooling of the air took place in a secondary heat exchanger before the process finished at the fuel/air heat exchanger. To cool components within the airframe bleed air was drawn from small intakes mounted on the engine nacelles during low-speed flight, while at higher speeds there was a further air bleed located within the intakes themselves. A further cooling option became available

once the main undercarriage legs were lowered since the two jet pumps in the main-gear bays could be used to supplement the ram airflow, while at higher altitudes and speeds the fuel/air heat exchangers undertook the same role.

Upstream from each primary heat exchanger air regulation was carried out by using a ram air valve which modified the inlet flow upstream of the cold-air unit. This maintained an ambient temperature of 100°C when the inlet temperature was below 25°. The fuel/air heat exchangers provided further air cooling in supersonic flight. Should there be overheating in the primary or secondary heat exchangers, the downstream duct closest to the heat exchanger or in the duct downstream of the cold-air unit, the conditioning valves closed and latched shut. Should there be over-pressurization in the system downstream of the bleed valve, a similar action was made by the bleed valve. The conditioning valve would close should there be an indication of high differential pressure between the cabin and the cold-air unit.

Cabin pressure control was managed by using the discharge valves and the ground-pressure relief valve which regulated the outflow of conditioned air from the pressurized zones. On-board control was governed by identical systems known as SYS1 and SYS2; these in turn controlled two discharge valves positioned fore and aft on each system. Both systems were automatic in operation and governed by the cabin altitude selector, throttle settings and weight switches. There was a degree of limited manual control for each pressurization system which allowed the flight engineer to shut any of the discharge valves manually if required. The settings for the cabin differential pressure ranged between 10.7 and 11.2psi (0.75–0.78kg/sq cm), the lower limit was gained from the amplifier of the selected system while the upper was the value set by the pressure limiter on each discharge valve. Cabin altitude was set to 11,000ft (3,400m) by the cabin altitude limiter on each valve although this increased to 15,000ft (4,500m) when all four valves were in operation. Should there be a requirement to dump cabin pressure there was provision for it, restricted to the pressure range of the cabin altimeter limiters.

Although air conditioning for crew and passengers is the most apparent aspect of a comfortable aircraft environment, there were further cooling enhancements on

Concorde. These were aimed at cooling the aircraft's equipment racks and initially took their airflow via two extractor fans from the passenger cabin. The expelling of the air required the use of three fans which covered the forward electronic racks, instrument panels, weather radar, TRU and INS crates. The residual air finally left the aircraft through the forward discharge valve. Additional fans, two primary and one standby, were used to extract air from the rear equipment racks, which, in turn, vented the air to the aft discharge-valve region. A non-return valve allowed for the extraction of the air from the underfloor area into the extractor ducting, which moved it to the forward discharge valves. To back up the primary system there was a forward emergency relief valve to ensure the extraction of air under abnormal flight conditions. Surplus cabin air was also used to cool and ventilate the main landing-gear bays and the flying control chassis; the former used air bled from the cabin underfloor area, while the flight-control chassis hydraulic system had its own ventilation valve, controlled by a barometric pressure switch. The hydraulic bay located to the rear of the aircraft was normally ventilated with air drawn from the cabin, this being assisted by a fan drawing air from outside the aircraft when the cabin differential pressure was low, such as during the landing phase.

When Concorde was parked on the ground it could be either heated or cooled, as needed, by the use of an external conditioning unit which plugged into the main distribution manifold, the connection for which was in the lower rear fuselage. This input supplied conditioned air direct to both the passenger cabin and the flight deck while the equipment bays, home to much of the avionics, used an indirect supply drawn through by electric fans. Further cooling was provided by using expelled cabin air to cool the main undercarriage bays and the hydraulic-system bay.

Electrics and Hydraulics

Since many of the systems aboard Concorde were electrically driven it is not surprising that it was well equipped with power generators, with one per engine rated at 60kVA each. For use on the ground, the aircraft had external power sockets under access panels, which allowed for the plugging in of an external power

With an external power cart plugged in to provide ground power, this Concorde is prepared for a post-maintenance flight test. Adrian Falconer

Complete with a tug more suited to towing Boeing 747s, this Concorde awaits its next series of functionals. Note the access steps for ground-engineering staff. Adrian Falconer

supply. The 28V DC on the aircraft was supplied by four transformer rectifier units and backed up by a pair of 25A/hr batteries. A further power supply back-up was supplied by an hydraulically-driven emergency generator that was capable of supplying the aircraft's essential services until a safe landing could be made. This part of the power supply system kicked in automatically should one of the main electrical busbars fail; a similar response also happened should either No.1 or 2 engine fail in flight and should there be a busbar failure on the ground, although for the automatic system to engage the engines had to be running at 58 per cent thrust.

The hydraulic system on Concorde operated at pressures between 4,000 and

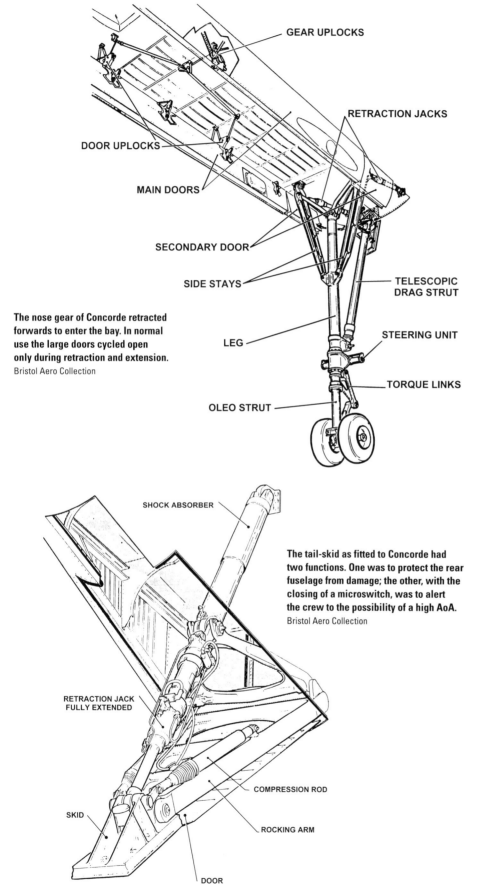

GEAR UPLOCKS

RETRACTION JACKS

DOOR UPLOCKS

MAIN DOORS

SECONDARY DOOR

SIDE STAYS

TELESCOPIC
DRAG STRUT

LEG

STEERING UNIT

TORQUE LINKS

OLEO STRUT

The nose gear of Concorde retracted
forwards to enter the bay. In normal
use the large doors cycled open
only during retraction and extension.
Bristol Aero Collection

SHOCK ABSORBER

The tail-skid as fitted to Concorde had
two functions. One was to protect the rear
fuselage from damage; the other, with the
closing of a microswitch, was to alert
the crew to the possibility of a high AoA.
Bristol Aero Collection

RETRACTION JACK
FULLY EXTENDED

COMPRESSION ROD

SKID

ROCKING ARM

DOOR

4,500psi (280 and 320kg/sq cm). Systems driven by hydraulics included the powered flying control units, artificial feel units, landing gear, wheel brakes, nose-wheel steering, windscreen visor, nose-cone droop and raising mechanism, engine intake variable ramps and the fuel pumps located in the aft fuel transfer tank. Services to these several sub-systems were provided by three independent systems designated green, yellow and blue. The first two were recognized as the primary systems, while the third was treated as the aircraft standby. Although each system reservoir was pressurized during maintenance, an auxiliary pump was available to recharge the reservoirs, which would eliminate the possibility of pump cavitation that could be caused during engine start. In the event of a main hydraulic system failure, Concorde was equipped with a two-bladed ram air turbine, which had the ability to drive two hydraulic pumps. For use in ground operations, there were two hydraulic pumps that could be used to pressurize all three hydraulic systems, which allowed for the functioning of the aircraft's systems.

Outside the flight-control system PFCUs, the aircraft's undercarriage was of primary importance. This was of the conventional, hydraulically-operated type and consisted of a twin-wheeled nose leg assembly and a pair of main legs that had a bogie mounting four wheels and brake units each. Located in the rear fuselage tail-cone was a tail-wheel unit whose task was to protect the rear fuselage from ground scrapes. This unit had a pair of small tail-wheels that replaced the skid of the earlier prototype and pre-production Concordes. Each main undercarriage unit retracted inboard while the nose unit retracted forward; as each unit began to move to the retracted position, the greater part of each nose door opened to let the leg enter the bay, while the main-gear doors cycled through open and close functions as the legs moved into their own bays. When the undercarriage was selected down, the reverse happened so that only the legs were exposed to the airflow. While the main and nose units were cycling through either the up or the down function, the tail-wheel unit was also moving into the bay or extending. Since Concorde had a powerful hydraulic system, the retraction or extension of the undercarriage units happened almost simultaneously. When the undercarriage units were up and locked into their bays they were held in place by hydraulic pressure and mechanical locks. As would be expected, the primary hydraulic undercarriage system was supported by a standby circuit that operated outside the main systems and increased the undercarriage lowering options available to the crew.

Should Concorde suffer a total loss of hydraulic function, there was one final option available, this being an emergency release of the undercarriage locks with the descent of the undercarriage units themselves under gravity and in free-fall. The operation of the mechanical release for the undercarriage was via a release handle in the cockpit. When operated, the uplocks retracted and allowed the legs to drop. Although gravity was held to be enough to force the legs into the locked-down position, should this fail to occur pneumatic pressure could be diverted from the hydraulic reservoir to complete the extension of the gear struts. Aircraft braking was applied hydraulically to the main wheels, each brake unit being a multistator assembly. To prevent brake lock-up and subsequent brake fires and damage, there was an anti-skid system fitted which cycled the brakes to prevent this. When Concorde was on the ground, nose-wheel steering was hydraulically powered, operated through an electronic controller linked to the rudder pedals and hand wheels. In the event of a system failure, the braking system was equipped with a brake accumulator that had enough braking energy for one landing.

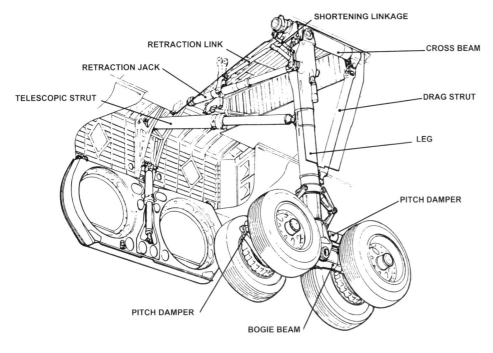

Accommodation, Fittings and Safety

To the passengers boarding Concorde, their first impressions might not be completely favourable since the fixtures and fittings were not palatial, all being designed to fit within the cabin; that hefty premium on the

ABOVE: Concorde's main gear was fairly complicated in operation, although a bonus was that it had only one operating door per bay to cycle during retraction and extension. Bristol Aero Collection

LEFT: The main gear fitted to Concorde is substantial. This view of the right-hand assembly shows the main retraction jack and shortening assembly. Adrian Falconer

BELOW: Each main wheel on Concorde was fitted with one of these multistator brake units. The tool used to align all the tangs before the wheel's refitting is known as a spider. Adrian Falconer

ABOVE: Viewed from the rear, the tail-wheel bumper in the rear fuselage was a neat installation. In the development aircraft it was no more than a skid; for the production machines wheels were added.
Adrian Falconer

RIGHT: The Concorde nose gear: affixed to the rear upper part of the leg is the fixed fairing, and midway down above the torque links are the jacks for the nose-wheel steering assembly. The framework over the wheels themselves was used for rain dispersal and to protect the airframe from foreign object damage. Adrian Falconer

LEFT: With a crane attached to the slings, the completed forward fuselage of F-WTSS is almost ready for shipment to Toulouse. The close spacing of the stringers under the skin is clearly evident.
Bristol Aero Collection

ticket was for speed. The passenger cabin was 115ft (35m) long and 8ft 7in (2.6m) wide at its maximum. The seating arrangements were based on four-abreast seating, split into two banks separated by a 17in (43cm) aisle. Originally an arrangement of 108 passengers, pitched at 38in (97cm), was put forward for premium-class passengers and an economy-class layout catered for 128, pitched at 34in (86cm). A final, alternative arrangement was for a higher density layout that would carry 144 passengers pitched at 32in (81cm). Eventually, after much market research and consideration, both Air France and British Airways would settle on a passenger number of just 100, the cabin being split into sections by a divider to accommodate them. In the forward compartment the seating arrangement housed forty passengers with the remainder in the rear compartment. To service both cabin sections there were a pair of compact galleys and similar-sized toilet facilities. To convey the passengers' baggage and any high priority freight there were two holds under the passenger floor.

Other equipment installed in Concorde included anti-ice and rain protection and dispersion systems. Both the wing leading edges, the leading edges of the intakes and the air spill doors all benefited from anti-icing, as did the engine inlet guide vanes. Rain dispersion and anti-icing were also available for both the visor and the inner windshield assemblies, although the former operated only when the visor was fully up and locked. Both were electrically operated, as were the anti-ice systems installed in the static vents and galley drain masts. To keep the windscreens clear, Concorde used a combination of windshield wipers, deflectors and rain repellent, although the last became effective only above 100kt. To keep the screens clear from rain was only one requirement for the crew's visibility, since at low level insects and dust became another hazard to deal with. For this purpose Concorde had a screen-wash system installed which operated in conjunction with the windscreen wipers.

Although Concorde spent much of its time operating at high speeds, it too had to comply with the regulations regarding the carriage of emergency equipment. In flight,

ABOVE: With the lower half of the shipping container in position, the forward fuselage of the first prototype is lowered in. Clearly visible underneath is the bay for the nose gear. Bristol Aero Collection

BELOW: Inside the Brabazon hanger at Filton another protective case section is lowered into position. Before development of the Super Guppy for air shipment, airframe sections travelled on specially constructed, flatbed trailers. Bristol Aero Collection

Given its importance, sections in transit required special-to-type containers.
They were also billboards for some subtle advertising. Bristol Aero Collection

fire is regarded as the major enemy and therefore Concorde was fitted with both audible and visual warning systems to alert the crew. In the main, these systems were centred around the engine nacelles and concentrated upon engine overheating or conflagration, but they also provided the means to extinguish any fire. There were further protection and detection systems whose sensors were situated in the air-conditioning ducting, passenger cabin and freight holds. Surrounding the engines and the nacelles was a dual-sensor system that warned of overheating or fire outbreaks. Before the fire suppression system operated, a set of secondary fire-damping doors were activated with the purpose of starving the fire of oxygen. A further fire-detection system was installed in the fuel tanks. This used flame detectors linked to a vent ignition suppression system, which automatically discharged extinguisher into the fuel system vent pipe, thereby preventing any ignited fuel vapour from blowing back into the system. Should fire break out in the vicinity of the fuel tanks there were four extinguishers; these could be operated manually from the flight deck by the crew, and should there be a cabin emergency involving smoke or fumes Concorde was fitted with two oxygen systems. Both function on low pressure, one for the passenger cabin and the other for the flight deck. Should there be a need for the crew to move about under such circumstances, there were portable oxygen packs available for use. To alert the crew that there was an emergency, the aircraft was well equipped with visual and aural warnings activated at all stations when the auto arm switch was operated on the flight deck. With the crew alerted, they could prepare the passengers and the cabin for evacuation. Once an emergency landing was made, the order could be given to deploy the escape slides fitted to each cabin door. Most of these could be used as rafts as well as slides. Other emergency equipment on Concorde included smoke masks, fire extinguishers, cots for infants and a defibrillator for heart-attack resuscitation. In the event of Concorde surviving a ditching, rafts were stowed, equipped with rations and other survival equipment.

Throughout the life of Concorde much of this equipment remained essentially unchanged, except for modifications and upgrading, although this changed radically after the crash in July 2000.

Parked at Filton before entering the Brabazon hangar for maintenance, this BA Concorde had its way blocked by a unique gate across the perimeter track. Adrian Falconer

CHAPTER FOUR

Flying the Fastest Airliner

Training the Crew

To get Concorde into the air was quite a complicated process. Both the flight and the cabin crew underwent rigorous training to prepare them for all emergencies. Training one of Concorde's three-man flight crew normally took about five months and all the applicants were already highly experienced in all aspects of commercial jet flying. Before even entering the cockpit, each new member spent at least six weeks in the training school classrooms where much of the theory of supersonic flight was discussed; however, only the aspects relevant to the aircraft were presented since the complexity of an aircraft such as Concorde would take years to master properly. One theme that pervaded all the training lectures was safety which was seen as paramount, and thus each exercise was studied under normal, abnormal and emergency conditions so that comparisons could be made. Further analyses were provided by computer which showed in graphic form the actions undertaken by each crew member. Supporting the training programme were extensive audio-visual aids, which in France centred around each trainee with his individual terminal. In Britain the original training regime was based around electronic working models, although technology finally caught up and computer terminals were incorporated later.

The ground-school part of the course was provided by British Aerospace and Aerospatiale and both pilots underwent this process for six weeks while the flight engineer course lasted seven weeks. Throughout this period study of all Concorde's systems was undertaken, many were already familiar to each crewman since they were variations on equipment already in use. Where intensive training was needed was in the handling of the engines and their associated systems plus an understanding of the fuel system. Once the study of texts and slides had been completed, the trainees moved on to a flight-deck mock-up where procedures could be practised and a familiarity with the instruments and controls and their behaviour

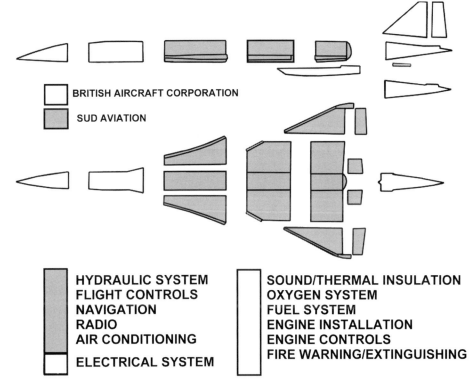

BRITISH AIRCRAFT CORPORATION

SUD AVIATION

HYDRAULIC SYSTEM
FLIGHT CONTROLS
NAVIGATION
RADIO
AIR CONDITIONING
ELECTRICAL SYSTEM

SOUND/THERMAL INSULATION
OXYGEN SYSTEM
FUEL SYSTEM
ENGINE INSTALLATION
ENGINE CONTROLS
FIRE WARNING/EXTINGUISHING

This diagram illustrates the division of work by the Anglo-French partnership, the airframe split eventually became 60–40 in favour of France, with the powerplant work swinging the other way. BBA Collection

built up. Once the end of course was reached each crew member underwent a thorough examination set jointly by the manufacturers and the European Joint Airworthiness Authority.

All successful candidates then went to a flight simulator either in Paris or Filton. As with all flight simulators, each is a complicated machine housed in an air-conditioned room. Externally they are box-shaped structures mounted on a series of hydraulic rams whose purpose is to simulate movement around all three axes. Entry to the flight deck was by an access ladder where each crew member was faced with Concorde parked on an airport ramp and visible through the simulated cockpit windows. In

common with the real aircraft, the simulator featured all the equipment fitted into Concorde, even down to the electrically-driven crew seats. Once the crew were seated in their simulated aircraft they could go through the full pre-start sequence before starting engines. When the Olympus powerplants began their start sequence, a familiar rumble, whine and vibration began to assert themselves. Once a simulated air traffic clearance to depart had been given, the simulator could give a distinct impression of nose-undercarriage bounce as the brakes were tweaked during the taxi sequence. Such was the depth of reality that the simulators created that the trainee crews soon forgot they were 'flying' a simulator.

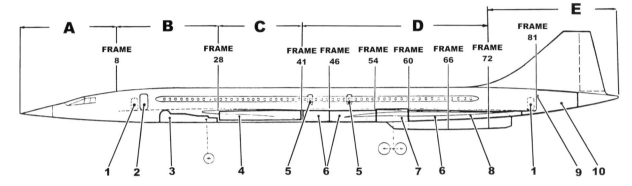

Many of the diagrams issued for Concorde were in English and French, emphasizing the joint nature of the project.
BBA Collection

NOSE FUSELAGE	A	POINTE-AVANT
FORWARD FUSELAGE	B	PARTIE AVANT DE FUSELAGE
INTERMEDIATE FUSELAGE	C	PARTIE INTERMEDIARE DE FUSELAGE
CENTRE FUSELAGE	D	PARTIE CENTRALE DE FUSELAGE
REAR FUSELAGE	E	PARTIE ARRIERE DE FUSELAGE

SERVICE DOOR	1	PORTE DE SERVICE
PASSENGER DOOR	2	PORTE PASSAGERS
NOSE GEAR BAY	3	SOUTE DE TRAIN AVENT
BAGGAGE HOLD	4	SOUTE A BAGAGES
TYPE 3 EMERGENCY EXITS	5	SORTIES DE SECOURS TYPE 3
FUEL TANK	6	RESERVOIR DE CARBURANT
MAIN GEAR BAY	7	SOUTE DE TRAIN PRINCIPAL
EQUIPMENT BAY	8	CAMPARTIMENT EQUIPMENTS
REAR PRESSURE BULKHEAD	9	FOND DE CABINE ETANCHE
FUEL TRANSFER TANK	10	RESERVIOR DE TRANSFERT

Enhancing the 'feel' of the simulator was the task of the computer system which operated the hydraulic rams. It succeeded by tricking the inner ear into believing that it was experiencing the sensations of flight; thus minor movements stimulated the feelings of climbing, diving, accelerating, turning and decelerating. The rams would move the simulator in the direction that the pilots selected by using their control yokes, and thus the crew seemed to experience a climb or dive, while an outside observer would see the simulator assembly move in small, jerky movements. Although on a day-to-day basis the simulator normally behaved itself, there was a back-up system integrated into the control circuit should the motion control system move violently outside its normal working parameters. To cut power to the simulator should it perform incorrectly there was an emergency power cut-off switch on the flight deck which, when operated, stopped the simulator in its tracks.

Having established themselves in the cockpit, the trainee crew undertook a sequence of nineteen 4-hour missions,

increasing in complexity as the course went on. Many of the actions were repeated over and over again, many for practice, others to reinforce the safety aspects of flying and handling Concorde in an emergency. The complete range of actions was undertaken under the scrutiny of an instructor who had the dual role of also acting as the air traffic control centre. The instructor was able, via his computer terminal, to select the flight parameters so that the trainees could have their simulated flight changed to practise the more difficult parts of aircraft control, such as landing. Regarded by all crews as the hardest part of handling an aircraft, that practised in the simulator centred around a landing under ILS guidance. Although the simulated landing could cover all the techniques needed, this is one phase that required flying in the actual aircraft to develop its finer points properly.

The first simulator mission was a straightforward, subsonic cruise where the crew went through the first, basic, systems usage and handling phase. It was during the second mission when simulated supersonic flight was undertaken. During this run the

flight engineer practised fuel trim balancing, which, in turn, prompted the pilots to add the centre of gravity (c.g.) meter to their constant scanning of gauges on the pilots' panels. Unlike on most modern subsonic airliners, the c.g. meter was one of the most important instruments on Concorde since its trim position governed the whole behaviour of the aircraft. Having grasped the importance of this, the crew then moved on to experiencing the trim changes at Mach 1 and 2, these manoeuvres being followed by an investigation of the autopilot. Again, unlike subsonic airliners, the autopilot on Concorde was used in preference to manual flying. As this system had seventeen flight and three autothrottle modes, there were numerous flight combinations available, many of which automatically functioned during an in-flight emergency; for example, should there be an engine shutdown on take-off, the rudder trimmed out the change in direction. Although this system may seem miraculous to some, there were pilots who left the conversion course since the importance of the autopilot as an extension of their skills escaped them.

Getting to grips with the autopilot real-ly started with the third simulator mission, where the entire flight was flown super-sonically, although this one had an auto-stabilization failure thrown in for good measure. As delta aircraft have a tendency to rise and fall in flight, there is a predis-position for pilots to overcorrect this. Returning the controls to neutral will stop the motion and therefore pilots can try again. Following on from this fairly gentle introduction to systems failure, there fol-lowed a sequence of missions where more and more incidents were added to test the crew's knowledge. During the eighth sortie the instructor would fail an engine at Mach 2; having recovered from this, the instructor would then restore the missing engine, only to be followed by a shutdown of the pair on the opposite side. The final stage was to practise three-engined land-ings which has stood crews in good stead while flying the real thing. From the eleventh simulator sortie the crew practise flying and operating the aircraft from dif-ferent seats, thus the flight engineer gets to land Concorde from the co-pilot's posi-tion. During this sequence the engineer also lands Concorde with just two engines, which is easier than most due to the reserve of power available from the after-burners. Having played musical chairs, the crew should by now have been forming a team and therefore the next series of sim-ulator runs concentrated on bonding them together to operate efficiently under pres-sure. Practices covered in this phase included autothrottle failures, the droop nose stuck at 5 degrees (which blocks much of the runway), instrument failure and emergency go-rounds in the face of changing weather conditions. The last three sorties covered noise abatement pro-cedures for operating out of New York, a full daylight sortie and a complete night flight from ramp to ramp.

Flight-Deck Layout

Having completed the simulator conver-sion training, the new crew moved to the real thing. As before, entrance to the flight deck was up the high set of flight steps to compensate for the height of the undercar-riage. Entering the flight deck, the crew saw the seats for the pilots and the engineer, plus two for supernumerary crew members, such as crew flight checkers, all fitted with full oxygen and communications equipment.

From any angle the flight deck of Concorde was cramped. Within this restricted space were the two pilots and the flight engineer. Adrian Falconer

This view of the second pilot's position reveals much detail, including the INS selector switches, visor controls and the Mach meter and airframe c.g. trim strip indicator. Bristol Aero Collection

75

Once seated, the pilots faced a left and a right dash panel containing the flight instruments, and the centre dash panel with the engine instruments. Above the centre dash panel was the glare shield panel, which housed the autopilot, autothrottle mode selector, plus the VOR/ILS frequency selectors for each pilot. The right and the left pilot console housed the controls for the nose-wheel steering, weather radar and the switches for the panel lighting. The centre console contained the throttles, thrust reverser controls, visor and droop nose standby controls, parking and emergency braking selectors, standby landing-gear controls, communications and navigation control panels.

The centrally-mounted roof panel between the two pilots, which stretched back towards the flight engineer, held a series of stepped sub-panels rounded off by a flat panel. The former housed the master warning indicators, external lighting switches, warning lights for the de-icing and de-misting controls, flying control inverter switches, autostabilizer, auto trim,

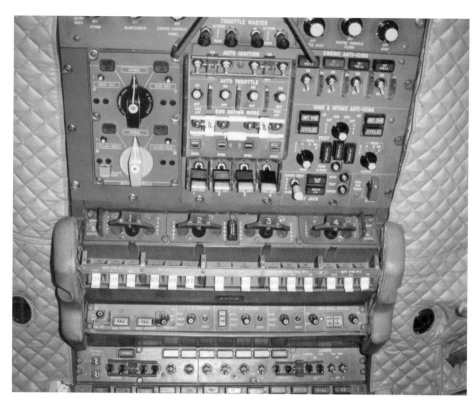

ABOVE: Located between the two pilots, this overhead panel controls many of Concorde's systems. Those to the rear were accessible to the flight engineer since the panel was stepped to present the controls in the best possible manner. Adrian Falconer

The main pilot's panel, showing the plethora of switches, knobs and dials. Prominent in the centre are the gauges connected with engine monitoring. Bristol Aero Collection

artificial feel switches and engine shutdown controls. The rear flat panel could be reached by all three operating crew members and was home to the throttle system switches, HP valves, ignition controls, flying control hydraulic switchovers, system heater controls and anti-icing switches.

To the rear of the co-pilot were the system management panels operated by the flight engineer. Some of these controls were deemed of such importance that they are also accessible to the captain, should he reverse his seat fully aft. The panels displayed information covering the powerplants, fuel system, hydraulics, electrical systems, air conditioning and pressurization, oxygen, fire detection and anti-icing systems. To aid the engineer, and to some degree the pilots too, the systems, where appropriate, were displayed in a logical layout which was etched and highlighted in white.

All the primary systems were equipped with audible and visual warnings, which were divided into four categories: Class 1, which covered warnings of serious faults or an emergency requiring the immediate attention of the crew and their immediate action; a Class 2 warning indicated a less serious problem that still needed to be brought to the attention of the crew, although immediate action was not required; a Class 3 indication covered any abnormality that required monitoring and needed to be dealt with before the situation became a Class 2 fault; a Class 4, and final, warning classification covered minor, miscellaneous indications. Class 1 and 2 warnings were presented by both audio and visual indicators on both the master warning panel and the systems management panel; audible warnings were broadcast over the flight-deck speakers, some could be cancelled while others needed their faults to be rectified before cancellation was possible; visual warnings were classified by colour: red indicated Class 1, amber Class 2, yellow Class 3 and green Class 4. The associated master warning system (MWS) was oriented towards giving warnings for Class 1 and 2 failures; not only did the relevant colour lights come on, but a single-stroke gong also sounded to emphasize the seriousness of the problem. Each master warning light on the MWS monitored a number of warning sources. The light itself could be cancelled by pushing the relevant light switch, although the gong would continue to sound until the fault was dealt with.

Should the crew continue to ignore an MWS light, a single-stroke gong would sound every 10sec until rectification had been carried out. The primary gongs were backed up by a secondary gong system which sounded if the MWS failed; this was part of the aircraft health monitoring system and sounded at 1sec intervals. The MWS amber lights, some of the red lights and their associated primary gongs could be inhibited via the MWS panel, although there was a recall system that reactivated any outstanding fault warnings should the relevant system still be indicating a defect. Certain primary red warning lights were marked with a 'T'; this indicated that they had a 'push-to-test' facility available.

The Crew's Seats

The three main crew seats for the pilots and engineer were mounted on rails and electrically operated. A fourth seat was also on rails and manually operated and was used by the first supernumerary crew member, frequently a flight checker or pilot on a live conversion course. A less palatial fifth seat was available and could be used by a further supernumerary crew member. The rail layout of the primary crew seats meant that all three crew members were provided with maximum mobility about the flight deck. In practice, this meant that the captain's seat could travel

far enough aft to monitor the systems management panel. The co-pilot or first officer's seat could also track rearwards to stop behind the centre console, which allowed access to the crew position. Height adjustment for both seats was electrically actuated, although there was a manual reversion facility if needed. Other adjustable parts of the front two seats included the pan, back and arm rests. The flight engineer's seat had two primary directions: outboard towards the systems management panel or forward to assist in operating the throttles. The seat floor-rails for this seat, electrically-powered fore and aft, gave it easy access to the centre console. It too could be electrically adjusted vertically, with manual reversion. In the event of a crash, the seat had to be within 2in (5cm) of the right-hand side of the aircraft's centreline otherwise the crash lock pin would not disengage. If at any time better access were needed to parts of the flight deck, the engineer's seat could be tracked forward under the systems management desk. To prevent the possibility of a clash between the captain's and the engineer's seat, an inter-seat strut was positioned on the inboard rail to the rear of the pilot's seat. Should the seats approach each other, a striker on the strut, when compressed, operated a limit switch which electrically disarmed both seats. Should the captain need to move further rearwards and the area was clear, an override pedal, operated on the engineer's seat, reset power to the pilot's seat. A similar, but removable strut, could be fitted to the captain's seat to stop it colliding with the occupant of the supernumerary's seat. Contact between the seats was prevented by a micro-switch's being tripped on the pilot's seat, which broke the tracking circuit of the pilot's seat. The first supernumerary seat was completely manually operated and mounted on sliding rails. The manual adjustments possible included fore and aft movement, height adjustment and partial rotation. When not required for use, the seat pan could be lifted up and folded upwards to the seat back, where it was held in place by the safety harness. To provide further clearance, the seat could be disengaged from the latchplate, which allowed full rearward movement and thus stowage in the left-hand rear corner of the flight deck. The second supernumerary seat was stowed flat against the left-hand equipment rack when not in use, being held in place by a claw arm catch. Releasing the catch allowed the seat to be swung

This view of the flight deck encompasses part of the flight engineer's position on a BA aircraft (BA seats were blue and Air France seats grey). BBA Collection

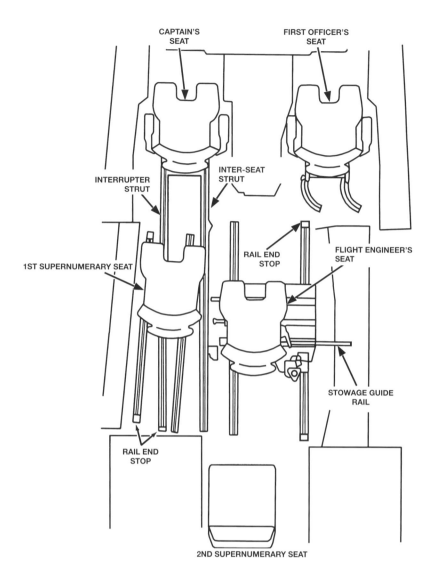

down, its legs to engage with floor latches and the back to be raised into the vertical. To reverse the process, a lever mounted on the forward leg freed the legs from the floor catches and allowed the seat back to fold for stowage. The safety seat harnesses fitted to the captain's, the co-pilot's, the flight engineer's and the first supernumerary seat were provided with inertia reels, while the second supernumerary seat had a fixed harness mounted to a single anchorage point on the floor and three seat anchor points.

Lighting

The flight deck and passenger cabins were well supplied with internal lighting, these being a mixture of fluorescent, electroluminescent, instrument integral, spot and flood. For general illumination purposes a pair of fluorescent lamps were fitted in the forward racking area and controlled by switches close to the circuit breaker panel and the cabin crew forward control panel. Two spotlights were mounted as boarding lights in the forward vestibule and a fluorescent light was mounted in the roof of the flight-deck compartment. Lighting at each crew station was controlled by the individual and covered both panel and general illumination.

During some flights there was the risk of encountering lightning storms which could overpower the cockpit lighting and leave the crew unsighted. To counter this, Concorde had storm lighting installed – high intensity, fluorescent lighting which operated in combination with a roof-mounted floodlight, both of which provided intense lighting to the dash panels and overcame any intense glare through the windshields.

Looking down the length of the passenger cabin of Concorde reveals the narrowness of the fuselage. Although it was never fitted with the latest hi-tech seats due to weight restrictions, such a lack did not bother the passengers as they were paying for speed, not excesses of comfort. Adrian Falconer

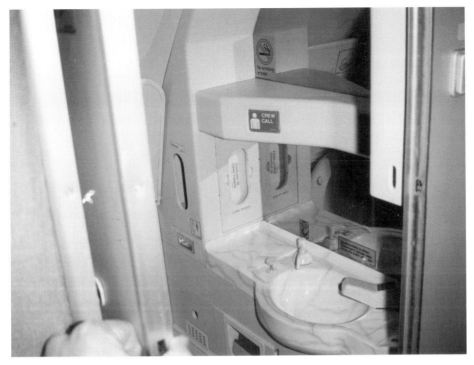

Toilets on Concorde were just big enough for their purpose, due to the size of the fuselage. Adrian Falconer

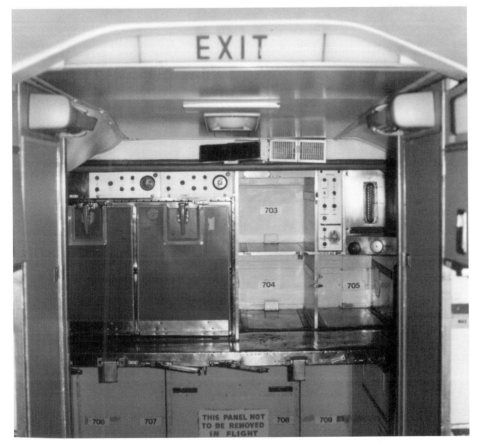

Given the restricted size of the Concorde main cabin it is hardly surprising that the galley is an excellent example of integrated minimalist design; even so the menus were of the highest quality. Adrian Falconer

Concorde was also provided with a wide range of external lighting intended to cover most eventualities. There were three anti-collision lights installed at the tip of the tail-cone and wing-root leading edges, all of which flashed simultaneously. Lights were also installed on the left- and the right-hand side of the front fuselage for taxi purposes. To assist Concorde during night landings there were landing taxi lights mounted on the left- and the right-hand nose-gear doors. To confirm that the gear was down and locked, the lamps would not illuminate even if already selected to. To control the heat generated by these lamps on the ground each one had a 400W filament controlled by a weight-on-ground microswitch. Once airborne, the release of the microswitch allowed a 600W filament to illuminate. As this happened the lamp rotated slightly downwards to compensate for Concorde's approach attitude. Supplementing the nose-mounted lights were a further set mounted on the leading edges of the main undercarriage doors. As with the nose-mounted lamps, the main-gear lights would not illuminate until the leg was down and locked, even if preselected to. There was an automatic blow-back system that operated should the legs still be down at a speed of 365kt. The final lamps on the airframe include navigation lights: one mounted on the tail-cone and two at the leading edge of each wingtip.

Crew and passenger comfort was also a priority, not only to justify the cost but for safety as well. The air-conditioning system consisted of four independent groups, each of which took high-pressure air from the engines and conditioned it by cooling, heating and dehumidification. The resulting air was used to pressurize the relevant areas and to cool and ventilate equipment racks. On the ground, Concorde could be supplied with preconditioned air through an external connection in the rear fuselage which was supplied direct to the distribution manifold. When the air conditioning was operating correctly the four groups supplied air to parts of the airframe. Group 1 supplied the flight deck, group 2 fed into the forward cabin and the remaining two supplied the rear cabin. Temperature control was normally automatic; thus the group 1 selector controlled the flight deck area, group 2 covered the forward cabin and group 4 managed the rear cabin. Semi-automatic control of the temperature in each group was possible through a standby temperature control for each group.

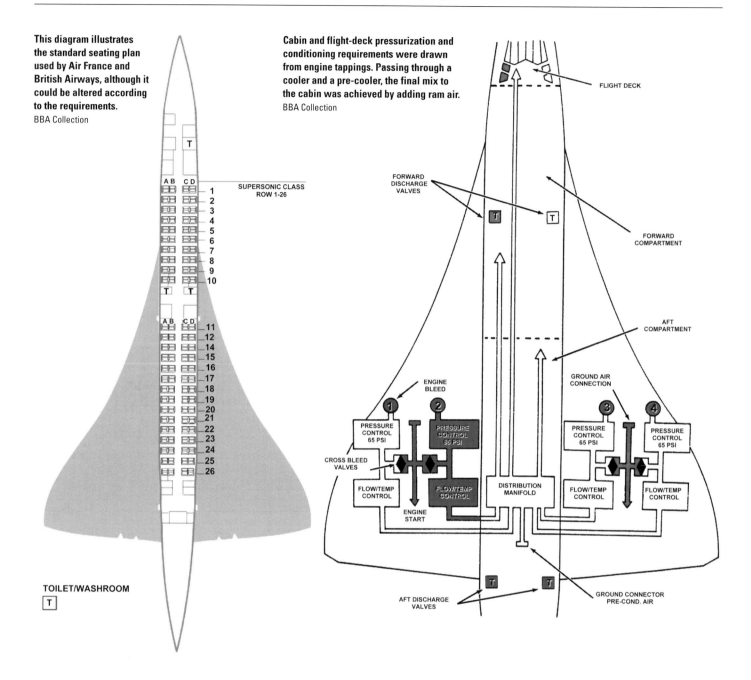

This diagram illustrates the standard seating plan used by Air France and British Airways, although it could be altered according to the requirements.
BBA Collection

Cabin and flight-deck pressurization and conditioning requirements were drawn from engine tappings. Passing through a cooler and a pre-cooler, the final mix to the cabin was achieved by adding ram air.
BBA Collection

The Systems Take Over

During their simulator training the tyro pilots and engineer were introduced to the automatic aspects of operating Concorde. These were centred around the automatic flight control system (AFCS) which had the capability for hands-off flight during the climb, cruise and let-down phases of flight and had the ability to fly Concorde during a go-around. Such was the reliability built into the AFCS that it could quite easily manage a Cat III landing in the foulest weather. Integrated into the AFCS were the autothrottle, autopilot, warning and landing displays, plus an interlock failure and monitoring test system.

The autothrottle sub-system provided control over the engines' thrust during the approach and cruise phases of flight. Within the autothrottle black box was circuitry that managed airspeed and Mach control modes, the latter including datum adjustment provisions. There was also an airspeed acquire mode which could capture a selected speed in the range of 130–400kt, although it was subject to a longitudinal acceleration limit of 0.1G. The autothrottle system also had a protection provision built in that guarded against engine over-speeds when the autopilot was engaged in maximum cruise mode. During an automatic landing the throttle setting was automatically retarded by the autopilot. The autothrottle system comprised two separate channels, selected by separate switches. During flight both channels were normally engaged, although channel 1 acted as the primary controller with the other acting as a synchronized standby. To safeguard against malfunction, each channel was self-monitoring and would switch out should there be a self-detected failure, a failure in the air data system or in the INS which supplied manometric and attitude data. The auto-

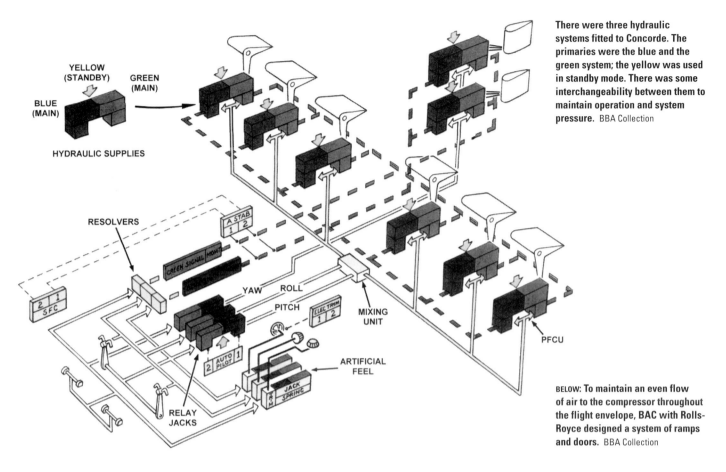

There were three hydraulic systems fitted to Concorde. The primaries were the blue and the green system; the yellow was used in standby mode. There was some interchangeability between them to maintain operation and system pressure. BBA Collection

BELOW: To maintain an even flow of air to the compressor throughout the flight envelope, BAC with Rolls-Royce designed a system of ramps and doors. BBA Collection

throttle system was rate-limited to 5 degrees of lever movement/sec and by a command authority limiter which required the throttle lever to be within the −1 to −36.5 degrees range. Should the autothrottle be engaged outside of the −36.5 point they would automatically move to this point. To give a greater range of sensitivity to each throttle lever's position, there were switches that isolated each lever so that individual tweaks could be made. Other switches, known as instinctive disconnect switches, were fitted to the outboard throttle levers. These would disengage the autothrottle system, while, as a final safety measure, there were slip clutches in the autothrottle drive mechanism which allowed direct manual override.

Controlling Concorde in flight was the purpose of the autopilot and flight director, there being two separate, integrated channels for each. The input signals and computing were common to each autopilot and flight director; those of the autopilot operated the pitch, roll and yaw relay jacks in their autopilot mode, during which the mechanical inputs were locked, while the electrical system was energized. During normal operation both flight director system channels

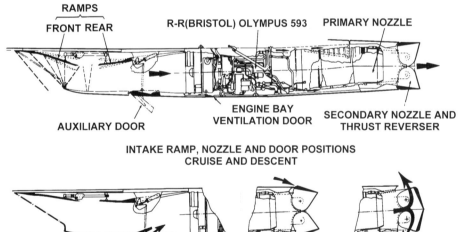

INTAKE RAMP, NOZZLE AND DOOR POSITIONS
CRUISE AND DESCENT

INTAKE RAMP, NOZZLE AND DOOR POSITIONS
TAKE-OFF AND LANDING

were engaged and the autopilot had only one channel in full operation, although both could be selected when 'land' mode was engaged. The selection of modes for both the autopilot and the flight director was under common switching control; therefore, should an autopilot mode be

engaged while the flight director was in operation, the mode reverted to 'pitch hold' and 'heading hold', although in 'land' mode the autopliot would also engage the 'land' mode. There was a proviso, however, regarding the 'go-around' mode which would return the autopilot to basic operating modes. If the flight director was engaged after the autopilot, then the already selected modes would be accepted by the flight director. Modes that could be engaged before automatic capture were indicated by 'prime' lights, which illuminated to signal successful arming. A subsequent selection of 'pitch hold' would disengage the 'primed' mode, thus extinguishing the 'prime' light. The autopilot was authority-limited to plus or minus 0.15G and 30 degrees of roll, although this increased to 35 in a controlled turn. There was also a rate limitation of 0.10G/sec at a rate of 5 degrees/sec, although this is increased to 0.25G/sec during land mode after glide-slope capture and in 'go-around' mode. The autopilot servo loops were self-monitoring at all times; however, should there be a need to disengage the autopilot, there was an instinctive disconnect button on each control yoke, and as a final safety measure the mechanical linkage between the relay jack and the control column contained a compressible strut that allowed the pilot to override the autopilot command direct.

The autopilot approach modes were fully self-monitoring; thus when both channels were engaged during land mode a state of full failure survival was possible should the primary No.1 channel fail. Its switching-out would allow the fully energized No.2 channel to take over automatically. Failure of any peripheral systems would cause the autopilot to disconnect if it were engaged in a mode that required the use of data provided by that system. However, there were exceptions; thus a failure of the ILS data feed during an approach would not cause a disconnect, although the radio altimeter readings must have exceeded 600ft (183m); this obviated nuisance disconnects. Simultaneous failure of both glide-slope receivers between 200 and 75ft (61 and 23m) radio altitude, or both localizer receivers below 200ft would also not disconnect the autopilot, although an auto-land warning light would illuminate to warn the crew of a sub-system failure. To allow for minor adjustments of the speed hold modes, the autopilot had a datum adjust unit installed. The pitch datum adjust was zeroed and inhibited in 'max. cruise' mode, while in heading hold an autopilot turn knob allowed adjustment of the heading at a fixed roll rate.

The autopilot provided information on the operational status and functional capability of the AFCS in the automatic approach and landing mode and displayed any warnings for both the autopilot and the autothrottle during the cruise phase. This particular arrangement had two data channels which operated at the same time; thus No.1 fed the captain's display and the No.2 channel operated the first officer's display; however, the most important warnings were cross-fed to both displays so that both crewmen received key information even if one channel had failed. Certain malfunctions that occurred within the latter stages of an automatic landing would cause the auto land light to illuminate, which, in turn, prompted the crew either to initiate a manual take-over or allow an automatic go-around to take place.

A further warning system built into the AFCS/autopilot was that which protected the altitude setting. This was indicated by both audible and visual warnings when the altitude deviated from that selected on the AFCS control panel. Although the altitude alert was integrated with the autopilot/flight director to make operation easier, the system was, in fact, completely isolated from the AFCS engagement modes. The altitude-alert system was inhibited when the undercarriage was in the down position.

Backing up the autothrottle, autopilot, autostabilization, trim and the flight director was the interlock failure monitor and test system which constantly surveyed the engagement state of these modules with their peripherals and data streams and flagged up a failure to the crew. Should there be an unintentional disconnect the disengagement was analysed to determine the cause, displayed to the crew and held in memory for subsequent retrieval by the groundcrew; this function was still available even after power had been removed from the aircraft and then restored.

The surfaces controlled by this myriad of electronics included the elevons on the wing trailing edges which provided roll and pitch control, while yaw control was covered by the use of the multipart rudder. Each of these control surfaces was driven by an independent powered flying control unit (PFCU). The control of these surfaces was by conventional yoke and rudder, although they were actually linked by three signal channels: the two electrical ones are notated green and blue and the third labelled mechanical. Each of the electrical channels had its power supplies delivered by their own inverter, colour-coded to match the channel. Each electrical channel generated a signal via a synchro transmitter, referred to as a resolver, to the PFCU's servos. Each of the flight control groups, the middle, outer and inner elevons and the rudders operated through its own resolvers; those handling the wing flight control providing the relevant mixing for the pitch and roll senses. The mechanical channel could also transmit the relevant pilot control inputs to the PFCU's servos; this circuit became declutched when either of the electrical channels was engaged. When the mechanical channel was engaged its inputs were delivered to the PFCU's servos via linkages and cables through a relay jack incorporated into the circuit to compensate for linkage inertia. As the elevons were dedicated to both pitch and roll axes, the system required a mechanical mixing unit which was located downstream of the pitch and roll relay jacks. Built into the mixing unit was the capability to limit the range of movement of the inner elevon sections, which, in turn, minimized the aerodynamic interference of these sections on the fin and rudder, thus reducing the yaw moment in the roll sense. The maximum range of each set of elevons through the front and rear mixer units was set at 15 degrees fully up and 17 fully down in pure pitch, although there was an override facility to fully up which would give a deflection of 17 degrees, should the situation warrant it. This, however, required some application of force to move the control surfaces. In the roll sense the outer and the middle elevon section could move 20 degrees each way, while the inner sections were limited to 14 degrees each way. The rudder had its limits set at 30 degrees each way. The mechanical stops at the elevon PFCUs limited the inner elevons to 19 degrees each way, while the other sections were limited to 23.5 degrees in either direction. The hydraulic systems that normally supplied pressure to the PFCUs, relay jacks and artificial feel units were the green and blue circuits, although in the event of either a blue or a green system failure the yellow circuit could be switched in, although its application was limited to the PFCUs and the relay jacks only. Selection of the hydraulic systems was carried out using the servo controls' panel.

The monitoring of the flight control systems covered the behaviour of the flight control inverters, the pressure within the hydraulic systems, operation of the servo controls and the operation of the electrical control channels. Should there be a failure in one of the control channels, the monitoring system would automatically switch over to the next available channel. Also monitoring the behaviour of the aircraft's flight controls was the comparator which observed the input of either the pilot or the autopilot and the resultant control surface displacement. Should there be a disagreement between the control channels the comparator defined the suspect before switching over to the good channel, although this was negated should there be a high rate of control input or the flight control surface feeds back inaccurate data due to the sudden application of high aerodynamic loads. Further protection from over-control was provided by the neutralization system which engaged in the transonic speed region at high indicated airspeeds and locked the outer elevons into the neutral position at VMC plus 25kt. When it was safe for the outer elevons to be re-engaged there was a time-delayed transition before they became operable, thus reducing the chances of airframe disturbance. This protection system was available only through the blue and the green electrical channel, not in the mechanical channel selection.

The relay jacks were twin-ram, electrohydraulic actuators whose ram displacement, direction and speed were controlled by a spool valve. As each spool valve was controlled by both the blue and the green hydraulic systems, there were indicator lights for each relay jack and its pair of hydraulic systems; therefore, should the spool valve lock up for any reason, the alternate, hydraulic system would take over operation of the relay jack while the affected selector valve was shut, thus removing hydraulic power from the jammed circuit. This fail-safe ensured that any jammed relay jack would not affect the operation of the flight control system. Moving the actual control surfaces was the purpose of the PFCUs. These were twin-ram actuators that were also controlled in a similar manner to the relay jacks, via a spool valve. Should there be an indication of a spool valve jam, the defective side of the valve would automatically switch out to leave the working side of the system in operation.

Integrated into the flight control system was the auto-stabilization system whose other purpose was to minimize the effect of turbulence and reduce the resulting flight path disturbance following an engine shutdown. The autostabilization system consisted of two separate channels for each control axis, thus maintaining control of pitch, yaw and roll. Each channel for each axis could be selected by an individual

This view along the wing trailing edge shows the location of the thrust reverser buckets in the up position. Unlike most other aircraft, the augmentor assemblies are shaped to conform to the shape of the nacelle box instead of being round. Adrian Falconer

When the system hydraulic pressure is fully dissipated the elevons droop against their limit stops, as shown here. Note the static discharger wicks on the outer elevon section and the open rear service door. Helio Coelho

switch, all were engaged during normal operation, although Channel 1 was the primary while Channel 2 was in synchronized standby mode. The autostabilization system generated signals in pitch, roll and yaw as a function of the aircraft's speed and Mach number from the ADC. These signals were independently supplied through both electrical channels direct to the PFCU servos, although there was no feedback to the pilot. As well as the basic autostabilization functions, the system also provided a roll/yaw turn co-ordination function that reduced side-slip angles at lower speeds in response to large lateral control demands. The autostabilization Channel No.1 was normally linked to the blue electrical channel, although this would switch across to the green control channel in the event of a failure. A similar process also governed the No.2 autostabilization system.

In a similar manner to the other control systems on Concorde, the artificial feel units also operated on two separate channels, pitch, roll and yaw all being controlled by individual switches. During normal aircraft operation all six feel channels were engaged, although Channel 1 for each axis acted as the primary. The mechanical unit that controlled the range of movement available to the pilot was a spring rod that increased the control stiffness in relation to the aircraft's speed. The Channel 1 jacks were powered by the blue system and those in the No.2 Channel were fed by the green hydraulic system. Jack system pressures were governed by speed signals generated by the ADC. Throughout the flight envelope the pitch artificial feel maintained a constant load factor, while the roll artificial feel channel kept a constant relationship between the rate of roll and the control-wheel force during the full flight envelope. The yaw artificial feel limits were governed by the rudder requirements matched to the aircraft's structural limitations. Should there be a failure in either the blue or the green hydraulic system or either of the air data computer channels there would be a corresponding loss of the artificial feel system channel. Such a loss would cause the system to default automatically to the back-up system. It should be noted that failure of the No.2 Channel in standby mode had no effect on the behaviour of the artificial feel system. Integrated into the pitch channel artificial feel was the stick wobbler function of the anti-stall system; thus it was a primary requirement for this channel to remain operable at all times.

Concorde not only had fuel system trimming available, the flight controls were also fitted with a conventional trim system available for roll, yaw and pitch axes. The operation of the trim system cancelled the load of the artificial feel by altering the feel datum, which, in turn, altered the neutral position of the flight controls. The trim system fitted to the pitch channel was electric in nature and comprised two separate channels. During normal operation both engaged, with No.1 channel having authority and No.2 being maintained in a synchronized standby condition. Control of the electric trim system was either by the pilot using the 'pitch trim' selector on each control yoke or via the autotrim when the autopilot was engaged.

Concorde was also provided with automatic pitch stability correction which covered four separate modes. The first was Mach trim which came into play during transonic flight when the aircraft's centre of pressure moved rearwards, reducing pitch stability. To restore this, the Mach trim function automatically signalled an up-elevon demand which was related to any Mach number between 0.69 and 1.34. The second mode was incidence trim which compensated for changes to the centre of pressure when the aircraft altered its angle of attack. This mode began operation at 10.5 degrees and reached its maximum point at 19.5. This mode also had a secondary purpose in that it would increase the stick force required to reach high angles of attack; thus as the nose-up angle increased, the incidence trim applied a nose-down pitch trim. As the speed rose, pitch stability correction was introduced, integrated with the Mach trim channel and automatically signalled an up-elevon demand related to an airspeed input between 200 and 600kt. When the aircraft passes into the supersonic part of the flight envelope a further speed trim mode came into play, proportional to the Mach number. The auto-pitch stability correction modes were also activated when autopilot Mach trim was engaged. Should there be a failure or disengagement of both electric trim systems, the autopilot system would also disengage, although this was negated should Concorde be below 100ft (30m).

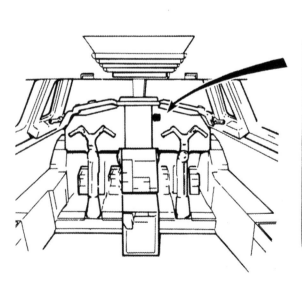

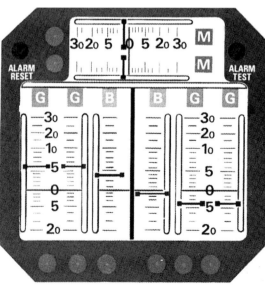

This gauge was one of the most important on the flight deck. It showed the positions of the flight control surfaces, the hydraulic system being used for operation and the c.g. for the aircraft at any given moment. BBA Collection

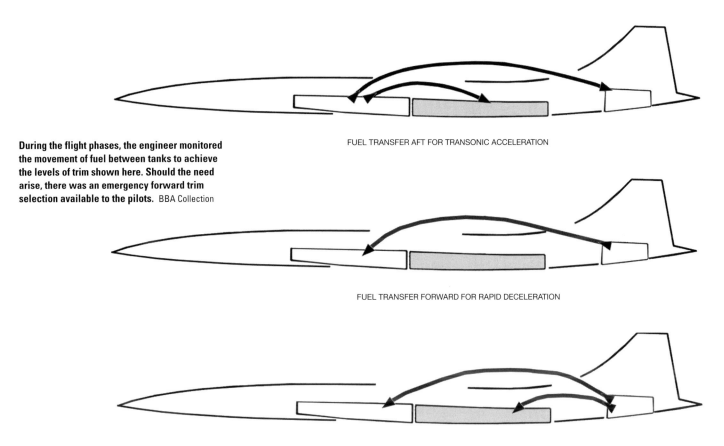

FUEL TRANSFER AFT FOR TRANSONIC ACCELERATION

FUEL TRANSFER FORWARD FOR RAPID DECELERATION

FUEL TRANSFER FORWARD AS SPEED REDUCES

During the flight phases, the engineer monitored the movement of fuel between tanks to achieve the levels of trim shown here. Should the need arise, there was an emergency forward trim selection available to the pilots. BBA Collection

Further protection for Concorde throughout varying angles of attack was provided by the high-incidence protection system, comprising an incidence trim mode, a stick shaker and the anti-stall system. The incidence trim mode was integrated into the automatic pitch stability correction system and operated at angles of attack above 11 degrees. Should the nose rise above 16.5 degrees, a stick shaker operated on the captain's control yoke, although the input was felt across both yokes since they were interconnected via mechanical linkages. The stick shaker gained its input signals from either channel of the air data computer, as needed. Cancellation of the stick shaker was possible by pushing the control yoke through the trim neutral position. Protecting Concorde from 10sec after take-off was the anti-stall system which came into play at 270kt. When the aircraft reached a high angle of attack the anti-stall system augmented basic pitch stabilization with a super-stabilization function that generated a positive warning to the crew during the approach to very high angles of attack via the artificial feel unit. As the anti-stall system was vital to protect Concorde, it had

two channels, with No.1 as the primary and No.2 in synchronized standby mode. The super stabilization function became active when the angle of attack exceeded 13.5 degrees; this in turn generated a down-elevon deflection through the pitch autostabilization channel, this being proportional to the angle of attack, the nose-up pitch rate and the aircraft deceleration. The deflection of the elevons was limited to 8 degrees down and 0 degrees up-elevon.

Should the flight control system experience any form of control jamming there was an emergency system that operated in both pitch and roll axes. The operation of the emergency flight control system was via strain gauge bridges within the control yokes which measured the pitch and roll forces generated against the jam by the pilot. When a control jam was detected the command signals were input direct to the electrical flight control systems. It should be noted that there were no emergency flight control functions in the yaw mode. When the emergency flight control system was engaged the control forces experienced were similar to those with the artificial system disengaged.

Communications

Given that Concorde was a highly complex aircraft it should come as no surprise to find that it was fitted with an extensive range of communications equipment. The basic system consisted of VHF and HF radios, SELCAL, ATC transponder, interphone systems to the ground service point and the cabin/galley and passenger address systems. Also part of the communications suite was the cockpit voice recorder, installed as a safety measure and matter of record should an incident occur.

The VHF suite comprised two identical radio installations which are provided to cover the 118–135.975MHz frequency range, there being a 25kHz channel spacing between each selectable channel. The HF system was similar to the VHF in that it too had two separate installations which provided single side-band and amplitude-modulated operation to give two-way communications at 2,182kHz and in the 2,800kHz–25MHz band. The SELCAL (SELective CALling) was used in conjunction with the aircraft's VHF and HF radios and permitted a ground station to contact a particular aircraft; this removed the need for the pilots to monitor the radios continuously. When SELCAL was initiated a flashing light indicated to the pilot which communications channel the broadcast was on; there was a two-tone chime which repeated every 5sec until the call was answered. Also fitted in duplicate to Concorde was the ATC transponder system. The secondary radar enabled a ground controller to identify the aircraft and determine its height.

Each flight-deck audio selector panel provided integration of the radio communications and radio navigation systems and the crew's interphone network. The flight interphone system allowed communications between the flight crew stations internally and between the stations and the groundcrew handling connection mounted on the nose landing gear. The flight interphone system could under some circumstances be connected to the service interphone system. The latter was provided to allow communication between flight crew stations and cabin crew stations. The system also permitted communication between crew stations and between all internal and external communication points. Another system available to both flight and cabin crew was the public address system. The PA could be operated from the flight deck and the three cabin attendant points in the passenger cabin. This allowed a tape reproducer to be connected and thus routine announcements, such as safety demonstrations, could be played automatically. Similarly, announcements which came into play when the emergency oxygen masks were deployed in the passenger cabin could be played automatically (it could also be used to broadcast music).

For communications between the cabin and the flight-deck crew this interphone station in the main cabin was used. Adrian Falconer

One later addition to the communications suite was the cockpit voice recorder (CVR) which recorded any communications from the captain, the first officer or the flight engineer on to tape. In addition, the CVR recorded any verbal communications generated through the boom microphones, regardless of any communications switching, and any flight-deck noises picked up by an area microphone.

Given the speed of Concorde it is hardly surprising that its navigation system was extremely accurate. The system included both ground-dependent and independent position-indicating systems, which displayed data to the crew. This information was provided by the air data system whose inputs came from the ADC No.1 and 2 computers. These, in turn, gained their data from the pitot probes for total pressure and readings from the relevant sensors: temperature from the temperature probe sensors, droop nose angle from the transmitter units, static pressure from the static ports and aircraft weight from the FQI selector and the c.g. channel selector. Each of the ADCs had a built-in servo monitor which checked for altitude, airspeed, Mach number, temperature, vertical speed and

This view of Concorde's nose was rarely visible to boarding passengers. Observation reveals that close to the chine under the windows are the secondary sensors that came into their own when the nose was drooped. BBA Collection

incidence. To ensure that there were no discrepancies in the data provided, each of the ADC units cross-checked for any disparity.

The actual navigation was handled by three separate INS systems whose tasks were to provide navigation, heading and altitude information. The No.1 system provided data to the left dash panel and the AFCS No.1 and No.2 INS did the same for the right-hand panel and AFCS No.2. The third platform had the capability to transfer data to either dash panel, although it had no input to either AFCS. Each of the INS platforms had a programming module in the centre console which could be used to retrieve data in digital form and load it for any desired route. On the ground, the INS platforms took 15min to align, this being initiated by a mode selector unit. There was one MSU for each platform, these being on the flight engineer's panel. Once the selector had been operated in navigation mode it needed not be operated again unless there was a failure of the INS. Protecting the AFCS platforms was a comparator able to detect whether there had been an INS failure; should this happen the relevant AFCS or INS would disconnect and display a warning to the crew. Should there be a failure of the No.1 INS to the captain he was able to switch to the No.2 system to regain data; a similar facility was afforded to the first officer.

Also aboard Concorde was a duplicated radio navigation system whose purpose was to give bearings to the VOR or the ADF beacon or the distance to the nearest ADF beacon, localizer and glide slope indications. Other systems available to the crew included the horizontal situation indicator, with inputs from the VOR, the ILS and the INS. At low level Concorde was protected by two independent radio altimeters that yielded low-altitude information in the range 0–2,500ft (0–760m). This system was integrated into the automatic landing system and the low-altitude flight system. To ensure that there was no hidden failure, this most important of systems was monitored three times per second. Supporting the radio altimeters was the ground proximity system which warned of any impending collision with the terrain. This had five warning modes: an excessive rate of descent, excessive ground closure rate, loss of altitude below 700ft (214m) after take-off, closeness to the ground with the aircraft in landing configuration and a duck under of the

glide slope. When the first four were activated, a red flashing light was illuminated accompanied by an audible 'whoop, whoop pull up'. When mode five was activated the warning was aural only and consisted of the wording 'glide slope'.

Concorde was also provided with a weather radar system comprising duplicated radar displays, transceivers and a single radar antenna, managed through a single control unit. The radar system produced continuous information on the approaching weather and could be used for ground mapping if required. The radar scanner angle could be adjusted to match that of the nose droop angle.

Nose Operations

The droop nose assembly was required on Concorde to allow good visibility during landing and take-off. The visor was maintained in the up position by a mechanical uplock, while the down position was maintained in position by hydraulic pressure

and mechanical springs. The nose assembly had three positions: up and locked, 5 degrees deflection and fully down at 12.5 degrees. The nose was held in the up position by two mechanical uplocks, at the 5-degree point two jacks and their internal locks held it in place and the fully down position was achieved by the use of hydraulic pressure, aerodynamic loads and weight. Operation of the nose and visor came from the green hydraulic system; this also supplied power to release the nose and visor locks. Should the green system fail it could be replaced by the yellow system, although its input was limited to lowering the nose and visor, the former requiring assistance from the assembly's weight and aerodynamic forces since the hydraulic power released only the locks. Should there be a total hydraulic failure the nose could be released by a mechanical release on the flight deck. This released the locks and allowed the nose to drop to the 5-degree point, at the same time this operation also released the visor, which was lowered in sequence.

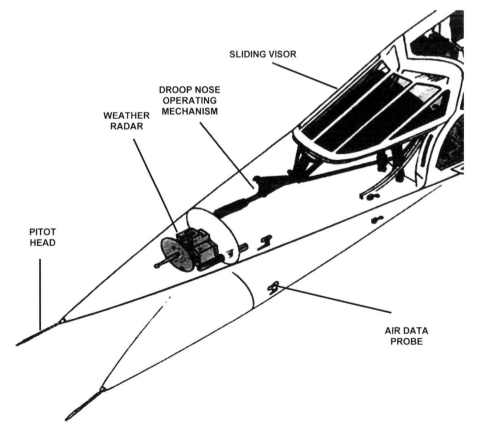

The droop nose and sliding visor ensured that the flight crew had a reasonable sight of the ground during take-off and landing. BBA Collection

**TAKE OFF AND INTERMEDIATE APPROACH
NOSE TO 5 DEGREES VISOR DOWN**

**SUBSONIC AND SUPERSONIC FLIGHT
NOSE AND VISOR UP**

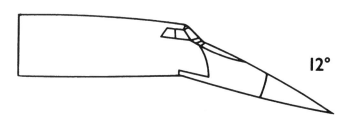

The droop nose greatly benefited crew vision; however, under certain flight conditions it could set up a disturbing harmonic buzz. BBA Collection

**FINAL APPROACH AND LANDING
NOSE DOWN AND VISOR DOWN**

BELOW: Safely ensconced in the purpose-built nose dock at Filton, this frontal view of Concorde emphasizes the almost dart-like shape of the nose. Adrian Falconer

OPPOSITE: This shows the range of movement selectable for the nose-droop mechanism, the method of locking the nose in position and the position of the visor at each point. BBA Collection

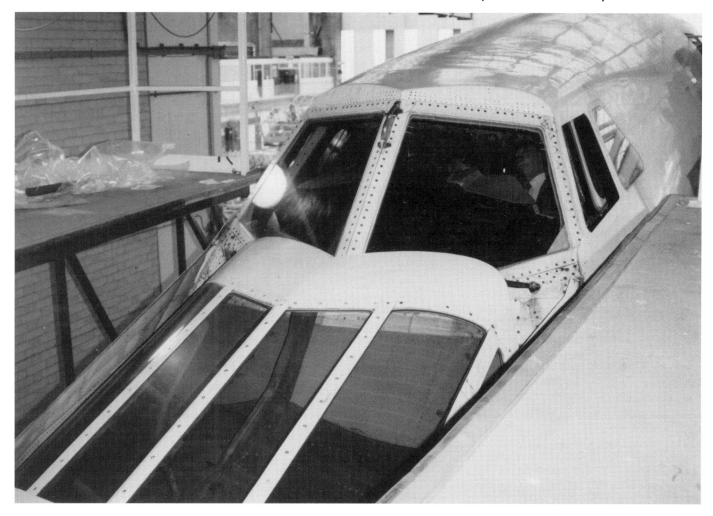

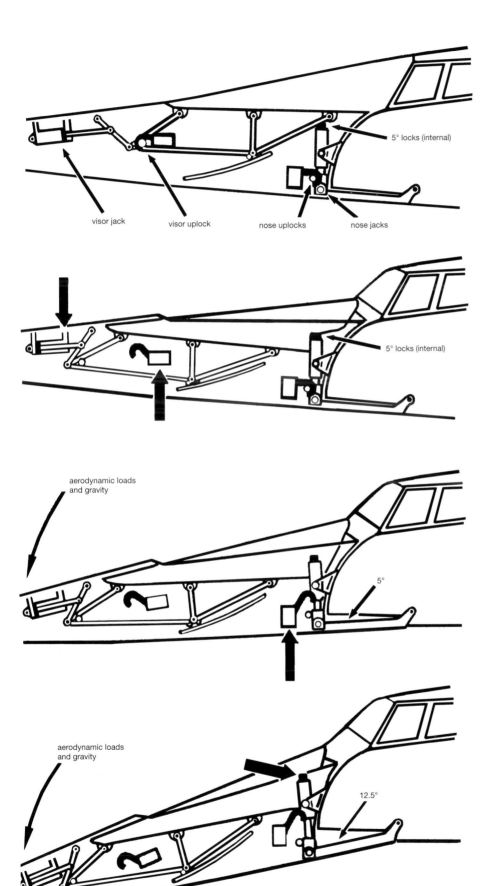

visor jack   visor uplock   nose uplocks   nose jacks

5° locks (internal)

5° locks (internal)

aerodynamic loads
and gravity

5°

aerodynamic loads
and gravity

12.5°

More on the Electrics

All the equipment on Concorde required a large amount of electrical power; this was provided by four engine-mounted integrated drive generators (IDGs) and a hydraulically-driven emergency generator for essential supplies under failure or emergency conditions. External ground power could be connected to the power distribution system through a single-point ground connection. The primary electrical system was a.c., with d.c. power from transformer rectifier units and batteries.

The a.c. system normally had its ground power supplied from an external generator, during which operation it was monitored for voltage, frequency and direction of rotation. When ground power was applied, a circuit breaker closed, which directed power to the split system breakers, the bus tie breakers (BTB) then to the a.c. main bus-bars. When Concorde started its engines, the output from each IDG was automatically directed to the a.c. main bus-bar as soon as the minimum requirements for voltage and frequency were reached and frequency synchronization had been achieved. Frequency control for each generator was provided by individual constant-speed drive (CSD) units. These could be disconnected in flight should the need arise; however, the CSD could be reset only on the ground with the relevant engine stopped. Each generator was protected at all times by a fault detection system that tripped should any limits be exceeded. Each IDG was connected to its relative bus-bar via a generator circuit breaker. All the generators could be operated in parallel and in any combination between two and four outputs; in this arrangement the bus-bars themselves were then connected via the relevant BTB and split system breakers (SSB). The SSBs connected the left-hand main a.c. bus-bars to the right-hand main power system. Normally the a.c. essential bus-bars were powered by the associated a.c. main bus-bars, however, in the event of the failure of a main bus-bar, the emergency generator would start automatically and connect to the dead essential bus-bar thus restoring power.

Should there be a failure of the primary electrical generators the emergency power generator would kick in. This hydraulically powered supply was driven by the green hydraulic system and could supply enough power to maintain power to all essential services. This generator would start should there be a total failure of any of the main

The rear service door and the cabin windows were reduced in size to comply with American FAA regulations. Helio Coelho

This view along an Air France Concorde shows the curves engineered into the fuselage and wings by the aircraft's designers. Looking to the rear, one of the aft access doors is open to allow the cabin to be serviced before the next group of passengers board. Bernard Charles

a.c. bus-bars or if Nos 1 and 2 engines be shutdown in flight.

The d.c. power generating system was governed by four transformer rectifier units (TRUs). Nos 1 and 4 were powered from the a.c. essential bus-bars, while the remainder draw their power from the a.c. main bus-bars. The on-board battery connected to each essential d.c. bus-bar via the essential main isolate breakers also provided d.c. power.

More on Safety

Although Concorde has had a generally exemplary safety record in comparison with subsonic aircraft, it had ample safety and emergency systems and equipment. Included in this category were the emergency evacuation alert system, emergency safety equipment, passenger and crew oxygen supplies and escape equipment.

The emergency evacuation alert system gave aural and visual warnings for both the flight and the cabin crew, this also permitted the cabin crew to operate the cabin warning system by remote control from the front passenger door position. The indicator system included a bleeper and a flashing light in the flight compartment and in each of the three vestibules. The warnings were automatically actuated at all stations whenever the flight-deck control switch was set to the 'on' position. If an emergency were signalled, the crew, both flight and cabin, had access to emergency equipment. This included a torch at the flight engineer's stations, smoke goggles for all three flight crew, plus a portable oxygen pack stowed in the miscellaneous equipment rack. In case of a fire there was a carbon dioxide fire extinguisher, asbestos gloves and a fire axe. Similar equipment was stowed in the miscellaneous equipment rack and in rack 215. Should there be a need for them, ropes and lifejackets were also available.

The passenger cabin was equipped with carbon dioxide fire extinguishers at the forward, centre and rear left-hand doors and there was a water/gas extinguisher at the centre right-hand door. Should there be a need for Concorde to ditch, there were ditching lines, one located to both port and starboard in the centre amenity stowage and in the forward amenity stowage was the escape rope. Each of the six cabin doors had slide packs installed in them, those at the forward passenger and centre doors also doubled as rafts. Another raft was positioned at the rear of the passenger cabin on the right-hand side. Emergency packs were in the forward amenity store: two at the rear of the forward cabin and one more at the rear of the cabin on the left-hand side. Emergency transmitter equipment included two radio beacons to the rear of the forward cabin and one to the rear of the aft cabin. Should there be a need for them, there were first-aid kits located in the forward, right-hand centre and rear amenity stowages. As in other aircraft, each passenger had a lifejacket under his seat and a further six were carried for the use of infants; the cabin crew also had lifejackets. Other equipment carried included a battery-operated megaphone, a fire axe and cabin crew portable oxygen sets.

The slides and combined slides/rafts could be used during the evacuation of the aircraft; those designated as slides/rafts could be detached for use as rafts, and the slides would also float, although they were not designed for long-term use. To supplement the slides/rafts were a thirty-six-man raft complete with an emergency pack; further emergency packs were available for use with the combined slides/rafts. To signal that a Concorde was down, it was fitted with two radio beacons, each of which was self-buoyant, dual-frequency and battery-operated. The escape ropes could be used in several ways to assist the passengers and crew to escape from a ditching or a crash landing. During any emergency there were emergency lighting systems available that could be armed from either the flight-deck overhead panel or the steward's panel. These lights came on automatically should there be a failure of the d.c. essential bus-bar.

The emergency oxygen systems fitted provided for both crew and passengers. The crew system was of the gaseous pressure breathing-on-demand type, the gas for which was held in high-pressure storage cylinders. Oxygen was delivered at a lower pressure suitable for human use via a control regulator which was operable up to a cabin altitude of 32,000ft (9,800m). Above this, the crew were supplied with undiluted oxygen at a progressively increasing pressure, according to the cabin altitude. The passenger system was supplied from three cylinders via a system control panel. Regulation of the gas was maintained at 40psi (2.8kg/sq cm) via a distribution panel that had an emergency override to deliver a pressure of 90psi (6.3kg/sq cm) if required. Not only could the passenger system be used for emergencies, there was a medical/therapeutic point in the passenger cabin, this having its own mask. The emergency pressure was supplied automatically should cabin altitude exceed 14,000ft (4,300m) and resulted in the passenger masks being deployed without manual intervention. The use of fixed-point oxygen systems was augmented by the provision of some portable sets, which allowed crew members to move freely about the cabin.

Concorde was also protected from the airman's greatest fear: fire in the air. A multiplicity of systems were installed on Concorde, thus there were smoke detection systems in the air generation ducts as well as in the cabin and the freight hold area. Both audible and visual alerts warned the crew of any problems. The fire detection system in the engine bays consisted of a dual-loop sensor which required that both loops must detect a fire before giving a warning to the crew. This ensured that, should there be a failure in one loop, no spurious warning was indicated and that a failed loop could be switched out, leaving the other to provide cover. Supplementing the fire detection system was that covering engine overheating, although this was specific to certain parts of the engine and not general like the fire detectors. Outside the general fire detection system in the engine nacelle there was a similar double-loop system with similar redundancy to detect a torching flame. A further overheat detection system was located in the nacelles; this consisted

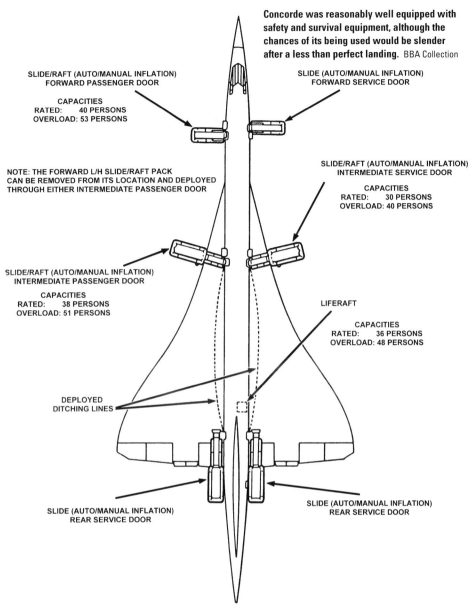

Concorde was reasonably well equipped with safety and survival equipment, although the chances of its being used would be slender after a less than perfect landing. BBA Collection

SLIDE/RAFT (AUTO/MANUAL INFLATION) FORWARD PASSENGER DOOR

CAPACITIES
RATED: 40 PERSONS
OVERLOAD: 53 PERSONS

SLIDE (AUTO/MANUAL INFLATION) FORWARD SERVICE DOOR

NOTE: THE FORWARD L/H SLIDE/RAFT PACK CAN BE REMOVED FROM ITS LOCATION AND DEPLOYED THROUGH EITHER INTERMEDIATE PASSENGER DOOR

SLIDE/RAFT (AUTO/MANUAL INFLATION) INTERMEDIATE SERVICE DOOR

CAPACITIES
RATED: 30 PERSONS
OVERLOAD: 40 PERSONS

SLIDE/RAFT (AUTO/MANUAL INFLATION) INTERMEDIATE PASSENGER DOOR

CAPACITIES
RATED: 38 PERSONS
OVERLOAD: 51 PERSONS

LIFERAFT

CAPACITIES
RATED: 36 PERSONS
OVERLOAD: 48 PERSONS

DEPLOYED DITCHING LINES

SLIDE (AUTO/MANUAL INFLATION) REAR SERVICE DOOR

SLIDE (AUTO/MANUAL INFLATION) REAR SERVICE DOOR

ALL SLIDE/RAFT PACKS CAN BE DISENGAGED AT THE DOOR SILL TO SERVE AS RAFTS AND FLOTATION AIDS

of simple temperature sensing elements connected in series to form loops on the engine-bay doors. Their primary purpose was to detect hot gas or air leaks. Beyond the engine nacelles there were further systems, one located in each wing leading edge and providing coverage of any hot-air leaks from the air-conditioning system.

Having detected a fire or high overheating, there were four extinguishers available for suppressing any conflagration. There was one extinguisher bottle in each engine bay, these being controlled from the flight deck by electrical initiation. Each extinguisher had two firing heads and was capable of

suppressing a fire in its own or the adjacent engine bay. When an extinguisher was discharged, its contents were dispersed around the bay by nozzles around the periphery and its operation closed a fire valve that shut off the flow to the air-conditioning primary and secondary heat exchangers. Further protection for the engine bays was provided by fire flaps whose operation sealed off the engine bay to starve it of oxygen. These normally acted as secondary air doors and engine-bay vent doors in the engine fire zone. These were operated in an emergency by an engine shutdown handle in the cockpit. Protecting the fuel tanks was the purpose of the fuel tank vent ignition suppression system. This used a flame detector that automatically triggered a discharge of agent into the vent pipe between the detector and the fuel tanks. This ensured that any ignition of the vented fuel by any external source could not feed back to the fuel tanks. Further protection was provided by smoke detectors in the air generation ducts and the passenger cabin and freight holds.

Handling the Fuel

Unlike the design of subsonic aircraft, the fuel system on Concorde had two functions, the unusual one being to provide trimming throughout the aircraft's speed range. The fuel was housed in thirteen sealed tanks integral with the wings and fuselage and divided into three distinct groups: engine feed, main transfer and trim transfer. Arranging the fuel in these groups meant that it was delivered to the engines at flow rates, temperatures and pressures to comply with the engines' operating parameters. The trim group was the means of controlling and adjusting Concorde's centre of gravity throughout the flight envelope and also compensated for the differing centres of pressure experienced during transonic acceleration and deceleration. The fuel system also acted as a heat sink for excessive heat generated by the hydraulic system and cabin conditioning and that generated by kinetic energy. As the fuel was stored in separate tanks, this reduced the possibility of fuel surges and the devastating effects of hydraulic dieseling. A further precaution to compensate for Concorde's steep climb-out angle was the de-aeration system which ensured that air in the tanks did not become a hazard.

Each of the Olympus engines had its own fuel feed from a dedicated collector tank, but there was a cross-feed system that allowed any engine or group of engines to be supplied from any other collector tank. To cover the possibility of low pressure in the fuel lines there was an accumulator which delivered fuel until the pumps took up the slack. Between the low pressure valve and the engine-driven pump was an LP protection system which allowed fuel to bypass the air conditioning and hydraulic heat exchangers in the event of low fuel pressure. When the bypass circuit was disarmed a constant flow of fuel passed through the heat exchangers.

The main transfer group of fuel tanks included Nos 5, 6, 7 and 8 tanks, which operated in sequence to reduce the disruption to the aircraft's c.g. while supplying fuel to the engine collector tanks. The main transfer sequence was manually selected and used the pumps in Nos 5 and 7 tanks; the former fed fuel into No.1 tank via the left-hand pump and No.2 tank via the right-hand pump, while the latter fed fuel to No.3 tank via the left-hand pump and to No.4 tank via the right-hand pump. As soon as Nos 5 and 7 tanks had emptied, their role was taken over by Nos 6 and 8 tanks. Before Nos 5 and 7 tanks switched out, they were replenished by Nos 5A and 7A tanks.

The trim transfer system was used to redistribute fuel in the trim tanks and main transfer tanks so that the c.g. could be moved to its optimum position for take-off, subsonic and supersonic flight. Under normal operation, the system was automatically controlled from the engineer's panels; however, there was a forward transfer override control available to the pilots for use under abnormal circumstances which might require a rapid transfer forward of fuel.

To reduce the possibility of fume explosions, the fuel tanks vented into a ring main gallery which then fed a scavenge tank that subsequently vented to the atmosphere through the rear fuselage. A scavenge pump automatically removed any fuel that had entered the scavenge tank and returned it for reuse in No.1 tank. When flying at high altitude, the aircraft's tanks were pressurized to between 1.2 and 1.5psi (0.08–0.11kg/sq cm) which prevented the fuel from boiling off. This increased differential pressure was required to maintain a minimum pressure as the altitude increased. Should there be a need for it, there was a fuel-jettison system installed which was part of the trim transfer group; the dumping of fuel was through a vent pipe at the rear of the aircraft. To ensure that sufficient fuel remained for the engines, the system monitored the amount being dumped before switching out. To combat the possibility of aeration in tanks 10, 11, 6, 8, 5A and 7A, whose contents remained mainly static during the climb-out, there was a special pump in tank No.10; the others used the built-in system pumps. These de-aerated the fuel in the tanks, thus reducing the chance of pump cavitation or transients in tank pressure.

Fuel contents were measured by the fuel quantity indicators which worked through capacitor-type gauging channels. These gave indications of each tank's contents at the flight engineer's fuel management panel and at the refuel control panel during refuelling. The fuel gauging system supplied data to the central dash panel and the management and refuel panels, and also provided tank limit control during trim transfers and refuels, as well as c.g. data at the cockpit panels, Mach limits to the same panels and warnings in the cockpit should the c.g. limits be compromised. The load control system pumped fuel from tanks Nos 9 and 10 into Nos 11, 5 and 7 to provide a rearward c.g. transfer, and to gain a forward trim, fuel was transferred from tank No.11 to Nos 9, 5 and 7. The trim tank contents were preselected using the load limit selectors, there being settings for tank Nos 9, 10 and 11. Any fuel excess outside trimming requirements was automatically transferred to Nos 5 and 7 tanks. Since this was a vital service, the trim transfer system had duplicated electrical control circuitry whose No.1 channel was the primary and No.2 monitored it and would switch in if No.1 failed.

The c.g. was indicated in the cockpit by three distinct channels. The primary one was the main channel which drew its data from all the fuel tanks and used it to compute the c.g. Standby channel No.1 gained its data from the tanks on the left-hand side of the aircraft and channel A of tanks 9, 10 and 11. For computational purposes, the resultant figure was doubled and presented to the crew. The No.2 channel took its data from the right-hand tanks plus channel B of tanks 9, 10 and 11 and presented its results in a similar manner. The setting of the c.g. limits by the crew was by the use of 'bugs' which defined the forward and aft limits throughout the Mach range. These were set on the Machmeters in the cockpit and moved relative to the aircraft's speed and c.g. range. The limits were displayed by two separate channels, one was contained in the No.1 standby c.g. pack and delivered data to the captain's position and the other channel was contained within the No.2 standby c.g. pack and delivered its indications to the first officer's and the flight engineer's indicators.

Since Concorde was sensitive regarding its c.g., it had a c.g. and Mach limit warning system. The first level of warning indication activated as the set boundary limit was reached and should the set boundary be breached. The warnings were initiated through the standby Nos 1 and 2 c.g. packs and activated lights on the master warning panel and the flight engineer's station.

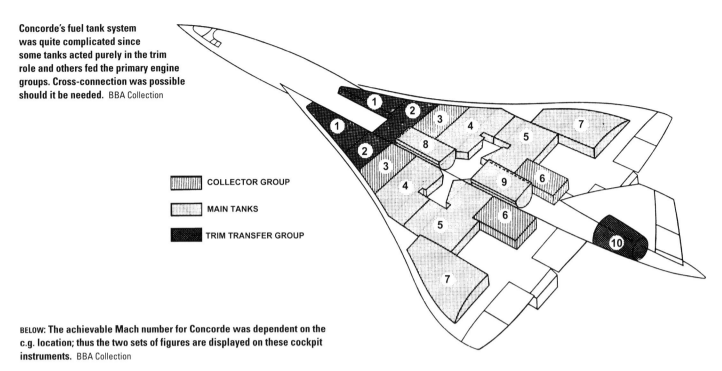

Concorde's fuel tank system was quite complicated since some tanks acted purely in the trim role and others fed the primary engine groups. Cross-connection was possible should it be needed. BBA Collection

COLLECTOR GROUP

MAIN TANKS

TRIM TRANSFER GROUP

BELOW: **The achievable Mach number for Concorde was dependent on the c.g. location; thus the two sets of figures are displayed on these cockpit instruments.** BBA Collection

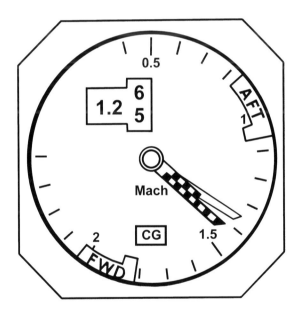

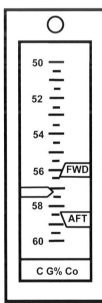

More on the Hydraulics

Hydraulic power was at the heart of Concorde operation. It was provided by three independent systems; two, blue and green, acted as the primaries and there was a yellow system designated for standby purposes. Each of the three was powered by two engine-driven pumps per powerplant and emergency power came from a ram air turbine. The pumps mounted on engines Nos 1 and 2 delivered hydraulic power to the green system and those on Nos 3 and 4 engines delivered it to the blue system; pumps on Nos 2 and 4 engines covered the yellow system. During normal operation the three hydraulic systems operated at a pressure of 4,000psi (280kg/sq cm) and there was an overpressure limiter that allowed for a maximum pressure of 4,500psi (316kg/sq cm). To prevent cavitation of the hydraulic pumps the three systems' reservoirs were pressurized and there was an auxiliary air compressor that could be run to ensure that the reservoirs were pressurized before the engines started. The emergency hydraulic

system was powered by a two-bladed ram air turbine which in use would drive two hydraulic pumps should the main power-plants' windmilling speed be insufficient to drive the hydraulic and the electrical systems in the event of a four-engine flame-out. To supply hydraulic power for ground servicing purposes there were two electrically-driven pumps that would pressurize both the main and the standby system.

The green hydraulic system supplied power to the No.1 and 2 engine air intake ramp and spill doors, plus one ram each of the power flight controls and the relay jacks. It also supplied pressure to the artificial feel, one No.11 fuel tank pump, droop nose and visor, landing gear, main wheel brakes, anti-skid units and the nose-wheel steering jacks. The blue system supplied power to Nos 3 and 4 air intake ramps and spill doors, the alternate rams for the power flying controls and the alternate feeds to the relay jacks. The blue system also provided the second supply to the other artificial feel channel and the remaining No.11 tank pump. Standby power was supplied by the yellow system, which could, if needed, supply hydraulic pressure to all four intake ramps and spill doors, the flight controls, the droop nose and visor, landing-gear deployment, wheel brakes and anti-skid, emergency and parking braking, without the anti-skid system being operative, and nose-wheel steering.

One of the primary systems driven by the green and the blue hydraulic system was the

Even surrounded by ground equipment, Concorde looked a purposeful, sleek aircraft; and its dramatic sweeps and angles are emphasized in this photo. Nick Challenor

landing gear. This consisted of the two main gears, the nose leg and the tail bumper wheels, plus the gear doors. In the event of an emergency, there were two standby systems: one was the independent hydraulic system and the other used a mechanical release and free-fall under gravity to drop the undercarriage into the locked position. Concorde's braking system comprised dual, hydraulically-powered, multi-disc wheel brake units, governed by an anti-skid system, all being mounted on the main legs. Should there be a loss of primary hydraulic power, emergency braking could be sustained by an accumulator which provided pressure for a short period. The final undercarriage system was the nose-wheel steering which was electrically controlled and hydraulically driven through the rudder pedals and the hand wheels on the flight deck.

This then was the complex machine that our tyro crew would fly for either British Airways or Air France.

LEFT: Looking more like an insect with everything out and down, an Air France Concorde approaches Paris Charles de Gaulle after another transatlantic journey. Bernard Charles

BELOW: The end result – high above the clouds, BA Concorde G-BOAG flies on its way to a landing at Heathrow. BBA Collection

CHAPTER FIVE

Trials and Tribulations

The outward face of Concorde was the cabin crew, moving about, efficiently dealing with the needs of their passengers. Although this supersonic marvel was slightly cramped inside because its purpose was to achieve flight speeds above Mach 1, the service aboard it more than amply justified the price tag. Included in the ticket price was a meal excellent in every way.

Handling Emergencies

As well as dispensing meals and drinks, the cabin crew were well versed in the disciplines related to the safety of the aircraft. Before take-off the cabin crew went through the customary safety routine and then described what passengers might need to do in emergencies such as a crash-landing or a ditching. They then ensured that the passenger luggage bins were closed and that those marked 'CREW USE ONLY–RESERVE A L'EQUIPAGE' did not contain any metallic objects that could interfere with the flux valves by a magnetic disturbance. Part of the briefing also concerned smoking areas, which were restricted to the passenger cabin zones and the flight-deck; smoking was not allowed in the toilets and there were hard-wired smoke detectors installed to warn of infringements.

Should there be a need for an emergency evacuation all the cabin crew assisted. Once the aircraft had stopped the crew guided passengers towards the forward cabin exits after which they were to shepherd their charges clear of the downed machine. Should neither of the forward escape slides be available, at least one crew member used the escape rope in the forward vestibule to leave the aircraft and attempt to realign any of the door slides/rafts for escape usage. Should the aircraft have to ditch, the flight crew would have already transmitted a mayday which included the disposition of the crew and passengers, intentions on landing, location and a description of any dangerous cargo, plus the remaining quantity of

High above the clouds, a BA Concorde, G-BOAA, cruises towards the point where the thrust augmentation can be selected to push it up to Mach 2. BBA Collection

fuel still on board. While this was happening, the cabin crew would have advised the passengers to put on their uninflated life-jackets, an action that they themselves would have already carried out. These actions completed, the flight crew would begin to discharge fuel and pull the circuit breakers that controlled the ground proximity warning and landing gear warning

indicators, this would be followed by an audio cancellation at 180kt otherwise the pulled undercarriage circuit breaker would set the warning system off. Once these parts of the checklist had been completed the aircraft would be depressurized to below 10,000ft (3,000m). Once this had been done both the cabin and the actual altitude should be roughly the same, which

When Concorde touches down, tyre contact generates a large amount of smoke, as this view of a British Airways aircraft shows. Alpha Echo wears the Chatham Dockyard flag motif on its fin and rudder. Nick Challenor

British Airways and Air France Test Crews

British Airways			Air France		
Captain	Senior Flight Officer	Senior Flight Engineer	Captain	Senior Flight Officer	Senior Flight Engineer
AR Meadows	CJD Orlebar	WD Johnston	G Jacob	Metias	Frot
HC McMullen	BR Oliver	J Stanbridege	M Gilles	R Puyperoux	R Duguet
AJ Massie	M Bannister	TB Dewis	F Rude	A Colloc	Cuechiaro
JD Eames	D Whitton	P Eggington	P Dudal	Marchand	Roiganbach
JD Cook	WI Smith	PJ Phillips	M Butel	Holbecq	Ranty
JC Hutchinson	CD Green	DA MacDonald	M Chemel	Chambrier	Poulain
JL Chorley	RJ Taylor	JA Rodger	M Caillat	J Marcot	Diou
NA Britton	B Holland	RC Bricknell	Lalanne	Lorisch	A Blanc
BO Walpole	JR White	P Ling	G le Gales	JC Delorme	H Perrier
JW Burton	PW Horton	RN Webb	Machavoine	J Schwartz	M Vasseur
J Bradshaw	MR Withey	TJ Quarrey	C Marty	Y Pingret	
P Duffey	AI Heald	SG Floyd	Leclerc	V Venchiarruti	
KD Leney	WD Lowe	IF Smith	P Dudal	B Vialle	
J Hirst	K Williams	M Cooper	J Franchi		
NV Todd	BR Holland	WJ Brown	JL Chatelain		
BJ Calvert	DC Rowland	IV Kirby	G Defer		
DG Ross	WJ Piper	PJ Newman	A Quilichini		
C Morris	B Irven	W Dobbs			
MA Riley	DG Mitchell	J Groatham	**BAC Test Crew**		
BGT Tichener	BJ Calvert	AA Brown	Pilots	Flight Engineers	Observers
JC McNeilley	D Cobley	SL Bolton			
HJ Linfield	B Harmer (F)	JE Lidiard	EB Trubshaw	DFB Ackary	AA Driver
JM Rendall			PP Baker	A Heywood	RG Campbell
A Winstanley			A Smith	BG Watts	D Corbyn
D Brister			G Wilkinson (CAA)		
P Allan					
J Lowe					
M Bannister					

allowed the emergency depressurization selector to be engaged.

All these actions would happen in a very short period and would be followed by the final ditching briefing delivered by the captain. This would be followed by the pred-itching checklist which required the seat-belt signs and no smoking signs to be on while the emergency lighting system was set to arm. The flight crew would then begin their final checklist which included

the landing gear, nose and visor being in the up position and the intake ramps at 0 per cent, the ramp masters on manual and the bleed and ditching valves selected shut. The final call would be to lock the seats and power them down. Completing these steps would lead to a descent to 1,000ft (305m) where the PA call of 'Take up ditching positions' would be given to be followed by 'Brace, brace' at 200ft (61m). Should the PA system be unavailable, the

same signal could be given by cabin signs. As the 50ft (15m) altitude point approached, the autothrottle would be dis-engaged, the throttle setting being held manually. At a signal from the captain, the flight engineer would pull all engine shut-down handles. Having survived such a touchdown, the crew would begin passen-ger evacuation by the most convenient door. While the flight crew were carrying out their tasks and passing on instructions to the cabin crew, they too would be carry-ing out their own actions to prepare for ditching. Having acknowledged the instruction to prepare to ditch, the senior cabin crew member ensured that col-leagues were fully aware of their duties, after which the passengers were fully briefed on the situation and the cabin lighting would be turned to maximum. The cabin crew then secured all loose hand bag-gage and equipment, locked down the gal-ley trolleys and equipment and turned off the galley electrical systems. Since the fit-ting of lifejackets could be difficult with small children, the cabin crew needed to do this, after which blankets and pillows would be given to passengers, who by then would have been redistributed. The reason for this was to place able-bodied passengers next to the disabled, the physically unsta-ble, children and young people. Before the final stage of the descent the cabin crew would check that the lifejackets fitted cor-rectly, the seats were in the upright posi-tion, any high-heel shoes removed and

TOP: Pictured soon after its maiden flight is the French Concorde prototype 01, F-WTSS, complete with short tail-cone, later extended to improve stability. Alongside is an Armstrong-Whitworth Meteor NF.11 of the CEV acting as a photo/chase aircraft.
J.A. Todd Collection via Lee Howard

ABOVE: The next Concorde to fly was the British prototype G-BSST. Typical of the Olympus engine is the dirty exhaust, a problem that nearly saw Concorde banned from landing in New York. Unlike the production machines, the prototypes had an unusual paint scheme applied for photographic recording purposes. BBA Collection

RIGHT: Although much of Concorde was white, the engine nacelles and wing leading edges on the British prototype were painted black. The latter had white photo-calibration marks imposed for data recording purposes. BBA Collection

TOP: **Shock cones from the thrust augmentors feature strongly in this view of the British preproduction G-AXDN. A close look at the tail-cone, under the rudder, reveals the location of the brake-parachute door.** BBA Collection

ABOVE: **With everything out and down the French prototype F-WTSS, sporting the Paris show number 375, comes in to land.** BBA Collection

FOLLOWING PAGE
This dramatic angle emphasizes the slenderness of the Concorde airframe. Note the deflected upper rudder segment (and pity the paint team applying the Air France tail logo). Bernard Charles

THIS PAGE
TOP: Concorde 02 on the ground at RAF Fairford, which was used as the test base. Although the aircraft is the centre of attention, the surrounding vehicles and ground equipment are noteworthy, since they are bedecked with the full range of government-furnished colours. Adrian Falconer

ABOVE: Possibly the most unflattering aspect of the Concorde droop nose is its first position, with the visor retracted; the angle mars the dart-like appearance of the aircraft. Adrian Falconer

OPPOSITE PAGE
TOP: When British Airways accepted its first Concordes they retained their white overall finish, over which was applied a blue cheat line. The fin sported a red-based play on the Union Flag. This machine is G-N94AD, registered for use in the combined Braniff/British Airways flights. BBA Collection

BOTTOM: A further change in the colour scheme for the British Airways Concorde fleet saw the major colours switch places. Thus the cheat line became red, with the speedbird incorporated at the leading edge, the stylized flag on the fin became more pronouncedly blue and the titling featured capital letters for both words. BBA Collection

ABOVE: One of the most unusual colour schemes applied to a Concorde was this Pepsi design on Air France F-BTSD as product promotion by the company. Jose M. Palacios

LEFT: Written large on the forward fuselage is the Pepsi titling. It would appear that the aircraft was painted with the visor raised since the area normally hidden in supersonic flight is still white. Jose M. Palacios

ABOVE: Air France Concorde F-BTSC wears the first and short-lived, original colour scheme; a similar one was carried by such aircraft as the Comet. BBA Collection

BELOW: Captured on film in New Zealand, this British Airways Concorde glistens after recent rain. Rob Neil

ABOVE: Caught just before touch down at Farnborough is the preproduction aircraft G-AXDN. The unusual markings were required for use by cameras recording the behaviour of the aircraft in flight. BBA Collection

BELOW: Only one British Airways Concorde was allocated to the Singapore Airlines run, this being G-N94AD, but even this was half-hearted as the Singapore scheme was applied to only one side. BBA Collection

ABOVE: Instead of the more rigid airline scheme, British Airways later adopted a series of styles known as 'ethnic'. That applied to Concorde was based on the Chatham Naval Dockyard flag. This proved to be one of the more popular schemes. By the time this picture was taken the airline's full title had been restored to the nose, the previously applied 'British' having been subject to criticism. BBA Collection

BELOW: Air France used essentially only one basic finish on its Concordes. This was based on the tricolour with the EU star symbol over the flash on the fin. Here F-BVFB prepares to touch down at a snow-covered Charles de Gaulle airport. Bernard Charles

stowed, seatbelts secured, ties and collars loosened, spectacles and dentures removed, all sharp objects removed and that the bracing position was understood by all passengers. The cabin crew's final action would be to turn the lights to dim and tell the captain that cabin preparation was complete; at this point they would take up their own ditching positions.

The cabin crew were also trained for crash-landings. There are two types of these, unpremeditated and premeditated. The former was defined as one that takes place without warning, such as during landing or take-off, and the latter is defined as giving ample time to prepare for evacuation. During either of these the most important factor is time, and thus the cabin and the flight crew are drilled so that their actions almost border on the automatic. Any landing that could involve fire or the breaking of the aircraft's structure required that the cabin staff be warned as quickly as possible so that they could evacuate the aircraft as soon as it came to rest. Should there be a landing involving a hung-up undercarriage leg, the cabin crew had to be aware that the aircraft could either be resting on a wingtip or, more awkwardly, on its tail. In either case a quick decision had to be made regarding the deployment of escape slides to ensure that passengers could slide to the ground safely. During a night evacuation the cabin lights were required to be dimmed so that crew and passengers could adjust to outside conditions quickly.

Type Certification Air Data Sheet No.A45EU

This type certification was issued by the Federal Aviation Authority on 9 January 1979, with copies going to British Aerospace at Weybridge and the Bristol Division and to the Société Nationale Industrielle Aérospatiale, at 37 Boulevard de Montmorency in Paris.

The first section described Concorde and included the fuels and oils available for unlimited usage. These included ASTM 1655-57 Grade JET A1 aircraft fuel, this having the French specification AIR 3405 C Issue 4, and the British equivalent being D.Eng RD2494 Issue 7; the Canadian specification was given as 3-GP-23h. Only one fuel additive was specified as mandatory: Shell ASA 3 antistatic additive. Others that could be added included anti-icing, corrosion inhibitors or a combination plus automate yellow for use in fuel-system leakage detection. Oil types approved for the Olympus engines included the products of BP, Esso, Mobil and Shell, and Esso were approved as the only supplier of the oils required for the integrated drive generator.

Performance specifications concerning engine limitations were the next defined items, these included maxima concerning thrust outputs at several altitudes, such as the maximum overspeed of 110 per cent being available for only 2sec. Oil system parameters were then set out, these including temperatures and pressures, and similar data for the fuel system was listed next. The certificate then laid out the flight restrictions, these including several speeds and altitudes, although many of the figures were to be found in the pilot's manual. Further handling data was also defined; this including the c.g. range, datum, maximum weights, the minimum crew (always the pilot, the co-pilot and the flight engineer), the maximum passenger number and baggage weight.

The capacities of the fuel tanks were given at maximum contents with a specific density of 6.68lb/US gal. Also laid down in this table were the usable and unusable fuel totals, unusable fuel being that which was either trapped in the tanks, in the sumps and in the fuel galleries. Oil capacities per engine were given as 26 US quarts (28ltr), of which 11 (10.5ltr) were usable (6.5 US quarts [6.2ltr] being required for starting).

The maximum operating altitude of 60,000ft (18,300m) came next, after mention was made of the control surface range of movements (the pilot's manual was the source for these). The all-important Certificate of Airworthiness for Export/Certificat de Navigabilite pour Exportation carried aboard each Concorde was mentioned in the next paragraph, these being serially numbered between 01 and 16. This document had its own reference number: Concorde Document No. 408.106/78 Issue 2, including revision 1. All modifications carried out by British Airways and Air France and approved by the CAA and the DGAC were laid out in Air France Document No. AF-01-TSS, the index of Air France originated modifications and Civil Aviation Authority letter 9/30/CON 10FH, dated 15 December 1978. Additional paperwork needing to be carried on Concorde included the FAA Standard Airworthiness Certificate, which was based on the two documents issued by the British and the French airworthiness authorities.

Concorde's certification was based on FAR 21.29 (a)(1)(ii), which, in turn, was based on the Anglo-French Supersonic Transport TSS Standards, as defined in contents list No.29, dated 26 March 1976, portions of FAR 25 effective from 1 February 1965 (which included all amendments appropriate to a supersonic transport), portions of the US Special Conditions for Concorde No.25-43-EU-12, dated 21 June 1972, plus FAR Part 36. The aircraft was approved with respect to optional certification requirements relating to ditching, ditching equipment and ice protection that corresponded to FAR 25.801.25.1415 and 25.1419. The type certification was applied for on 15 July 1965 and approved on 9 January 1979.

This view of an Air France Concorde shows the undercarriage units retracting as it leaves Paris. The glow of the afterburners can just be seen in Sierra Delta's jet pipes. Philippe Noret

Possibly the most difficult event to deal with is the unpremeditated crash-landing. For there to be survivors the crew need to act quickly and decisively. If time is available the captain will order an immediate evacuation of the aircraft and define which doors and escape slides are to be used. The unpremeditated crash-landing is normally announced over the PA that all aboard must 'Prepare for crash-landing'. The passengers are warned via either the PA or the flashing of cabin signs to strap themselves in. On the descent the first officer would call 'Brace, brace' or flash the cabin lights at 200ft. Exit doors are not opened until the aircraft comes to rest, after which the crew are expected to help the passengers to evacuate, having defined which set of doors to use. The cabin crew have their own duties to perform before a crash-landing (similar to those for ditching), thus all loose items of whatever nature need to be secured and stowed away. Passengers are also warned about their clothing and other items, after which the senior cabin attendant will report that the passenger cabin is ready for the events to follow. Once the aircraft has stopped the crew would operate only those doors unaffected by fire or other hazard. The passengers would then be directed out of the doors and the crew authorized to use reasonable force to ensure that the evacuees are kept moving. As the passengers approach the forward door and its slide they would be urged to 'Jump, jump, jump', although the instructions for the centre and rear doors are slightly modified to 'Walk to the slide and jump'. When assisting passengers down a slide the crew are expected to move them physically along, but only below shoulder level, the foot or the knee could be used in the small of the back to tip them down the slide. Although to slide down on the buttocks is the preferred means of departing, to hurry up the process an ejection in any position is recommended. Obviously the crew could not fully evacuate the aircraft on their own and so assistance in the shape of four-able bodied persons would be needed to help people off the slide and away from the aircraft. Once all the passengers were clear, the crew make their departure.

Not all flights in Concorde were revenue-earning, some flights were for training or delivery purposes. Since most of the occupants during these trips were aircrew, the evacuation instructions were completely different. During these flights only the

forward passenger cabin was in use, normally only sixteen people were on board and thus evacuation, guided by the senior cabin crew member, was by the left-hand, forward door. Once the warning of a crash-landing had been given those in the cabin needed to be briefed, the galley equipment to be turned off and the cabin dividers placed to open and the doorways kept clear of such things as the aircrews' 'nav' bags. Once completed, the lights were set at dim and the captain informed that the cabin and its occupants were ready for crash-landing. Once the aircraft had stopped, the selected door must have its emergency lights on, after which the occupants could evacuate.

Not every incident on board an aircraft involves collision with the ground; however, there are occasions when the emergency equipment needs to be used. The most likely item to be used is the oxygen system, which comes into play when the cabin altitude exceeds 14,000ft (4,300m). When this happens the regulator pressure is increased to 90psi (6.3kg/sq cm) and the therapeutic valve also opened. Once the pressure line was open it forced the passenger cabin masks to be presented and provided a continuous flow of oxygen. Once the cabin altitude stabilized below 10,000ft (3,000m) the oxygen flow was reduced to normal pressure. While this system was in use the crew needed to monitor

a warning light that flashed amber should the line pressure exceed 70psi (4.9kg/sq cm). Once the pressure increased above 85psi (6.0kg/sq cm) the warning light should go out. Should there be a failure in the oxygen system there was a manual override knob available that would mechanically override the barometric control, which in turn would pressurize the oxygen system. This would be the case until the emergency override returned to normal. The cabin crew were fully briefed in the use of the oxygen system under emergency circumstances and in individual cases where an ill passenger might require the gas.

Concorde had two doors for passengers and four service doors. All were outward opening, although only the forward passenger and service doors had observation windows. Other doors on the aircraft included an upper baggage compartment door which could be accessed from the outside, although there was a means of opening the compartment from the inside by an emergency handle. The other hatches covering the lower baggage hold and other miscellaneous compartments could be accessed only from the outside. The flight-deck access door was electronically locked through a striking plate controlled by a switch on the flight-compartment roof panel; this ensured that only the crew could open the flight-deck door from the inside, although it was

Magnificent is the only word that describes this view of a BA Concorde leaving London Heathrow on another flight to JFK Airport, New York. BBA Collection

possible to open it from the passenger side by a key. This might seem like a point of vulnerability; however, there was also a mechanical bolt, an observation mirror in the ceiling and an observer-scope built into the door. By contrast, the toilet doors we manually locked but could be opened from outside by using a special tool.

Although much of the foregoing may seem like a catalogue of potential accidents and disasters, the hardest battle Concorde would ever face would be that of gaining permission to fly into New York. On 21

determine the effects that such an aircraft could have on the quality of the human environment. Making the Europeans' joint case to William Coleman, Secretary of Transportation, were representatives of Air France, British Airways, government officials from both nations and representatives from the airframe and engine manufacturers. Standing in opposition was a collective of environmentalists who would attempt to portray the Anglo-French Concorde as a singular source of excessive pollution that would poison North America, while

going supersonic over any part of the continental USA.

Other parts of the judgment handed down by Coleman covered many aspects of Concorde operations; thus Britain and France would be most careful to comply since the economic impact on the countries and their airlines would be grievous should Concorde be banned from landing due to any infringement. Should such an event happen it would, however, lay the USA open to claims of favouritism with regard to their own airlines, which had

BA Concorde G-BOAA with its visor in position for high-speed flight; not long after, the afterburners would be engaged and the aircraft accelerate across the Atlantic. BBA Collection

January 1976 at 11:40hr GMT, simultaneous departures took place from London Heathrow and Paris Charles de Gaulle airports. These were not ordinary flights since the stars of the show were both Concordes.

Routes and Sales

Getting to this momentous point had been an uphill struggle since the American authorities made strenuous efforts to ban the aircraft from landing anywhere within their borders. The legislative tool employed to confound the Anglo-French proposal was the National Environmental Protection Act of 1969, requiring that a full evaluation be presented and investigated to

completely and carefully avoiding the impact that the existing fleets of subsonic airliners, produced mainly by Boeing and Douglas, were having on the environment due to their use of inefficient turbojet engines. In the event, Coleman granted a limited, sixteen-month access for Concorde to conduct scheduled flights to the USA, beginning on 4 February. The criteria as laid down allowed for two flights per day into John F. Kennedy Airport in New York and one per day into Dulles Airport in Washington. Further restrictions placed upon the aircraft meant that it could not land within the USA earlier than 07:00hr nor depart after 22:00hr local. In common with the authorities in Britain and France, America would also ban Concorde from

also been objecting to the aircraft. A possible reverse effect involving trade between the USA and the Europeans was also seen as a potential consequence of such a ban. With the way clear for operations to start, both Concordes left their home airports and headed across the Atlantic.

Although a triumph of technical and operational achievement, the total production of Concordes, including prototypes and preproduction airframes, would total only twenty in all. The reasons behind such a short run stemmed from the original over-optimistic ordering by foreign airlines and an inaccurate estimate that worldwide requirements could reach 240. Illustrating this is the Pan Am order placed in June 1963 for six Concorde SSTs, this being

Concorde Orders and Options	
1984	
British Airways	1
1980	
Air France	1
1972	
Iran Air	2(+1)
Air France	4
CAAC	2(+2)
BOAC	5
1966	
Qantas	4
Eastern	6
1965	
Air Canada	4
Air India	2
American	6
Braniff	3
Eastern	2
JAL	3
Lufthansa	3
MEA-Air Liban	2
Qantas	6
Sabena	2
TWA	6
United	6
1964	
American	4
Air France	2
BOAC	8
Continental	3
TWA	4
1963	
Air France	6 – first order – final total is 8
BOAC	6 – first order – final total is 8
Pan American	6(+2)
Total	**81 incl. options, plus 16 delivered.**

quickly followed by TWA's, which tentatively placed an order for a further six. The total orders and options for Concordes are shown in the table (*left*).

Many of these airlines had placed their orders under the assumption that the creation of sonic booms over land would be acceptable. The study of the effects of such disturbances in Britain, France and the USA had proved inconclusive; however, the anti-Concorde movement had increased its influence especially as US Senator Proxmire had given his aid to the cause. As the pressure mounted against Concorde the enthusiasm of the airlines waned, leaving only Air France and BOAC (later British Airways) as the only confirmed customers. Not only was the contentious issue of sonic boom given as a reason to cancel by Pan Am and JAL, but their adherence to traditional accounting methods meant that they could not accurately determine any profits or losses from operating Concorde, although they were silent when asked the same question concerning the subsonic airliners due to be ordered by them. One of the strangest reasons given for cancelling an order was that the aircraft did not come equipped with an auxiliary power unit to provide independent power supplies and engine starting.

The initial take-up of the production airframes meant that of the sixteen production aircraft, five were placed in storage after test flying unsold. In Britain airframes 214 and 216 sat unused and in France airframes 203, 213 and 215 were parked, awaiting a buyer. An attempt to interest Singapore Airlines was only partially successful. Originally the airline required a wet lease, complete with crews, for four years. As the manufacturers felt unable to provide crews for the duration

of the lease, the deal fell through. Allied to manning problems were those of spares and maintenance costs and which party would foot the bill. Eventually British Airways stepped in to offer a form of counter proposal which required BA to supply an aircraft and crews to fly the route London–Bahrain–Singapore in return for a share of the profits. Only a single aircraft would be involved and it was painted in Singapore Airlines colours on the port side, retaining BA colours on the other side. By 1980 this service was cancelled since passenger loads were uninspiring and, more importantly, the flights were loss-making. While this was taking place attempts were being made to sell off the remaining five white-tail Concordes to the Philippines and South Korea. After many test flights and presentations by teams from Britain and France, both countries eventually rejected Concorde, although at least one passenger is reported to have increased her footwear collection considerably during this period. As the stored airframes were complete air-tested machines, they eventually entered service with British Airways and Air France, which gave each airline a seven-strong fleet.

One final attempt was made to sell the Concordes in storage; the expected operator was to be Federal Express which wished to use the aircraft in the high-speed freight carrier role. A study into the feasibility of such a conversion was undertaken during 1981–82. As this was to be a complete change in the aircraft's role most of the passenger-based equipment would be dispensed with; thus the cabin oxygen system and air conditioning would be removed and parts of the undercarriage emergency lowering system would need to be relocated since the freight pallets would cover their original access points. A certain amount of

Concorde G-N94AD wears the titles of Singapore Airlines on its port side as part of a combined operation to Singapore via Bahrain. This service was eventually cancelled as uneconomic. BBA Collection

structural strengthening would also be needed in localized areas of the cabin, which would need to withstand loads up to 9G. All the cargo nets were stressed to absorb the same loadings; both nets and mounting could be moved to accommodate various loads. Federal Express stipulated that they would require three modified airframes, supported by British Airways for a period of ten years, and added to this would be an extensive support contract supplied by Britain and France in which both airlines and manufacturers would be involved. Although the study concerning the structural modifications was undertaken successfully, the negotiations for the support contracts soon ran into trouble and eventually broke down altogether. The sticking point

BA G-BFKW starts its taxi movement towards the Heathrow runways. Eventually the aircraft was reregistered as G-BOAG. BBA Collection

British Airways Concorde G-BBDG was used for hot-and-high plus intake performance trials, hence the special datum markings on the fuselage to calibrate the tracking cameras. BBA Collection

was the ten-year support requirement – neither the British nor the French negotiators felt able to offer more than a five-year block of support; the other five years would have to be renegotiated to account for the possibility of rising costs. The final phase of negotiations ended unresolved in February 1983, the very month that Federal Express had hoped to start their new service.

During this period British Airways were operating their Concorde fleet fully subsidized by the government, although such a state of affairs, requiring taxpayers' money, could obviously not continue. The subject finally came to a head in the first years of the Thatcher government, when British Airways were given the option either to purchase the Concorde fleet outright or

dispense with it altogether. The deal between the airline and government allowed British Airways to buy five of the Concordes for £16.5 million each, while the other two were sold for the knockdown price of £1 each (for a fleet of seven that cost the taxpayer £164 million originally). Included in the arrangement were all the spares, including engines, that would be needed to operate the fleet for the foreseeable future, although separate contracts were negotiated with Rolls-Royce, British Aerospace, Aérospatiale and SNECMA for design engineering authority and major overhaul support. A further financial advantage was gained by British Airways during 1978–79 when an outstanding debt of £160 million was converted by the

government into an 80/20 profit-sharing scheme. This arrangement lasted until 1984 when the Concorde purchase deal was finally completed. Other financial arrangements covered repayments to British Aerospace and Rolls-Royce to cover development and support costs. Although British Airways readily accepted these to release them from an on-going financial commitment across the Channel, the French were shocked since this part of the Concorde development treaty had been overlooked by the government; after much Gallic shrugging and procrastination they too eventually paid up. While the obligatory financial manoeuvrings were going on, a number of production Concordes were still being used for development trials. On

Elegance and artistry are less than adequate words to describe this most striking of aircraft. Foxtrot Bravo of Air France is captured on approach. Those with keen eyes will already have noted the curving shape of the nacelles and intakes. Bernard Charles

BELOW: Surrounded by ground equipment, BA Concorde G-BBDG on the ramp at Tengah, Singapore. The aircraft, on loan from British Airways, was being used in trials required to refine the operation of the ramp control system. BBA Collection

6 January 1977 Capt Brian Trubshaw lifted Concorde 202, G-BBDG, from Filton's runway to undertake test flight no.428. The route took it to Tangier in 2hr 55min, of which just over 2hr were spent at supersonic speeds. The maximum height reached was 54,000ft (16,500m), the maximum speed achieved being Mach 1.85. Test flight no.433 was misnamed as it was, in fact, a CAA training flight which saw the aircraft flying between Filton and Fairford with a flight time of 1hr 10min. Aboard were Capt E. McNamara and Capt G. Wilkinson of the Civil Aviation Authority; the Flight Engineer was D.F.B. Ackary.

Pastures New (I)

While Concorde was scoring a range of enviable firsts, it was also involved in a series of development trials, but for these production aircraft were used in preference to the preproduction aircraft. The first trip

been taken to carry out of a series of upper atmosphere intake development trials in order to refine the behaviour of the intake ramps under various heights and flight conditions. During 1979 Concorde G-N49AE was flown from London to New York under the command of Capt Brian Walpole; from New York the aircraft was flown to Baltimore and Philadelphia to undertake Category 2 Instrument Landing System Validation flights.

In-service operation of Concorde by British Airways got off to a shaky start with the company's concern over the costs of operating the aircraft. The problem had its roots with the directors of BOAC, which had been subsumed together with BEA, into British Airways in April 1972. They regarded Concorde as an expensive luxury that would cost far too much to purchase and operate at any sort of a profit. Eventually the offer of public money helped the airline to make up its mind to exercise its purchasing options. Adding to the emerging British

July 1977. Two further flights were undertaken in 1978–79 when the then unsold airframes 214 and 216 undertook their maiden flights. The former, registered G-BFKW, left Filton on 21 April with Trubshaw at the controls. After a short trip round the Bay of Biscay and some roller landings at the Fairford test base, the aircraft returned there. During this run more than 1.5hr were supersonic. Airframe 216, registered G-BFKX, flew on 20 April with Trubshaw again in command. After going to the Bay of Biscay and 49min supersonic, the Concorde returned to Filton and went into storage; eventually British Airways acquired it. Outside its normal airline duties Concorde also assisted the RAF on 1 August 1979 in an exercise (*North Sea*); the aircraft involved was G-BBDG, simulating a supersonic target attacking over the North Sea.

When Concorde finally entered service with British Airways in 1976 the planned initial routes were quickly extended to

Concorde Alpha Echo parked at Heathrow with its nose fully up and its visor fully retracted. This photograph was taken when the unpopular 'British' titling was applied to the nose. BBA Collection

involved production Concorde 202 G-BBDG, which undertook a development trial to the Middle and Far East during August–September 1974. Trubshaw was in command for the 7 August departure, the flight taking in visits to Abu Dhabi, Iran, Qatar and Singapore. On 5 April 1978 Concorde 202, G-BBDG, was flown under Trubshaw's command from Filton to Casablanca to undertake a series of hot and high performance trials which would occupy the aircraft throughout April and May. The return flight to Filton was made on 5 May. In Casablanca the opportunity had

Airways' concerns was the excessive slippage of delivery dates, which would throw the airline's plans into disarray. Deliveries to British Airways saw G-BOAC leaving Filton for Fairford to undertake a series of shake-down flights before acceptance. Proving that a registration sequence had no bearing on deliveries, Concorde 206 G-BOAA left the British Aircraft Corporation test base at Fairford to fly to Heathrow on 14 January 1976, some months after 'AC'. Airframe 208, also known as G-BOAB, followed on 30 September, and G-BOAE, airframe 212, was delivered on 10

include two round trips to New York daily, although it would take until 1978 for local objections to be overcome. In contrast, the Washington/Dulles service was greeted with bunting and speeches when the first Air France and British Airways Concordes landed almost simultaneously on 24 May 1976. The fight for Concorde to operate into New York eventually spilled over into both the legal and the political arena as the New York Port Authority tried to ban it from landing there. Eventually the court ruled in favour of Concorde since it had successfully complied with all the demands laid

ABOVE: **Wearing the combined BA/Braniff registration G-N94AB, applied in 1979, this aircraft is at Heathrow undergoing pre-flight maintenance before flying to the USA.**
BBA Collection

A pair of Concordes touching down at Orlando International Airport on 18 October 1982. To the front is a BA machine with an Air France aircraft to the rear. They were going for the dedication of the British and the French pavilion at the Disney EPCOT centre.
BBA Collection

Concorde's Culinary Delights – British Airways in 2000

For those with enquiring minds and discerning palates, the appetizers consisted of a canapé selection which included foie gras mousse, smoked halibut, caviar and sour cream barquette. If this was not enough, the appetizer menu also offered mousse of salmon and trout enveloped in thinly sliced Scottish salmon, all being served with pinwheels of buttered brown bread. After struggling through this, passengers were given a choice of three main courses. The first was based around a prime fillet of beef dressed with herb butter and served with tomato, broccoli spears, hollandaise and baked potato. The second consisted of crayfish tails poached with white wine and finished in a cream and Dolcelatte cheese sauce, this, in turn, being garnished with sautéed pimento, asparagus spears and saffron rice pilaf. The third choice was lighter – honey-glazed duckling breast and country-style ham garnished with fresh

mango. For those final little spaces a mixed seasonal salad was served with a vinaigrette dijonnaise. To follow, the desserts included crème brûlée, flavoured with vanilla enriched with double cream and glazed with natural brown sugar. The obligatory cheese board had a selection of Stilton, Leicester and tomme de Savoie, with butter, crackers and crudités. To wash this down, coffee, with or without caffeine, and tea were available.

The catering department was especially proud of the airline's wine cellar, overseen by experts including Michael Broadbent and Hugh Johnson. The former is a Master of Wine, a director of Christie's and head of their wine department. He is one of the few Britons to have been awarded the prestigious French L'Ordre National du Mérite. Hugh Johnson is a Docteur de Vin of the Academie of the Confrerie des Chevaliers du Tastevin and the author of numerous books on wine. Given their

credentials, their wine choices were always of the best and thus passengers on Concorde could expect to choose from the champagnes Moët et Chandon, Cuvée de Dom Perignon 1980, Pommery, Cuvée Spéciale Louis Pommery 1981, G.H. Mumm Cuvée René Lalou 1982, and Krug, Brut, Grande Cuvée. White burgundies on offer included Chablis, Grand Cru Les Preuses, Domaine de la Maladière 1987, Puligny-Montrachet, Clos du Vieux Château Laboure-Roi 1986, Puligny-Montrachet, Truffieries Louis Latour 1985, Beaune, Clos des Mouches, Joseph Drouhin 1986. For those with a slightly different taste, a range of clarets was offered that included Domaine de Chevalier 1983, Grande Cru Classe Graves Léognan Les Forts de Latour 1976, Pauliac Les Forts de Latour 1978, Pauliac Château Talbot 1978, Grande Cru Classe Saint-Julien, Château Lynch Bages 1983, and Grande Cru Classe Paulliac.

on the operators concerning noise generation and pollution control. On a typical British Airways Concorde flight to the USA and back the aircraft left Terminal 3 at Heathrow departing at 13:00hr local, with an expected arrival at Dulles of 12:10hr local. The flight was scheduled in such a way that connections to several airports in the USA could be achieved without rushing too much; therefore passengers were able to connect to Atlanta, Boston, Chicago, Cincinnati, Cleveland, Dallas, Detroit, Houston, Kansas, Los Angeles, Miami, Nashville, New York, Richmond, San Francisco and Tampa.

Having obtained landing rights in the USA, attention turned to other zones of interest. The first to be looked at was Australia; however, this destination was never managed since the route extension reached only to Singapore, even though this was only a co-operative venture with Singapore Airlines, begun on 9 December 1977 as an extra leg to the Bahrain route, the dedicated aircraft being G-BOAD which had Singapore Airlines' markings painted on its right-hand side. The return leg was flown the next day, the pilots in command included Capt J.W. Hirst and Capt A. Meadows outbound; Capt B.J. Calvert and Hirst covered the return legs. But services were suspended after only a few flights since the Malaysian government raised strong objections to the aircraft's overflying the Straits of Malacca. Negotiations between airlines and officials allowed flights to resume in early 1979, but finally ceased by 1980 since the earnings and passenger loadings were deemed insufficient. Another joint venture involved services shared with Braniff Airlines; originally the whisper was that one side of the aircraft would be finished in Braniff colours and titles, although this was quickly dropped, given the airline's

propensity to finish its own fleet in bright, disruptive colour schemes. The first flight was undertaken on 12 January 1979 by an Air France Concorde routed from Paris to Dallas, Fort Worth, via Washington. The return trip was flown the next day. Yet again passenger revenue failed to live up to expectations and the relationship ended.

While BOAC, later British Airways, was dithering over whether Concorde would enter commercial service, Air France had no hesitation in accepting its allocation of the fleet since the French government held the majority shareholding in the airline. While British Airways and Air France had initially concentrated on breaking into the North American market, the latter was also looking towards the South American market to extend its available routes and generate more revenue. All the flights were routed via New York, from there two flights would continue on to Dulles while the remaining eleven flights continued on to Mexico City. Other flights would also land elsewhere in Latin America, at such destinations as Rio de Janeiro and Caracas in Venezuela. During the period in which Air France was instigating these routes to Latin America, it was suddenly hit by the responsibility for the day-to-day running and operating costs of its Concorde fleet. The resulting reduction in government subsidies was followed by a cost-cutting exercise to control expenditure and thus the Latin American routes ceased in April 1982. Further cuts saw the termination of the route to Miami in March 1984 and the Washington section ended in November 1994.

Where the Concorde fleets really made their profits was in the provision of aircraft for charter flights. Some were just round-the-coast-type pleasure trips, but others were of a more high profile nature. The former type, round-the-coast or Bay of

With its nose drooped to 5 degrees and its visor retracted, BA Concorde, G-N81AC, taxies away from the ramp at Heathrow before departing to the USA. BBA Collection

Biscay trips, were frequently advertised as 'champagne flights' and lasted about 1hr 40min, with a short supersonic burst as the highlight. The latter type of charter were normally booked by such companies as Pepsi who would hire F-BTSD from Air France and have it repainted in the company's house colours, in which guise it was rolled out in April 1996. A more unusual, but more restrained, venture was sponsored by the American lingerie company, Victoria's Secret, but little was changed externally, only a discreet logo applied to the tail, most of the decoration being reserved for the cabin. Adding spice to the occasion were a bevy of super models who had been invited to grace it.

Few realized that Concorde had a fan and a supporters' club, both of which booked the aircraft for trips in 1978. The first trip, involving G-BOAE, Capt Peter Duffey, took place on 14 November, lasted over 2hr and took in the delights of the Bay of Biscay, while a second flight with the same aircraft, crew and route took place seven days later.

In addition to regular and charter flights, both airlines provided Concordes for VIP flights on request. The first notable to take such a flight was Prince Philip who flew in Concorde 002 on 12 January 1970. In France President Georges Pompidou had a similar experience on 7 May 1971. While Concorde gained column inches from the tabloids for its rich and famous passengers, the aircraft frequently filled in on domestic routes to use up some capacity excess.

Air France Foxtrot Bravo is awaiting its next passengers for whom the forward access steps are in place. To the front of the aircraft is a power supply set and a vehicle to tow it clear once Concorde has been cleared to depart. C.P. Russell Smith Collection

BELOW: **Foxtrot Bravo lined up on the ILS for a faultless touchdown at Paris Charles de Gaulle. Even in daylight all the external landing lights are selected to on.** Philippe Noret

RIGHT: Taking the Pepsi challenge is this Air France Concorde, touching down in Madrid.
Jose M. Palacios

BELOW: The tailwheel, requiring less fluid, is safely stowed and the nose gear is following. Close behind are the main undercarriage units whose inner doors have cycled open to allow them in. Philippe Noret

BOTTOM: Foxtrot Charlie has everything stowed away to begin the climb before it reaches the acceleration point over the Atlantic. The thrust augmentors have been disengaged and will not be relit until the dash across the ocean begins. Philippe Noret

Pastures New (II)

Significant occasions in Concorde's history have included the first transatlantic flight from Washington to London on 25 May 1976, with British Airways flight BA378, this being the return flight after the 24 May trip; the aircraft was G-BOAC, Capt N.V. Todd in command. One of the earliest charter flights involved departing from London for San Juan, Puerto Rico, then a return to London which occupied a Concorde from 26 to 29 June 1976, with Capt Duffey. Although Concorde and its supporters had won the legal right to land in New York, the Port Authority insisted that test flights be flown to measure the noise levels generated by Concorde when taking off. This was done on 20 October 1977 and required that Concorde land with an on-board load of 174 tons (177 tonnes). Piloted by British Airways Capt Brian Walpole, Concorde left the 13,400ft (4,100m) runway at 230mph (370km/hr) generating a noise level of 88dB, as recorded by the Federal Aviation Authority, the Port Authority limit being 112. This was followed by a joint Air France/British Airways Concorde landing two days later. The first British Airways Royal Flight was undertaken on 2 November 1977 with the Queen on board aircraft G-BOAE for a trip to Barbados; the time taken chocks-to-chocks was 3hr 29min. Another such flight occurred on 12 February 1979 with the first leg departing Heathrow to Kuwait on aircraft G-N94AB. Five days later the aircraft was flown from Bahrain to Riyadh,

the pilot in command being Capt A.R. Meadows, with an airborne time of 49min. Five days earlier the same aircraft with the same pilot in command had been used to fly the Queen from London to Kuwait in 4hr 1min. The final leg of this tour was flown on 19 February by the same aircraft; the pilot in command was Capt A.J. Massie, with Meadows as supernumerary crew; the transit time from Dhahran to Bahrain was recorded as 10min, with a maximum speed of 391mph (630km/hr) being reached. The crew for this flight included Capt Norman Todd in command with Capt Brian Walpole as First Officer. Inaugural flights by British Airways continued unabated, one of the last undertaken in 1977 was on 23 November with Concorde finally exercising its right to land in New York as flight BA170. Operating under the guise of BA173, the twice-daily flights began on 1 June 1978, with aircraft G-BOAD, Capt John Hirst.

Chock-to-chock time was 3hr 52min, airborne time 26min shorter. British Airways also began British internal flights; the first trip into Birmingham and back was on 10 May 1981, using aircraft G-BOAA, Capt Lemay; the total airborne time was 65min for both legs, with a maximum speed of Mach 0.6 being reached. Scotland was the next destination, the first Glasgow and back to London flight taking place on 11 October 1987.

On 12 September 1982 Concorde G-BOAE, piloted by Capt J.D. Eames, made an inaugural flight to Rome, the flight taking 2hr 52min, with 36min at Mach 2. On a further trip Concorde G-BOAA flew to Larnaca, in Cyprus on 14 November 1984, the pilot being Capt Walpole with the return leg under the command of Capt Massie. Two days later Eames took G-BOAB to Seattle Tacoma, via Boeing Field, to show the aircraft off and secretly to show the Boeing Company precisely

This BA Concorde wears a united UK/USA registration, G-N81AC, for use on the combined Braniff and British Airways operation. BBA Collection

This excellent side view of Concorde G-BOAD shows the aircraft on the ramp before moving into position for loading at Heathrow. The nose is in the 5 degrees position with the visor partly retracted. BBA Collection

Surrounded by the Red Arrows' Hawks, a BA Concorde flies past an admiring audience. BBA Collection

what they had been missing after the cancellation of their own SST programme. Concorde would also reach places in the Far East and the Antipodes when G-BOAE, piloted by Capt H.C. McMullen, with J.L. Chorley, flew to Colombo then proceeded to Perth, arriving on 14 February 1985 as flight BA9060C. Having completed the turnaround in Perth, G-BOAE flew to Sydney under the command of Capt McMullen and Capt Leney. The following day the same Concorde left Australia to fly on to Bahrain taking 9hr 5min to do so. Aboard the aircraft were several senior pilots such as McMullen, Leney, Chorley and Massie, all taking it in turn to occupy the flight-deck. During this phase Mach 2 was achieved, with an altitude of between 57,000 and 60,000ft (17,400–18,300m) throughout. Having landed in Bahrain, the Concorde was then flown on to Colombo. The purpose of this position-

ing was to use G-BOAE to make an inaugural flight from Sri Lanka to London. The first leg was from Colombo to Bahrain, this being followed by that from Bahrain to Paris, Charles de Gaulle. This was an unscheduled stop since an unexpected headwind had reduced the aircraft's fuel safety margin. With refuelling complete, the final short stage to London was made. There was a contrast in styles when G-BOAB took a mixed load of international bond dealers and England football supporters to Helsinki on 22 May 1985 as flight BA9083C; the return flight was made the same day. A flight to New Zealand during early April 1986 saw G-BOAB land at Auckland. On the return flight on 7–8 April the aircraft was under the command of Capt John Cook, making the fastest flight from New Zealand to London in 19hr 6min, setting a world record in the process.

The USA and the world-famous Oshkosh air event would also be graced by Concorde. This time it was airframe G-BOAG under the command of Capt J.D. Cook who took it to the home of America's home-built and vintage extravaganza at the end of July 1985. This was not the first flight within North America since G-N94AA was flown from New York after delivering its passengers to the Canadian International Air Show at Toronto, flying past an impressed audience on 1 September 1979. Neither would it be the only visit of Concorde to airshows since it has frequently visited the Royal International Air Tattoo at RAF Fairford. Latin America had also been visited earlier that year when during 6–7 April G-BOAB under the command of Capt Walpole and Capt Massie arrived in London having staged through New York and Barbados to reach Rio de Janeiro. During the Barbados–New York return leg

Setting up Concorde for departure was quite complicated, as this view shows. To the rear are a pair of air starter trolleys to turn over the engines, while to the front are the access steps for passengers and another set for the external power leads. C.P. Russell Smith Collection

Concorde set a new world record of 2hr 7min for this distance, much of it flown at Mach 2 at 60,000ft (18,300m). The aircraft had been chartered by Cunard to collect passengers from the *QE2* liner after completing a world voyage. The outbound leg of this flight was made on 5 April from London to Brazil, this taking 8hr 45min with Capt Walpole, Capt Bradshaw and Capt Massie taking it in turn to be in command. Another trip to America would begin on 28 April 1986 when G-BOAC left Heathrow for the USA. The total airborne time was 4hr 54min, the first landing being in New York. After depositing the passengers to catch up with the *QE2* the aircraft staged on to Indianapolis, with Capt A.R. Meadows. The return journey was the next day, with G-BOAC staging via JFK Airport, before entering the supersonic track for Heathrow. The journey time was 4hr 41min, flown at 56,600ft (17,300m) with a maximum speed of Mach 2.02. Concorde has also been used to promote the 'Go British' week which was at its zenith in 1985; the aircraft arrived at Arlanda Airport, Stockholm on 28 September having flown low over the city to show off to as many people as possible.

The other Concorde operator, Air France, was also active in promoting its inaugural flights to unusual or new locations. One of the most adventurous trips was undertaken over 12–13 October 1992 when the airline attempted the fastest supersonic, round-the-world flight. Known as Sunchaser One, the publicity for the

flight promised that the Concorde would 'fly so fast around the world that the sun won't have time to set'. Before this, Concorde 001, F-WTSS flew to and from Dakar during 25–26 May 1971, the return flight taking 2hr 52min. This was followed by a training flight to South Africa over the period 23–24 February 1973 with Concorde 002. When the aircraft finally entered revenue-generating service with Air France, airframe F-WTSC undertook an endurance flight from Paris to Rio de Janeiro and back in January 1976, this being the airline's inaugural commercial flight with Concorde. A joint venture with British Airways followed on 24–25 May when Concorde F-BVFA, operating as flight AF053, under the command of Capt Pierre Dudal, went from Paris to Washington, Dulles, taking 3hr 50min to make the journey. The return leg involved a British Airways aircraft under the command of Capt Todd, which left Washington for London, using aircraft G-BOAG, the flight time was 3hr 40min. Air France flight AF002 was of great significance to the airline as this signified the entry of their aircraft into JFK, New York on 23 November 1977. Five years later an Air France first flight was not quite so dramatic since this involved a flight from Paris to Luxembourg and back on 20 May 1982, taking 28min. A slightly longer journey was undertaken on 1 October 1983 when F-BVFF flew from Paris to Dublin and back, under Capt G. Jacob, in 1hr 9min.

The following year would see the same aircraft making its first landing in Rome on 8 July 1984. Capt Gilles was in command the entire flight lasting 1hr 55min, of which 20min were supersonic. In the same year Air France took Concorde to Austria, when it flew a round trip from Paris, landing at Linz and Vienna on 26 October. Nuremberg was one of the next places visited by an Air France Concorde, when F-BVFF, operating as AF4860, landed on 19 July 1986. August of that same year saw Concorde landing at Tel Aviv International from New York on the 17th as AF 4160. The inbound aircraft was F-BVFF, while the Concorde used for the next departure to Paris was F-BTSC. In 1987 Air France Concordes visited Kathmandu and Delhi during October, and in December a short flight from Paris to Toulouse for charity purposes was made in support of a cancer trust. Concorde F-BTSD flew from Paris to Stavanger in Norway, transporting financiers for a meeting, returning to Paris the same day. During the period 1–17 November 1993 Concorde F-BVFA undertook a world tour via Barbados as flight AF4853, Capt Francois Rude. A change of flight number to AF 4857 covered the next leg from Kuala Lumpur to New Dehli, with the same pilot in command. The final leg became AF4859 and included a departure from Bahrain to Paris with Rude in command as before. On 24 August 1986 Air France flight AF4862 signalled another first for Concorde when it

ABOVE: This Air France Concorde, F-BVFC, has had many windows blanked out since it is on hire to the Institut Weizmann des Sciences for the study of a solar flare. BBA Collection

BELOW: Air France's Foxtrot Alpha flares out as the main gear touches the runway. Prominent in this view is the neat way the visor stows away when the nose is drooped. Philippe Noret

made a return flight to Hahn and back to Paris. Flight F-BTSC was chartered to fly French football fans to Liverpool for a European Cup game on 25 August 1979. Another charter involved a flight from Paris to the Island of Kish, or Jazireh Ye Queys, a luxurious holiday development off the coast of Iran, on 24 January 1978. This would be the start of a semi-scheduled charter flight that continued until the overthrow of the Shah.

Criticisms and Accidents

Although Concorde finally proved a money-spinner for both operating airlines, the reasons given for the cancellation of orders by other airlines extended far beyond political and media opposition. Some could squarely be laid at the door of the aircraft's designers, who had insisted on incorporating some features that the airlines did not require, such as a moving map display

which, in reality, was useless given that Concorde spent much of its time flying over water. Also viewed with some scepticism was the auto engine monitoring system that was designed purely for use on Concorde; the airlines suggested that they much preferred an existing system to be incorporated. Similar circumstances surrounded the INS, a product of Sagem-Ferranti, whereas potential customers had expressed a preference for a system manufactured by Delco and Litton.

ABOVE: **Complete with a shimmering smoke haze, an Air France Concorde taxies towards its parking slot. Even in these conditions the nose is slightly lowered to improve visibility.** Philippe Noret

BELOW: **A snow-covered Charles de Gaulle Airport is the venue for Air France Concorde F-BVFB, landing after flying from the USA.** BBA Collection

Engine starting was also a bone of contention, with the airlines requesting the use of an external air starter, whereas the prototypes were fitted with gas-turbine starters and the preproduction machines were fitted with an MFPU. Units were also contentious, many of the airlines being used to observing system pressures in pounds per square inch; however, the French, as is their wont, insisted that all measurements be displayed in bars. Doubts were also raised about the viability of the droop nose and visor assemblies and their continuous and safe usage, although extensive testing soon proved that the equipment was safe. When the airlines began their investigations into Concorde, they raised concerns about the visor in the raised position and the resulting lack of visibility. This was quickly explained away as being applicable to the prototypes only, and that the production machines would have visors with a greater visible area. Having had these fears assuaged, they then raised concerns with reference to the behaviour of the

ABOVE: With an air starter trolley plugged into Nos 3 and 4 engines, an Air France Concorde starts engines before departing on a post-maintenance trials flight. Bernard Charles

RIGHT: With its burners quietened, the ill-fated AF Concorde F-BTSC passes the camera with vapour plumes bleeding from the outer wing panels.
BBA Collection

nose radome assembly in the drooped position, the routing of the hydraulic system pipework and electrical looms in the vicinity of the engines. Three sets of modifications were required before all were satisfied that a catastrophic engine failure could be survived by these most vital of systems.

As with all aircraft, Concorde has evolved as time has passed and incidents have occurred. The first, a precursor of events that would follow, took place in June 1979 when an Air France Concorde leaving Dulles suffered a blow-out of tyres Nos 5 and 6 and the disintegration of the wheels, causing damage to No.2 engine, to three fuel tanks and the hydraulic system. The National Transport and Safety Board recommended that the undercarriage should always remain locked down in such circumstances and an emergency landing made as soon as possible. Similar incidents also occurred in July and September that year. In contrast, British Airways would not have a reportable occurrence until September 1980 when G-BOAF suffered a tyre blow-out. Other faults plagued the computerized engine monitoring system, which resulted in a British Concorde having to divert to Boston as a safety precaution on at least one occasion.

One of the most serious incidents to affect Concorde involved Air France aircraft F-BVFD, which was badly damaged during a heavy landing at Paris. Such was the extent of the distortion to the airframe that the aircraft was withdrawn from revenue service in December 1994 for spares recovery before being scrapped some twelve years later. During 1989 the British Airways fleet began to suffer a serious spate of mysterious failures to sections of their aircrafts' rudder sections. The first recorded incident was reported in April, being followed by similar incidents in January 1991 and March 1992. Other problems continued to plague the Concorde fleet, especially with regard to tyre failures on the main-gear bogies. In all these incidents damage was also suffered by the engines, fuel tanks and hydraulic pipelines, and on at least one occasion the sweeper bar for removing FOD on the bogie failed, turning the remnants into shrapnel that punctured the wing. Modifications were then urgently put in hand to fit strengthened undercarriage sweeper bars to the British Airways fleet and a further programme was begun to strengthen the rudder section mountings and reduce the potential for play in the operating control runs. Although much work was expended and the frequency of failures was reduced, they would never be completely eliminated as sections of the rudder continued to come off the airframe, the last case being reported in October 1998. Fortunately the elevons were more robust, although on at least one occasion a section was torn clear of its airframe in May 1998 from a British Airways Concorde, which result in the aircraft's making an emergency return to New York.

Concorde engine problems have been fortunately few, most being spurious, but all resulting in an emergency diversion for safety reasons. One of the most difficult for the engineers to diagnose concerned G-BOAG, which reported a low oil-pressure warning light illuminated for No.3 engine in transit from New York to London in May 1994. As a precaution the engine was shut down, however, the same light for No.2 engine also lit up, resulting in a precautionary shutdown. A successful landing was made at Heathrow and investigations revealed that incorrect servicing procedures had been followed, resulting in the engine oil tanks' being under-filled. During 2000 British Airways began to experience a series of engine failures. The first happened in January on a flight to Barbados which required that the engine be shut down and emergency vehicles be in attendance. A second engine failure occurred on a flight outbound from Shannon, when No.3 engine needed to be shut down, after which a return was made to Shannon. Following a similar pattern to the reported engine problems, near misses were unusual, although this happened in August 1998 when two Concordes came within 820ft (250m) of vertical separation in the vicinity of New York. Structural problems concerning Concorde were likewise fortunately few. Only one incident concerning fuselage integrity was reported, affecting an Air France aircraft in which cracks were found round a passenger cabin window. As a safety precaution the captain decided to return to New York and reduce the cabin pressurization to the minimum. Other cracks have been discovered in wing structures, these coming to light in August 1994 on a British Airways machine. In July 2000 British Airways began to subject their fleet to extensive NDT checks of the structure during maintenance. During this process minute cracks were discovered in the wing spars, which led to the temporary grounding of one aircraft for further investigation. In contrast, Air France carried out the same sequence of checks, but allowed their fleet to continue revenue operations.

All these incidents would pale into insignificance following the events that took place on 25 July 2000.

This rear view of an Air France Concorde shows the burners still alight after take-off and the slightly flattened under-fuselage near the main undercarriage units, plus the fairings covering the PFCUs. BBA Collection

CHAPTER SIX

The American SST

Transatlantic Interest

Having declined to join the British and the French in pursuit of a multinational SST, the USA gave every indication of forging its own path towards supersonic glory. Although the Americans had entered the jet age belatedly, their 'can-do' attitude allied to the information gained from the wreckage of Nazi Germany spurred them on to push forward with their own development programme. From these efforts the first of a series of straight-winged jet aircraft would appear, mainly powered by centrifugal jet engines. The adoption of the axial jet engine and its improved thrust output plus its improving reliability meant that the American aviation industry would advance the airframes they were mounted in. The first expression of this new technology was the seminal North American Aircraft F-86 Sabre single-seat fighter. With this the sound barrier could be comfortably breached. Having proved that a jet-powered airframe with swept wings was the path to follow, the military and the US Air Force made great demands on their manufacturers to produce supersonic fighters and strike aircraft; thus would be born the Century series of fighters, comprising the NAA F-100 Super Sabre, the McDonnell F-101 Voodoo, the Convair F-102 Delta Dagger, the Lockheed F-104 Starfighter, the Republic F-105 Thunderchief and the Convair F-106 Delta Dart.

TOP: The Convair XF-92 was built as the prototype for a new series of fighters. Due to the shape of the fuselage, it did not perform as well as expected and therefore went to NASA for trials use. Courtesy NASA

RIGHT: This nose-on view of the XF-92 reveals the pure delta shape of the wing and the tapered fuselage. To cure the XF-92 of its problems, it was redesigned, gaining an area-ruled fuselage and a revamped wing leading edge. The result was the XF-102. Courtesy NASA

The civilian branch of the aviation industry, on the other hand, was slow to get any benefit from the military developments being made available. One reason was the surplus of retired military transports available for the established and new airlines and the development of similar aircraft specifically for the same market, thus the Boeing Stratoliner, the Lockheed Constellation and versions of Douglas transports went into civil operation. Possibly de Havilland and its Comet airliner would be the spur for the appearance of a turbojet-powered machine in America.

All of the initial contenders, Boeing, Douglas and Convair, concentrated on similar-looking aircraft, with four podded engines mounted two per swept wing. The start of the Anglo-French project was first regarded with some scepticism in the USA, although NASA and its predecessor NACA had already undertaken extensive research into swept-wing behaviour. To prove these theories NASA developed the 'X' series of research aircraft to push the boundaries forward. Having explored the possibilities of high-speed flight, its application to the civil industry was quietly shelved

and all efforts were aimed towards the military. All this changed when the aircraft industry and NASA began to take notice of the Concorde project.

To stimulate the industry, the Federal Aviation Administration issued a request on 15 August 1963 for designs for a supersonic transport; this came from the 'Project Horizon' initiative sponsored by President Kennedy in an effort to stimulate the stagnant American economy. The aviation industry's remit was to outline a design for a home-grown SST. Giving backing and impetus to this effort were

In order to catch up with the rest of the world, the USA used air-launched, rocket-powered aircraft for its high-speed research. This is the Bell X-1 in flight. Although providing valuable data on the physics of flying above Mach 1, it was recognized from the outset that rocket propulsion was not acceptable for civil transport. Courtesy NASA

BELOW: After achieving Mach 1, the next step was to break the Mach 2 barrier. To that end Douglas built this X-plane; as before, the aircraft was air launched from a carrier aircraft. Courtesy NASA

Kennedy and the Congress. Before the appropriations were made the President decided that a full investigation into the costs to the government and the economy, and the benefits, should be made. To this end Vice-President Johnson chaired a cabinet-level committee, beginning its investigations in May 1963. The FAA, the driving force behind the project, made the strongest representations and its report stressed the great benefits to the economy. Their arguments were strong enough to convince the President that approval should be given and the competing manufacturers informed; thus on 5 June the SST programme was launched, although ironically Pan American Airways had signed a purchase option for six Concordes just two days earlier. Following on from this confirmation, Najeeb Halaby delivered an address to the American Institute of Aeronautics and Astronautics which was intended to promote the SST, not only from an economic view but also as a jump in technology that the project would bring. The stipulation presented to the major aircraft and engine manufacturers in August required that they take notice of both the commercial and the technical aspects and applications of their designs; the resulting aircraft had therefore to be a superior, commercial, supersonic transport, appealing to the world's airlines, not only from the point of view of technology but of operating economics. Other points requiring attention included the price per aircraft that each customer could afford to pay, safety, and a reasonable delivery date for entry into service. The aircraft projected by the FAA needed to have a sustainable cruising speed in the region of Mach 2.2, carrying a payload of 30,000 to 40,000lb (13,600–18,00kg), this total including 125 to 160 passengers over a range of about 4,000 miles (6,400km). The accompanying advertising conveyed the impression that the aircraft would be far safer than and superior to any other available from elsewhere.

The development of the American SST was seen as requiring a three-stage plan. The first would encompass the design competition itself and was scheduled to begin in January 1964. The second part of this stage would begin once the engine and airframe manufacturers had been chosen, and required that the FAA, manufacturers and airlines get together to move to the next stage. In the second stage the chosen manufacturers would begin to flesh out

their original submissions, while the third stage would cover the development, design, manufacture and thorough testing of two preproduction prototypes. Funding for stage one would come mainly from the government; the second and the third phase would be supported by loans with repayments coming from the sales achieved. This did not guarantee any purchases by, or on behalf of, the US government; but it promised that it would provide all assistance necessary to capture sales overseas. At the end of the second stage interested airlines would be asked to pay a royalty of $200,000 per airframe ordered within six months, while those coming on-board afterwards would be asked to pay $850,000 per aircraft. Further payments garnered from the airlines after delivery would be a 1.5 per cent royalty on revenue generated by seat sales, which would be paid to the government as recompense for the development, which would last for twelve years.

The FAA Takes Command

The guiding agency charged with overseeing the development of the American SST was the Federal Aviation Authority, which set up the Supersonic Transport Development Office under the guidance of Najeeb Halaby, an FAA Administrator; this would work in conjunction with representatives of the interested airlines. This group would cover the first phase in great detail, their remit embracing the management, technology, operations and economics of operating an SST. Technical aspects were subdivided into six areas: aircraft systems, sonic-boom effects, aerodynamic behaviour, airframe design, propulsion and systems, plus certification and tests. Operations and economics covered flight operations, safety, economic parameters, ground operation costs and training planning. Management covered company competence evaluations, managerial organization, development and production facilities, development and production master planning, management control skills and subcontractor capability and competence. Successful completion of this phase would allow the start of the second stage; this was expected to last for twelve months. At the conclusion of both stages the final products would be revealed, these being mock-ups of complete airframes, partial airframe mock-ups, engine mock-ups and full experimental data. Although

the airframe and powerplants were given great prominence, there was also other development work being undertaken involving the avionics and flight control systems for whichever manufacturer emerged as the eventual winner.

With all these reference points established it appeared that the American SST was all set for take-off in 1963. However, the 75–25 per cent cost split led the aviation industry to complain about its level of financial risk. The alternative was a fixed cost plus incentive fee that would reduce the manufacturers' risk. In turn, the government rejected this proposal and stalemate ensued. Realizing that this state of affairs could not be allowed to continue, Halaby advised President Kennedy to ask the financial community for advice and arbitration. The chosen specialists were Eugene Black, retired president of the World Bank, and Stanley Osborne, chairman of Olin Matheson, to review the financial risk assessment of the SST programme. They delivered their report on 19 December 1963 to the now President Johnson. Their report resolved the difficulty and recommended that the risk split should be changed to a 90–10 per cent ratio in favour of the manufacturers, which included an easing of the penalties for any cost overruns incurred, although it was also recommended that the airlines should have a stronger voice concerning the overall conception of the SST. In addition to their financial recommendations, Black and Osborne also warned that such a crash programme as this could be dangerous both technically and economically. Their final warning was that to enter into a race with the Anglo-French consortium could prove to be far more costly than was at first realized. Although this was a strong recommendation it was not accepted outright; but Johnson, at the suggestion of the FAA Budget Bureau Director, set up a high level SST overview committee to keep an eye on proceedings. This Presidential Advisory Committee on Supersonic Transport consisted of Halaby, Douglas Dillon from the US Treasury, Luther Hodges from the Commerce Department, James Webb from NASA, John McCone from the CIA, plus Black and Osborne.

With the costing arguments close to resolution, the groups of manufacturers began to plan their initial submissions. The chosen airframe manufacturers were Boeing and Lockheed and the design of the engines was given to General Electric and Pratt &

Whitney. In early 1965 the preferred development teams had crystallized into two groups, these being Boeing/General Electric and Lockheed/Pratt & Whitney. Changing the way that the government, FAA and manufacturers looked at the American SST was one external factor – the cancellation of the BAC TSR2 by the British, which was seen as creating a delay in the development of the Bristol/Rolls-Royce Olympus engine for civil supersonic use. In response, the US government decided to extend the development time allocated to the SST.

Having stretched out the development period, the redesignated Phase 2A got under way; this now meant that the development period had been extended from twelve months to eighteen. This allowed all four manufacturers to resume their research efforts for the design/production part of the contract. Within this phase each manufacturing group was expected to provide detailed designs, mock-ups of major parts of the airframe and engines and experimental data. By the conclusion of both phases the government had estimated that development costs would be $24 million for the first stage and $10 million for the second, covering the airframe designs and the two engine designs. While the technical aspect of the SST was finally gathering momentum, the FAA was undergoing an upheaval, with senior and middle management changing and unforeseen funding problems coming to the fore. Once the FAA waves had settled, it resumed contact with other organizations, one of the first being NASA. The first request to NASA was for aircraft from

At the other end of the design spectrum, North American produced the massive, six-engined XB-70 bomber. Although capable of performing the tasks set for it, it never entered USAF service because of its prohibitive cost and the improvements to Soviet air defences. Courtesy NASA

Edwards AFB to undertake sonic-boom flights to determine their effects upon people on the ground, buildings and the environment in general. The aircraft involved with these trials included the Lockheed F-104, the Convair B-58, the North American XB-70 and the Lockheed YF-12A. The trials were intended to be run in two phases; however it became clear after the first series of flights that the second set would

not be required since the sonic boom runs had proved that they would be an unwelcome nuisance over populated areas. The trials were carried out over Oklahoma and lasted six months, and elicited over 8,000 complaints and more than 5,000 claims for compensation.

Evaluation

By September 1964 all four companies were ready to hand in their submissions for evaluation by the FAA and other interested parties. Comprising over 22,000 pages, they were read by over 200 experts from NASA, the USAF, the FAA and the Civil Aeronautics Board. The proposals from both groups were disappointing since neither was able to cover the range required and payload requirements, and both would also have higher than expected operating costs. The engines too would fall short of the design parameters; but both General Electric and Pratt & Whitney were lucky enough to be granted a further six months in which to improve their offerings. Given this situation, it came as no surprise that the Department of Commerce was asked to undertake a further financial study of the entire programme. By December 1964 Phase 2A had

One of the best-known exponents of the delta-wing planform in the USA was Convair, who successfully introduced the F-102 and F-106 fighters and the B-58 Hustler shown here. BBA Collection

evolved into Phase 2B without any obvious progress towards a final selection. Secretary of State Robert MacNamara and his departmental officials were also coming under pressure in early 1965 from Halaby to make a decision concerning the SST programme; but MacNamara was still insisting upon further feasibility studies.

Having survived numerous investigations, the study of the final submissions began in September 1966. After due consideration, the result of the design competition was announced on 31 December, with Boeing and General Electric being chosen as the preferred developers. However, even this part of the process was slowed as President Johnson would not give the final go-ahead until 29 April 1967. With Phase 2C successfully completed, the chosen manufacturers immediately began work on the development of their own parts of Phase 3. At the end of this phase the selected consortium would not only have two prototypes, it would also be on course to completing the airworthiness certification and a planned production schedule for the airlines. The funding arrangements were destined to remain at the same level of 90 per cent from the government, although it would insist that each interested airline should contribute $1 million towards the final programme cost that had been calculated to reach $1,444 million. Eventually ten of fifty-two interested parties agreed to stump up their share of the risk funding, which allowed Phase 3 funds to be released and the contracts to be issued to Boeing and General Electric on 1 May 1967. This in turn allowed the projected first flight date for a prototype to be set for the closing months of 1970. The Boeing design office started with a series of concept drawings of which sixteen were seen as having further development potential. The lead design was always the 2707-100 variable sweep aircraft, although it would appear that the company were already covering all the possibilities should this version fail. The internal model numbers for these designs were 964-404 for the swing-wing aircraft, 969-321, which featured a highly swept, cambered arrow planform with fold-out canards on the forward fuselage, while the final back-up proposal was known as Model 969-302, based around a plain delta wing. Altogether the new Boeing product had attracted options for sixty-three aircraft, an ironic twist being that BOAC had placed an option for four aircraft, which made the airline unpopular in Britain.

The Boeing Bid

Boeing's first attempt at the design was known as Model 2707-200 (Dash 200), the most outstanding feature of which was its variable-sweep wings. This innovation had been proposed since it would give the Boeing aircraft good performance and stability at all points of the speed and flight envelope. A further gain would be a lower landing speed, which, in turn, would reduce the length of runway required for both take-off and landing. The only proviso was that such a swing-wing mechanism should not exceed 4 per cent of the gross structural weight of the aircraft. The dimensions given for this version of the Boeing SST included a fuselage length of 318ft (97m), the wings in their swept-back condition would have a span of 106ft (32m) and in the fully forward position the wingspan would increase to 174ft (53m). The gross weight with 292 passengers and luggage was calculated at 675,000lb (306,800kg). The intended powerplants would be four General Electric augmented turbojets, each being rated at 60,000lb.st (267kN), this in turn was intended to give the Dash 200 a maximum speed of Mach 2.7. Since the Boeing SST would be a long, heavy aircraft, it was decided to incorporate a form of direct lift control which used spoilers placed in front of the flaps to improve flight control during the landing phase. The airframe would consist mainly of steel and titanium, thus allowing the designers to push for a top speed of Mach 3, should such an increase in speed be desired.

Overall, the Boeing Dash 200 was a far more exciting design than the competing Lockheed/Pratt & Whitney proposal; however, it had already been realized that the cutting-edge machine from Seattle was not in any state to be constructed as quickly as was first thought. It was at this time that problems started to arise. The first to appear was the swing wing, which, after further study by Boeing engineers, was not the boon it was first held to be. Not only was there an inherent balance problem caused by the rearward mounting of the engines, the close coupling of the flight control surfaces to the aircraft's c.g. meant that there was an unforeseen increase in the high trim drag coefficient and in the pitching movement at low speeds which completely negated the supposed safety benefits. It was later revealed that the swing-wing aircraft suffered from poor mass distribution due to the aft location of the engines, plus a high

pitching moment of inertia at low speeds. To offset these difficulties Boeing added a pair of canard wings to the nose which in themselves would pose problems. Wind-tunnel testing of the new combination showed that, contrary to expectations, the canards would make the handling worse as the longitudinal stability of the aircraft would become even more unstable throughout the complete flight envelope. Further in-depth analysis showed that additional weight and strengthening would be required to support the canards and counteract their installation and to reduce the airframe's aeroelasticity. This was beginning to develop into a catch-up situation where each modification generated its own set of problems which then required yet a further set of fixes to sort out, and this meant that, as each was applied to the design and the wind-tunnel models, the situation worsened.

Further studies involved moving the wing pivot points to various distances from the aircraft's centreline; but their optimum position was as close to the centreline as possible to gain the benefits of subsonic flight with variable-sweep wings. This option was not feasible from an engineering point of view; the alternative was to move the pivots outboard. And this brought further problems as there was an increase in the movements of the aerodynamic centre, with resulting changes in the flight speed and angle of attack. To counteract the outboard relocation of the pivots, the tail surfaces needed to be increased in area; this was also required even when canards were installed. From a practical point of view, the wing pivot position also caused the lift:drag ratio to suffer at both subsonic and supersonic speeds. Moving the wing pivots further outboard also reduced the benefits of wing sweep at lower speeds since there was a loss of available wing area to produce useful lift. Even after Boeing had introduced a drastic weight reduction the airframe was still 7 per cent above acceptable limits.

Structurally the Boeing 2707 consisted of closely spaced, shaped frames connected by numerous stringers, all being covered by a titanium skin which was deemed capable of accepting the kinetic generated by speeds of Mach 3; the airframe structure itself consisted of an alloy of 90 per cent titanium, 6 aluminium and 4 vanadium. The wing glove extensions which housed the wing pivot points were built around a closely grouped pressure web beam structure, to the front of which were leading edge slats. Aft of the wing pivots were the

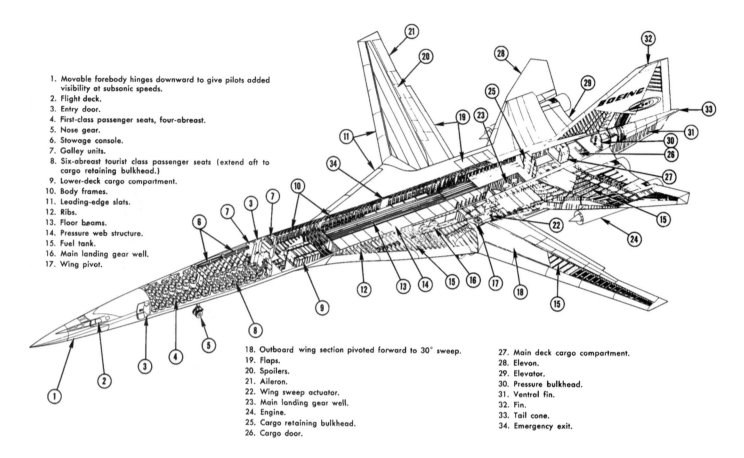

1. Movable forebody hinges downward to give pilots added visibility at subsonic speeds.
2. Flight deck.
3. Entry door.
4. First-class passenger seats, four-abreast.
5. Nose gear.
6. Stowage console.
7. Galley units.
8. Six-abreast tourist class passenger seats (extend aft to cargo retaining bulkhead.)
9. Lower-deck cargo compartment.
10. Body frames.
11. Leading-edge slats.
12. Ribs.
13. Floor beams.
14. Pressure web structure.
15. Fuel tank.
16. Main landing gear well.
17. Wing pivot.
18. Outboard wing section pivoted forward to 30° sweep.
19. Flaps.
20. Spoilers.
21. Aileron.
22. Wing sweep actuator.
23. Main landing gear well.
24. Engine.
25. Cargo retaining bulkhead.
26. Cargo door.
27. Main deck cargo compartment.
28. Elevon.
29. Elevator.
30. Pressure bulkhead.
31. Ventral fin.
32. Fin.
33. Tail cone.
34. Emergency exit.

ABOVE: This diagram reveals many of the internal fitments that Boeing proposed for the Model 2707-200 swing-wing SST (being at an early stage the drawing lacks the canards fitted later). BBA Collection

BELOW: The Boeing swing-wing SST was intended to have four main undercarriage units plus a nose unit to carry its immense weight. The multistage nose was intended to obviate the need for secondary external sensors as Concorde did when its nose section was drooped. The location of the engines and the swing wings ended this version. BBA Collection

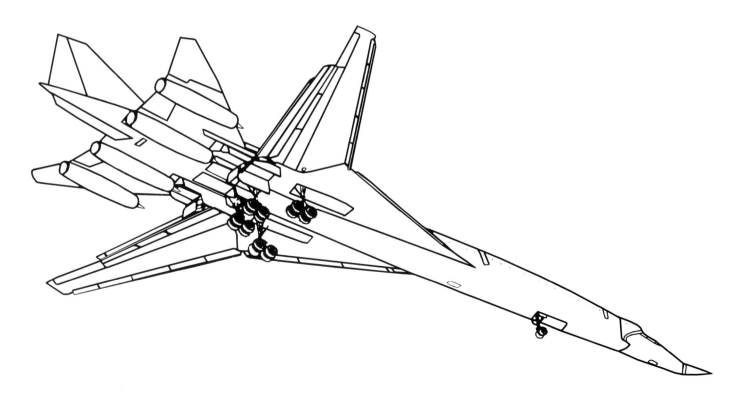

main-gear bays which were completely covered in flight, while, with the gear extended, the minimal amount of undercarriage bay was exposed to the airflow. Each of the four main undercarriage units was a bogie upon which were mounted four wheels, to allow for enough clearance upon retraction, and the main-gear units were slightly staggered, two forward and outboard of the aft pair. A similar arrangement applied to the twin-wheeled nose undercarriage, which was mounted well aft of the flight deck and would require some careful steering by the crew to remain safely on the taxiway. To the rear of the aircraft were the delta-shaped, fixed tailplanes, which were also home to the podded powerplants, two per side. A similar method of assembly was used in these structures, although they were made considerably stronger to absorb the thrust loading of the engines and the aerodynamic forces generated by the inboard-mounted elevators and the tip-mounted elevons. The wings were fairly slender in nature since in the swept-back position they formed a delta with the fixed tailplanes and in the fully forward position a full range of slats and

Fowler triple-slotted flaps would almost double the total area of the wing and extend over 85 per cent of the leading and trailing edges. Roll control was dealt with by ailerons mounted close to the tip of the wing. The wings themselves were mounted around a single pivot, having three selectable positions. In the forward swept position the leading edge sweep was set at 20 degrees for landing, the intermediate position was 30 degrees for take-off and at supersonic cruise the leading edge sweep was 72 degrees. There was an intermediate position between 30 and 72 degrees which could be selected for subsonic cruising. Mounted above the rear-most section of the fuselage and its tail-cone was the fin comprising a multispar structure interspersed with spacing and shaping ribs, all covered by a titanium skin. To the rear of the fin was the multisection rudder, each element being powered by its own PFCU. Flight control at low speeds in lateral mode was provided by conventional ailerons and the elevators catered for the pitching moments. Once the wings were fully swept back, flight control was achieved by the pivoted tips of the tailplanes, these being

the only means of control. The General Electric engines were GE4 turbojets rated at 60,000lb (267kN), each having an afterburner and variable inlet and exhaust.

On 15 January 1968 Boeing, after twelve months of trying, finally admitted defeat with the design of the Dash 200 aircraft and asked for extra time to revamp the entire design completely. In effect, the company had managed to create an aircraft that could easily cross the Atlantic, but empty. The FAA agreed to an extension until 31 March; not only was the prestige of the American industry at stake but the agency wanted a chance to recover some of the money already expended. Boeing took their SST back to the drawing board, although the proviso given by the FAA was that the new design must be ready for construction within twelve months and a prototype ready for a first flight in March 1972.

Boeing Try Again

Boeing's answer to its design crisis would be the 2707-300, which featured delta wings with a leading edge sweep angle of 51

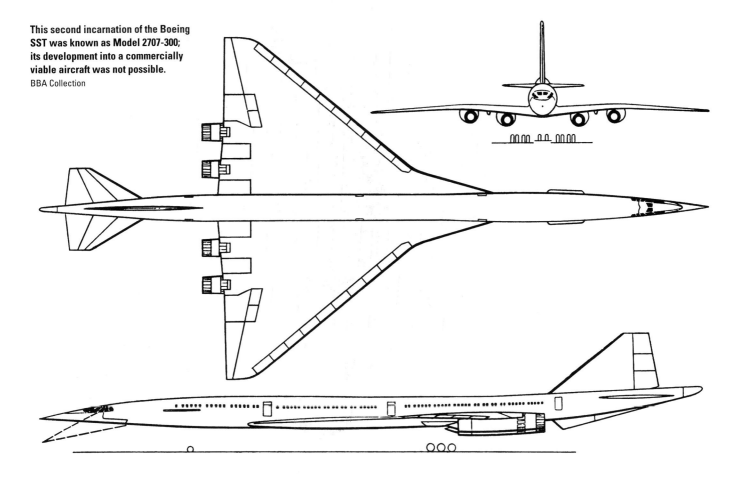

This second incarnation of the Boeing SST was known as Model 2707-300; its development into a commercially viable aircraft was not possible.
BBA Collection

degrees and a span that was similar in size to that of the Boeing 707, this being based on the Model 969-302. It was not dissimilar to the losing Lockheed proposal, a fact not lost on the design team at Lockheed. One of the hangovers from the earlier Dash 200 design was the retention of the all-flying tailplane assemblies. The deleting of the swing wings and the associated flight control system led Boeing engineers to design a high-lift system into the wings; this was based on trailing edge flaps and flaperons for improved roll control. At this point in the aircraft's development in June 1969 the projected aircraft weighed 750,000lb (340,900kg) gross weight with accommodation for 234 passengers, later to be increased to 250, and their baggage over a range of 3,575 miles (5,800km). Other innovations put forward by Boeing included a double-step, droop nose which gave the pilots an excellent view during the low-speed handling phases such as take-off and landing, while it allowed the detectors mounted on the nose assembly to remain pointed along the line of the aircraft instead of relying on a secondary set. The cabin layout meant that for tourist seating they could be carried six abreast, since this section extended fully aft to the cargo-

retaining bulkhead, although, in common with other aircraft types, it was highly likely that the 2707 in service would have a small section of the passenger cabin divided off for first-class passengers in less-cramped, four-abreast seating. Underneath the forward part of the passenger cabin would be a combined freight baggage hold and a further compartment aft of the cabin on the upper deck was set aside for the same purpose. Serving the passenger compartment were at least two galley units, matched in number by fixed toilet blocks that were provided with external cleaning points. Access to the aircraft was by four entry doors in the forward fuselage, which also allowed for cabin servicing trolleys to be exchanged. Should there be an emergency, two further doors were mounted above the wing gloves to allow escape.

Dimensionally the Boeing design would change as it evolved, growing larger with each modification. The original Boeing Model 733 had a wingspan of 98ft 5in (30m), an overall length of 271ft (82.6m), a height of 45ft 3in (13.79m) and a wing area of 5,019sq ft (466.3sq m). The proposed engines were four General Electric GE4/Js. These were needed to lift an airframe that weighed a maximum of

500,000lb (228,000kg), within which were to be seated 250 passengers, being pushed along at Mach 2.7 at a maximum altitude of 65,000ft (19,800m). The projected range was estimated to be 3,480 nautical miles/4,000 miles/6,440km.

The 2707-100 had an increased wingspan to 174ft 3in (53.1m), which thus increased the wing area to 9,000sq ft (837sq m). The fuselage length was also increased by a further 30ft to 306ft (93.27m). The powerplants remained the same, although the top speed had increased to Mach 3 and the passenger complement to 277. All these changes led to a growth in the maximum weight to 675,000lb (307,000kg). The travelling time between New York and London was given as just under 2hr and from Seattle to Tokyo via Honolulu was estimated to take just over 3.5hr.

The appearance of the 2707-200 airframe saw the wingspan rise by a further 3ft 2in, but in contrast the fuselage length was reduced to 298ft (91m), although enough of a redesign had been carried out to allow the passenger loading to increase to 292. Yet again, the changes led to an increase in the all-up weight to 680,000lb (309,000kg). Having admitted defeat with regard to the swing-wing version of the SST, Boeing

Boeing designed two versions of the 2707 SST. This is a mock-up of the second, the Dash 300. Gone were the swing wings, replaced by a delta planform. Had it been built, it would have been twice the size of **Concorde**. Courtesy Boeing

ABOVE: **A photograph of a NASA wind tunnel which dwarfs the scientist and the SST mock-up about to be placed inside.** Courtesy NASA

RIGHT: **This nose section was from the final Boeing SST submission; by this time the multistage nose had been replaced by an assembly similar to that on Concorde.** Courtesy Boeing

proposed a fixed-wing design. Designated 2707-300, the airframe had a wingspan of 141ft 8in (43m) while the fuselage was reduced in length again to 280ft (85m). Being a slightly smaller aircraft, the passenger complement fell to 234; however, the all-up weight had gone up again, to 710,000lb (322,000kg). The maximum speed was also dropped to Mach 2.7. When the first prototype drawings were delivered there had been a few changes from the Dash 300 prototype. The wingspan was extended by a further 4in and the fuselage had grown by a further 7ft. These alterations allowed the passenger number to increase to 250, commensurate with a growth of maximum weight to 750,000lb (340,000kg). As if the written details were not enough, Boeing produced a mock-up to the judging panel with the usual Hollywood razzle-dazzle to show it off.

Governmental Scepticism

The report was handed over to the government agencies. The FAA and its project office reviewed the design during December 1968 and found it much more acceptable, not only from a technical point of view, but also from the economic. To muddy the situation further there was a change of administration, with President Nixon returned to the White House. One of his first actions was to form a committee under the chairmanship of the Under Secretary of Transportation, James Begg, to review the entire SST programme in depth. One of those commenting upon the Boeing SST was Dr Raymond Bisplinghoff, who, at the time, was a well-respected aeronautical engineer and Dean of the School of Engineering at the Massachusetts Institute of

Technology, whose input concentrated upon the impact of sideline, not direct engine, noise from the SST, which could not be reduced without a further redesigning of the entire aircraft. Other areas of concern included the economic, national financial and environmental aspects and the technological fall-out. As well as the financial risks, the committee stressed the environmental issues, one of which was the safety of passengers and crew and another the contamination of the upper atmosphere by water vapour. The airlines were also causing problems since they had decided that the original six-abreast seating was too cramped and they preferred five-abreast instead. But as the aircraft had not proceeded much beyond the drawing board, Boeing felt able to comply with potential purchasers' wishes.

The report that this body delivered was negative in the extreme, but even so the Transportation Secretary, John Volpe, recommended, on the advice of the FAA, that on 1 April 1969 that the programme should continue. This decision was eventually ratified by Nixon in September, although with a reduced budget, which was approved by Congress by the end of the year. While Boeing was struggling to produce a workable SST, its press and publicity department was busy promoting the need and virtues of an American SST to counteract the threat of Concorde. The material pumped out at this time stated that the Boeing aircraft would easily capture at least $20 billion of the potential $25 billion SST world market by 1990. A further argument was that, even if the American SST were slow in coming into service, its ability to carry more passengers than its rivals would soon even up the market.

The following year was the turning point for the Boeing programme as numerous groups began to co-ordinate their opposition to the project on the grounds of cost and potential damage to the environment; not only were they complaining about their own home-grown aircraft, they were also turning their attention to the perceived threat posed by Concorde. As if to reinforce the feelings of the opposition movement, Nixon signed the National Environmental Policy Act, which committed all relevant government departments to protecting the environment. The supporters of the SST programme immediately began to lobby on its behalf as they feared that it would be presented as a sacrificial lamb on the altar of protecting nature. All of this came to a head in 1970 when the Senate voted on 3 December against the 1971 funding appropriations. Since two versions of the same bill had been presented to Congress, a reasonable compromise was reached that allowed development funding to continue, albeit at a reduced rate. However, a further twist was played out during March 1971 when both Houses voted heavily against spending any more money on the SST programme. Even this had a sting in it since termination costs did not come cheaply and eventually amounted to $171 million. This then would be the end of the American supersonic transport dream and all that remains are a few drawings, photographs and mock-up sections in museums. At the point of termination $1 billion and 8.5 million man-hours had been expended on creating nothing more than a paper dream. The financial

implications may have struck a chord with the media but the knock-on social effects were even more disastrous with Boeing laying off 7,000 in all departments almost immediately the announcement was made on 18 March. A similar effect was seen at General Electric where more than 6,000 were let go. Although these were the big announcements, the cancellation of the American SST was felt across the whole of the USA.

The Opposition

None of this impinged on the Citizens League Against the Sonic Boom, whose avowed intent was to first stop Concorde entering America by any means possible, after which they turned their attention to their home-grown products. Led by Senator Proxmire, the movement was growing in strength daily. Fighting a rearguard action against cancellation, was the unenviable task facing Secretary of Transportation William Magruder, whose department had assumed responsibility for the SST project from the FAA in April 1970. Possibly the final nail in the coffin was hammered home before the Transportation Sub-Committee, of the House Appropriation Committee, on 2 March 1971. Delivering this requiem for the American SST was Stewart L. Udall, who at one time had been the Secretary of the Interior. His status was that of representative of the Coalition Against the SST, based in Washington, DC. His opening comments were based around the original argument that the aircraft would be damaging to the environment, a statement based on the belief by some anti-SST scientists that supersonic transports would cause irreparable damage to the ozone layer. This view had a few holes in it since the current subsonic airliner fleet had engines that generated vast quantities of pollution, a stark contrast to the efforts made by the SST engine manufacturers to reduce hazardous outputs. Udall then moved on to state that the efforts of American technology could better serve people materially and with regard to their environmental health. During his period as the Secretary of the Interior Udall had appointed a team of scientists whose primary aim was to rubbish all SST projects.

Three statements were put forward by Udall on behalf of the Coalition. The first stated that the American airline industry was in a parlous state, especially as the oil crisis was beginning to bite; this in turn led

to a steep increase in fuel prices. Given these concerns, many airlines were reported to be unhappy with having to sign firm options for an aircraft which existed only on paper and was increasing in cost, as well as their confirmed orders for the subsonic fleets. At this point a comment by Charles Lindbergh on behalf of these concerned airline officials was read out. This telling declaration stated that:

> Although the SST is state-of-the-art technologically, it is not economical nor environmentally friendly. Seat per mile costs are now far too high due to rising costs, while the damage to the upper atmosphere is too dangerous on the basis of present knowledge. I believe it would be a mistake to become committed to a multi-billion dollar SST programme without the reasonable certainty that SSTs will be practical economically and acceptable environmentally.

At this time Lockheed Aerospace were in financial trouble and Rolls-Royce had just filed for bankruptcy; thus the chances of Boeing going the same way while still being involved in the SST project were extremely high. Unfortunately, the closing statement centred on the sudden loss of aerospace jobs that had afflicted Rolls-Royce and would hit the SST builders just as quickly.

The second argument placed before the committee centred on the environmental issues whose risks were not fully understood at the time for lack of research. Although scientists would be called to provide more expert testimony, their statements related to the potential damage caused by an SST, and the effects of subsonic aircraft and other fossil-fuel burners were overlooked. The final point placed before the committee concerned American national priorities. Correctly, Udall stated that, although the SST was technologically advanced, its benefits in the end would apply only to an elite, wealthy few, and was unacceptable, even if the SST were profitable from the outset. Such vast amounts of money already spent and promised should have been deployed in support of economic, social and environmental gains. This was also the time when many programmes, such as the Lockheed C-5A Galaxy, were overrunning their costs by great margins.

Having put forward a variety of arguments against the SST, Udall then raised the spectre of the pro-SST lobby. Whether this was diversionary was not revealed, but he did state that the committee should investigate the source of the $350,000 recently pledged to support this organization and whether it had been provided by the very corporations that would benefit from the continuation of the SST programme. But even at the time that he was speaking to the committee the fate of the SST was already decided.

The Other Contenders

While Boeing and General Electric had succeeded in gaining the SST development contract their rivals, Lockheed and Pratt & Whitney, were still investigating and developing their own submission. The Lockheed machine was designated the Model L-2000, with the company's designation of CL.823. This would feature revolutionary aerodynamic innovations that drew extensively on the work previously done by NACA/NASA. The basis of the wing centred upon a double delta-wing planform which would supposedly assist the aircraft in reaching a Mach 3 cruising speed. From this it would appear that everything about the L-2000 was revolutionary, but that would not be the case as Lockheed used their normal design philosophy of 'simpler, safer, better' to create their machine. To the rear of the double delta wing were a full range of elevons and a multi-section rudder and leading-edge slats that gave a total of sixteen flying control surfaces. By contrast, the Boeing 2707-200, with its variable sweep wings, was bedecked with fifty-nine flight control surfaces that included triple-slotted flaps, movable

With its afterburners blazing, this Lockheed SR-71 leaves Edwards AFB on a test flight. It was rumoured that Lockheed used this design to develop their own SST. BBA Collection

canards and the swing wings; none of these was in the Lockheed submission. The simpler airframe was also slightly smaller and so the L-2000's capacity of 230 passengers was smaller than that of the Boeing 2707.

The dimensions given for the L-2000 series included a wingspan of 116ft (35.4m), a fuselage length of 260ft (79.3m) and a height of 47ft 11in (14.6m). The wing area was specified at 9,026sq ft (838.5sq m). The original engines were four Pratt &

Whitney PW JTF17A-201s, although four General Electric GE4/J5Ks were proposed as alternatives, both sets being rated at 60,000lb (267kN) thrust per engine. Maximum all-up weight was given as 480,000lb (217,720kg), to travel at a maximum altitude of 80,000ft (24,400m). The projected range was around 3,480 nautical miles/4,000 miles/6,440km. The airframe was constructed mainly of titanium alloys with small amounts of steel being used in areas of high stress, such as the undercarriage mountings.

It was the L-2000's simpler design that won it friends among some of the airlines and some political supporters; however, as regards civilian transport aircraft Boeing had the greater influence and thus the swing-wing aircraft gathered the money, even though the Lockheed machine was seen as the one design that would allow America to produce an SST that would easily rival Concorde. Lockheed were also pushing their partner's engine, the Pratt & Whitney JTF17, as a far more able design which, because of its fanjet structure, would also achieve more success than the GE offering, which was a straight turbojet.

Lockheed also used its experience in both transport aircraft design and 'skunk works' aircraft to promote the L-2000 and many observers believed that the SR-71, a Mach 3, double-delta aircraft, was acting as a virtual prototype for the L-2000. Having

This slightly indistinct image is of the Lockheed L-2000 SST mock-up. Although it would appear to be the most viable design it would lose to the competing Boeing model. Courtesy Lockheed Martin

pushed their design as hard as they could, Lockheed were disappointed to receive the news that they had lost the SST competition on 31 December 1966. During the Lockheed design phase the aircraft underwent three initial iterations, known as the Dash 1, 2 and 3, before finally settling on the Dash 7 layout as the production version. Boeing's victory was seen as somewhat clouded since their aircraft would undergo multiple redesigns before being cancelled in 1971. Lockheed then stopped its development of supersonic transports, preferring to pursue a variety of military projects and subsonic wide-body passenger jets.

Only one other company put up a design for the SST project: North American Aircraft, who based their design on the existing XB-70 Valkyrie. This machine would be known as the NAC-60, which featured a conical, cambered, modified delta wing and fixed, forward canards, all derived from the Mach 3 strategic bomber. The known characteristics of this aircraft included a wingspan of 121ft 4in (37m), a length of 195ft 5in (59.6m), a height of 48ft 3in (14.7m) and a wing area of 6,417sq ft (597sq m). The accommodation was given as 170, travelling at Mach 2.65. Although the engines were never specified, it is safe

to assume that either the General Electric or Pratt & Whitney powerplants would be chosen. The projected range for the NAC 60 was given as 3,480 nautical miles/4,000 miles/6,4400km. North American eventually pulled out of the SST project since they needed to concentrate on the problems besetting the XB-70 bomber.

At the time the projects ended, the USA had spent $1,035 million on R&D, testing and mock-ups. Britain and France had both spent a similar amount of development funding, the difference being that Concorde was on the threshold of gaining full certification.

ABOVE: Although the XB-70 would not enter USAF service, it was the basis of an SST design put forward by North American Aviation. Courtesy NASA

LEFT: When the XB-70 was cancelled by the USAF, the prototypes were passed to NASA for use in exploring high-speed flight and the behaviour of the delta wing throughout its flight envelope. Courtesy NASA

This artist's impression is of the North American offering, closely resembling the XB-70 bomber from which it was derived. Courtesy NASA

CHAPTER SEVEN

So Close: the Tupolev Tu-144

Competition from the East

While the Anglo-French consortium was creating an SST that would be the most thoroughly tested aircraft ever built and the Americans were creating (only on paper) the most thoroughly untested SST never built, aircraft designers in the USSR were forging their own version of the SST and would beat them all into the skies.

Unlike the American and the western European offering, the Russian aircraft was very much politically driven; the others were expressions of a financial and technological need. The technology to create such an aircraft was already available since the military within the Soviet Union were flying delta-winged fighters such as the MiG-21 and the less than successful Myasischev

The MiG-21 was one of the most successful delta-winged aircraft built in the USSR, although it still reflected the belief that this wing planform required a tailplane for pitch control. BBA Collection

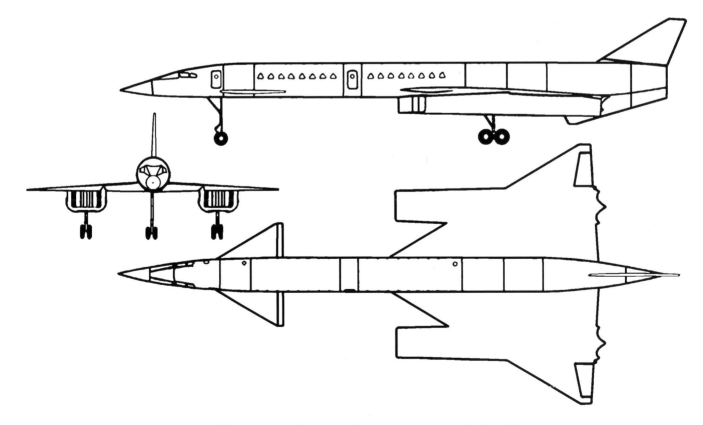

One of the first Soviet attempts at designing an SST is encapsulated in this layout from Tupolev, designated the Tu-4. BBA Collection

M-50 'Bounder' heavy bomber. In civilian air transports the Soviet Union was almost on a par with their Western opposition as several Ilyushin and Tupolev airliners would show. The Politburo became aware that Britain and France were beginning the design work necessary to build an SST, soon to become Concorde, and their arch rivals the Americans were also thinking of doing the same. In response, the Politburo convened a meeting in early 1962 in Moscow where Andrei Andreivich Tupolev, son of the famous designer Andrei Nikolaevich, and currently head of the Tupolev OKB, was approached to begin to investigate a Russian SST. This decision was ratified by Premier Kruschev on 26 July; he favoured the Tupolev OKB above the others and charged them with creating the aircraft soon to be known as the Tu-144, known to NATO as the *Charger*. Justification for the project, should such be needed within the Soviet Union at the time, was that the state airline Aeroflot needed to fly long-haul routes over some desolate parts of its massive empire

and that some of these flights were taking inordinately long.

Although Tupolev was the preferred developer of the Russian SST, the disgraced Myasischev, out of favour after the *Bounder* fiasco, was still developing his own designs for an SST even though his design bureau, OKB-23, had been shut and its participants dispersed. Some would progress towards aerodynamic models in the M-55 series, although none actually appeared as aircraft. Like Myasischev, the Tupolev OKB was approaching an SST design from scratch, after having rejected ideas of basing the new aircraft on the Tu-22 supersonic bomber. A similar situation faced the designated engine designers N.D. Kuznetsov, whose product, later designated the NK-144, developed from the engines assigned to the Tu-135P proposal, had been suggested by the designer S.M. Jager. These engines were two-spool turbofans with afterburners and had a specific fuel consumption in the supersonic regime of between 2.97 and 3.19lb/hr

(1.35, 1.45kg/hr). First runs of a testbed engine were undertaken in 1964. Although the Kuznetov OKB were fairly sure that their engine would work, an insurance policy powerplant was put under development. This would be a straightforward turbojet, under the guidance of the P.O. Sukhogo OKB. As the design load increased, some was passed out to other design bureaux such as Antonov, which would become heavily involved with the design and manufacture of the aircraft's outer wing panels. Tupolev, having assembled his preferred team, which included Yu N. Popov and B.A. Gantsevskiy, then went to meet the Politburo and be given their instructions regarding the project; these included the development timeline and the number of prototypes required. The former required that the prototype should be ready for its maiden flight in 1964, and the number of aircraft needed was determined to be two. To assist the Tupolev OKB in their development programme, the help of the Mikoyan Bureau was elicited. Its role would be to

Supporting the Tupolev development programme were a pair of modified MiG-21s whose main feature was the installation of the double-cranked wing as shown here. BBA Collection

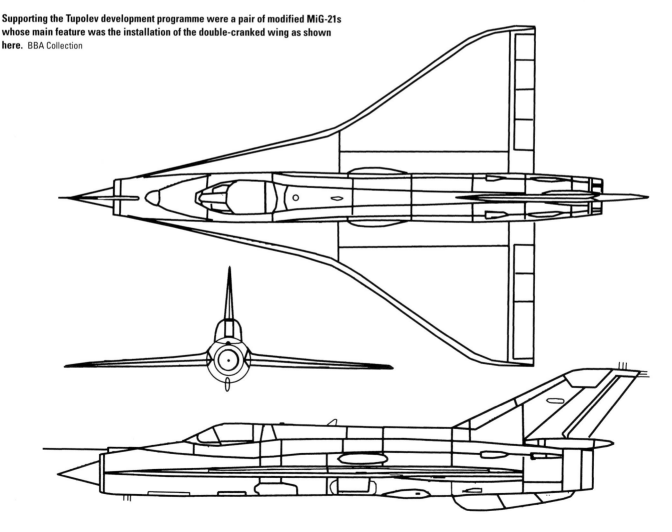

To assist the Tupolev OKB in designing their SST, a MiG-21 airframe was rebuilt to incorporate the proposed wing. After this conversion the machine was redesignated as the A-144 Analog.
Real Wings Photographs

provide aircraft based on the MiG-21 to trial any of the selected wing shapes. The converted MiG-21 was a tailless delta, designated as the A-144 Analog in its new guise, and to be built at the Voronezh Aircraft Plant, located some 370 miles (600km) south of Moscow, as would the airliner. Two Analog prototypes were built; the first was used to develop the elevon control system. In a similar manner to the Tu-144, the elevon sections would occupy the complete trailing edge of the wings, while the wing leading edges were swept back quite severely on the inner section and the outer wing panel had its angle of sweep reduced. To record the behaviour of the testbed in flight, recording cameras were placed in a fairing behind the cockpit and on top of the fin. To simulate the changes in c.g. expected with the full-sized airliner, a 640lb (290kg) balance weight was incorporated. This could be moved either fore or aft, as needed by controls in the cockpit to alter the c.g. The A-144 Analog, also known as the MiG-21I, made its maiden flight on 18 April 1968, the pilot being O.V. Gudkov.

By the end of 1969 at least 140 test flights had been undertaken in support of the Tu-144 project, during which a maximum altitude of 62,300ft (19,000m) was achieved. During these flights the A-144 reached a top speed of Mach 2.06 (1,317mph/ 2,120km/hr). Once the first Analog had completed its flight-test programme, it was used for general flying during which it was lost while performing aerobatics; the pilot on this occasion was V. Konstantinov. The second A-144 was delivered to the Gromov Flight Research Institute for development flying, after which it was used to train the first two pilots for the Tu-144, including E.V. Elyan, who pushed the aircraft to a maximum speed of 1,550mph/ 2,500km/hr. On its retirement, the aircraft went to the Air Force Museum at Monino, where it is alongside an example of the Tu-144. Such was the performance and stability of the A-144 Analog that serious consideration was given to developing it as the MiG-21LSH, heavy armoured attack aircraft (*Shturmovik*). The A-144 had a span of 37.72ft (11.5m), a fuselage length of

40.31ft (12.29m) and a height of 15.45ft (4.71m). The maximum take-off weight was 19,841lb (9,020kg). The fitted powerplant was the R-13F300 turbojet, rated at 8,972lb (39.92kN) dry thrust, while with reheat engaged the output increased to 14,307lb (50.32kN). Other characteristics of the Analog included a top speed of Mach 2.06 at altitude; at low altitude the speed was 745mph (1,200km/hr), the landing speed was 139mph (224km/hr) and the greatest altitude achievable was 65,656ft (20,025m).

The selection of such an aircraft wing layout had been the result of a hard-won battle against the more traditional aircraft and aerodynamic engineers within the Soviet hierarchy and ministerial vested interests who were originally bent on having an aircraft with a tailplane. To reach this point, extensive wind-tunnel testing of models with and without tailplanes had been undertaken, the collated data finally proving that a carefully designed and engineered delta wing would perform far better with the tailplane removed.

This diagram illustrates the prototype Tu-144, characterized by the closely grouped engines within one nacelle block. BBA Collection

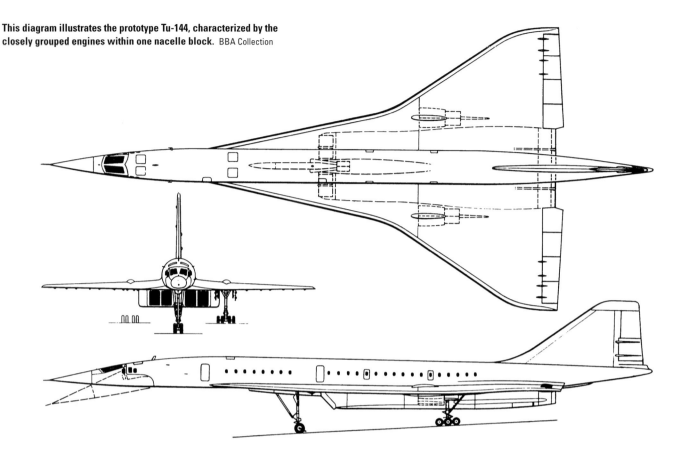

Dirty Work Afoot?

While the designers and engineers were working flat out, rumours were surfacing of espionage attempts by the the KGB. In the Western nations this possibility had already been brought to the attention of the Anglo-French Concorde design teams and to a lesser extent of the American SST designers. One of the first comments came from the press, which pointed to the appearance of an SST model on the stands of the Tupolev Bureau during the Paris Air Show looking 'just like Concorde', a patently untrue statement as subsequent events showed. However, the appearance of the rear-engined Ilyushin IL-62 airliner, which bore an uncanny resemblance to the BAC (Vickers) VC-10, seemed to reinforce the charge of espionage. Further incidents that emerged from this period were centred within France. The first concerned the head of the Aeroflot mission in Paris who was arrested while preparing to depart to Moscow with a briefcase allegedly full of Concorde blueprints. Another concerned attempts to bribe an airport worker at Toulouse to provide rubber scrapings from Concorde's high-speed taxi trials for analysis in the USSR. This one was apparently

stopped by the French Secret Service, who concocted a substance that resembled rubber-tyre scrapings, but would, upon testing, prove to be unsuitable for tyres capable of withstanding the rigours of an SST landing. Britain and its primary Concorde manufacturers were also not immune from attempts at espionage. One of the many and most blatant would be the visits to Rolls-Royce at Bristol by numerous Russian diplomats, attachés, journalists and other functionaries displaying an unhealthy interest in the metallurgical secrets behind the Olympus engine. The upshot was a display model of the Tupolev Tu-144 at the 1963 Paris Air Show at Le Bourget. At first glance it closely resembled Concorde and hence the press bestowed the nickname 'Concordski' on the project. However, close observation revealed that there were major differences between the two aircraft, including the grouping of the engines together as in the first prototype and a fuselage that was more oval in cross-section than that of Concorde.

While, at first glance, Russian design and development would appear to be drawing their inspiration from scraps of information garnered from the West, the Tupolev OKB was, in fact, following its own course of

design. Supporting Tupolev in their development efforts was the TSCAcGcl, the Institute of Aerodynamics, who studied in depth information picked up from Western sources and passed on the results to Tupolev. Both organizations presented their results to the Council of Ministers, who confirmed that the aircraft would be designated the Tu-144 on 16 July 1963 under Council Order 798-271; this was confirmed by contract order MAP276, dated 26 July. This contract covered the construction of five airframes during the period 1966–67; of these, two were intended for extensive fatigue testing. In a similar manner to their Western counterparts, the Soviet designers and engineers examined numerous layouts to determine which would be the most aerodynamically efficient. In charge of optimizing the aircraft's aerodynamics was G.A. Ceremukhin, whose counterpart in the engine department was V.M. Bulem. Initially, Tupolev and the Aerodynamics Institute investigated ten different layouts, some of which involved the fitting of a conventional tailplane, although this was quickly discarded since trials proved that it would destabilize the behaviour of the wing, especially in the low speed part of the flight regime. Many of the wing designs were trialled by pilotless aircraft capable of flying at Mach 2. These were designated the Tu-121 for high-speed research, while a further development would become the Tu-139. The final wing design chosen was that of an ogee shape of a composite compound nature. The result of this independence would be seen in the firming up of the Tu-144 specification, which gave a top speed of Mach 2.35, a range that would be over 4,000 miles (6,400km), with a passenger complement of 121 housed in two cabins, plus their baggage and some cargo. In a similar manner to that experienced by the Anglo-French Concorde team, those at the Tupolev OKB were also evolving their design, and so the final aircraft which appeared in 1968 had changed from the original layout when the design was frozen. In comparison to its nearest rival, Concorde, the Tu-144 had a slightly longer fuselage mounted upon an ogee-shaped wing.

It is interesting to note that both the Tupolev and the Anglo-French designers settled upon this wing for their design, and the American contenders would, discounting the Boeing swing-wing effort, settle on the double-cranked delta for their two models. The Tu-144 wing was a blended double delta in planform, where the forward section had a sweep set at 76 degrees, which would flare out to the outer wing panels, swept at 57 degrees. The aerodynamic complexities of an excessively multi-cambered wing were avoided by Tupolev by building the wing across a single plane, although a certain amount of wing leading-edge fixed droop was applied to the aerofoil to improve the airflow across the upper surface. Structurally the wing was built around a series of multispars, which gave the assembly great strength and provided mounting points for the engine nacelles and the main undercarriage legs. Connecting the spars were many

closely spaced ribs, all covered by aluminium alloy skins manufactured from ingots, the majority being of VAD-23, a light aluminium alloy. The trailing edge of the wing was lined by the elevon sections, of which there were four per wing, all driven by a pair of powered flying control units (PFCUs) each, the redundancy being required as a safety feature. Each PFCU could be driven by one of the three primary hydraulic systems, and thus only a total failure of a PFCU or a catastrophic systems failure would stop the PFCU from operating. As the elevons were in part placed in the gas stream generated by the engines, they were skinned with titanium to protect against overheating. Completing the flight-control system was the two-part rudder, which was also driven by PFCUs, these also featured a redundancy capability in a similar manner to the elevons and were also titanium-skinned.

In a similar manner to their American rivals, the Tupolev bureau tested their proposed designs in massive wind tunnels. In today's design environment powerful computers would be used for the same purpose.
Real Wings Photographs

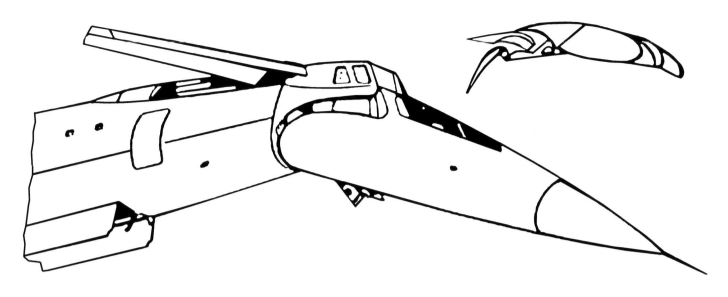

The production version of the Tu-144 was fitted with canards located behind the cockpit. These had both leading and trailing edge flaps that assisted the aircraft in take-off and landing. BBA Collection

Similar, Not Identical

One of the more obvious alterations from the models shown at the Paris Air Shows was that the fuselage cross-section had changed from an oval to one that was almost circular in shape with an external diameter of just over 11ft (3.4m). Punctuating the fuselage main cabin were twenty-five small windows and a pair of access doors each side. Forward of the passenger cabin was the flight deck with provision for three flight crew consisting of a pilot, co-pilot and flight engineer, and in front of the flight deck was the droop nose and associated retracting visor (the 'greenhouse') which gave the crew improved vision during the landing and take-off. Between the crew and the visor were the two direct vision panels, to the rear of which were side windows for lateral vision. This assembly was capable of deflecting downwards to a maximum of 12 degrees and was hydraulically driven in either direction with mechanical locks to hold it in position. The passenger cabin was nearly 87ft (26.5m) long with a maximum internal diameter of 10ft (3m) and a maximum height of 7ft (2.1m). Within this area was seating for 126 passengers and cabin attendant crew, a slight increase from the earlier specification, all carried on five-abreast seating. For the conveyance of freight and baggage the Tu-144 was equipped with holds at the front and the rear of the fuselage which could be

loaded by using either the ventral access doors or overwing conveyer belts. In common with Concorde the Tu-144 used mainly aluminium alloys throughout its airframe, although some use was made of steel and titanium. The former was required to handle the loads in high stress areas and the latter in areas of high temperature, the designer having realized from the outset that this would be a major problem. Unlike the Anglo-French consortium, the Tupolev OKB already had some experience with heavy aircraft travelling at supersonic speeds, having delivered the Tu-22 *Blinder* to the Soviet Air Force. Other than structural and engine considerations, attention was also paid to the development of lubricants, fuels and sealing compounds able to withstand drastic changes in temperature without breaking down. The powerplants also required reworking to withstand the temperature changes, although the Tupolev Bureau had already latched on to the idea that their aircraft and engines would operate at their most efficient at very high altitudes. This in turn brought its own problems, since new air-conditioning and pressurization units would also be needed for this far more rigorous environment. Since flying long distances manually would be very tiring, it was decided from the outset that the Tu-144 would require an autopilot, AFCS, autoland and an inertial navigation system to be created. Control of the aircraft was by electro-mechanical means, the departmental head for this

section being G.F. Naboyshchikova, ably supported by L.M. Rodnyanski who had undertaken similar work for the engine developers P.O. Sukhogo and for the Myasishchev OKB. The AFCS was developed from that installed in the earlier Tu-22 supersonic bomber. Other factors that Tupolev took into consideration were the existing airfields, aircraft handling facilities and air-traffic control systems, the replacement of which would have pushed the project cost up astronomically. The OKB also took account of upper atmosphere radiation and its effects upon both crew and passengers, and thus an attempt was made to protect the occupants by incorporating shielding in the fuselage structure.

Supporting the Tupolev Tu-144 was a most unusual undercarriage. The main-gear units consisted of twelve-wheel bogies, with the wheels grouped in fours along each axle. When the undercarriage was selected up, the leg would move forwards and as it did so the bogie would rotate to lie flat on top of it before disappearing into the slender undercarriage bays. Moving in the opposite direction was the nose undercarriage assembly, derived from an earlier Tupolev product, the Tu-114 turboprop airliner. This was fairly conventional in concept, having only two wheels mounted, one per axle. The braking system was applicable to the main wheels only and could be supplemented by a tail brake-chute mounted in the tail-cone, which could be deployed if needed. The

N.D. Kuznetsov NK-144 engines, developed from the earlier NK-8, and their afterburners were grouped in paired nacelles, the original single-box assembly having been abandoned as inefficient. Each powerplant was capable of developing a dry thrust of 28,600lb (119kN), which was increased to 38,580lb (172kN) with reheat engaged; the latter option was not exercised in cruise mode. During the early series of test flights the crew reported overheating and vibration problems with the engines operating in the subsonic regime. Overheating affected not only the engine nacelle assemblies but also around the rear fuselage. Rectifying the reported harmonic vibration was finally cured by replacing the prototype powerplant RD-36-51s with pre-series production engines RD-ZB-51, which were far better balanced. Further problems were experienced with the engines in that a change of fuel was causing corrosion to the combuster chambers, which, in turn, led initially to a degradation in performance and in one incident complete engine failure. The overheating problem would be cured only when the single engine-nacelle box was replaced by two separate and distinct units with improved cooling arrangements. To supply the engines a total fuel capacity of 19,230gal (87,500ltr) was available, being held in integral tanks in the outer wing panels, the leading-edge wing sections and the lower section of the fuselage. To allow for trim changes in flight, the Tu-144 was equipped with trim tanks in the fin and the forward fuselage, from which fuel could be pumped to maintain a correct c.g. throughout the full range of the flight envelope. The fuel consumption of the prototype engines was far greater than had been predicted. It had been expected that the reheat selection would increase consumption; however, the higher fuel usage in the subsonic regime came as a surprise and needed further investigation. The results of this revealed that the intakes and their secondary vent doors would need to be redesigned; however, given the short-turn usage expected from the first prototype, it was decided to leave any redesign to the preproduction and the production version.

First Appearance

With the first flying prototype and fatigue specimen steadily taking shape, construction having started in 1965, and a provisional date for its appearance, the amount of publicity concerning the new Tupolev product escalated. This adversely affected the maiden flight date that was already pencilled in by the state-controlled media and began to affect the aircraft's production and its flight-test schedule. To this end, the completion of the first and the building of the second prototype were hurried in an effort to keep up with the propaganda. The roll-out of the first prototype, CCCP-68001, took place in early December 1968, with the maiden flight set for later that month, once a full range of ground, engine and taxi trials had been completed satisfactorily. When ready for its first flight, the prototype was stopped by that familiar bugbear that besets many aircraft and their anxious design teams: the weather. Thus poised and ready, the Tupolev team had to wait until 31 December for the first flight, requiring 6,235ft (1,900m) of the runway at Zhukovski. Unlike Western airline test crews, those from Tupolev were seated on ejection seats, although they were not required to use them on this first uneventful flight of 38min. Initially the flight-test crew consisted of the standard trio plus a flight-test engineer (not required for the production aircraft). The crew for this first flight consisted of chief test pilot E.V. Elyan, later to be made a Hero of the Soviet Union, M.V. Kozlova as co-pilot, V.N. Benderova as flight test engineer, with flight engineer Yu T. Seliverstova. Throughout the entire flight the undercarriage remained locked down and this most radical of shapes in the Russian skies made a safe, untroubled landing. From this point, the flight-test schedule progressed smoothly, with the second flight, lasting 50min, taking place in early January 1969, once all the telemetry had been analysed. The first Tu-144 finally achieved supersonic flight on 21 May and speeds above Mach 1 were achieved a short time afterwards on 5 June. During test flying on 26 May 1970 the Tu-144 finally exceeded Mach 2 at an altitude

The second iteration of the Tu-144 saw the engines divided into two distinct nacelles, while the aircraft was supported on revamped undercarriage units. BBA Collection

of 53,480ft (16,311m). Further high-speed flying saw the test crew push to a speed of 1,242mph (2,000km/h) at 55,640ft (16,970m) and the maximum speed was attained later that year when 1,510mph (2,430km/h) was passed. Further development flights were undertaken to prove the behaviour of the environmental control system, the variable intakes, inertial navigation and the autopilot/autoland systems. The last was invaluable in returning the Tu-144 to the ground when all the Moscow airports were blanketed by a white-out and blizzards. The system was so accurate that the aircraft was landed completely in automatic mode. To assist the pilots, a CRT display was mounted in the centre of the main instrument panel, this

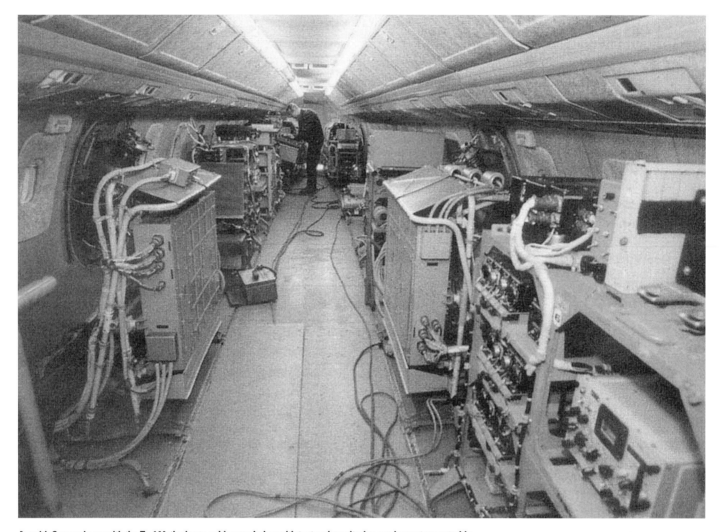

As with Concorde so with the Tu-144, the inner cabin was laden with test and monitoring equipment mounted in racks where passengers would later sit. BBA Collection

gave speed and locational and navigational data. Before the prototypes were retired, 150 test flights were undertaken. Many were made between Khabarovsk and Yuovosibirske, although to reach either destination required that the Tu-144 be as lightly loaded as possible, otherwise there was a chance that the aircraft could run out of fuel.

A public showing of the Tupolev Tu-144 had already been made in the USSR on 21 May 1970, at Sheremetvo Airport, near Moscow; however, other than intelligence reports the aircraft was little known in the West. During its development trials, the Tu-144 was flown extensively within the Soviet Union during May and June 1971. The first Western appearance was in May 1971 when the Tu-144 was revealed at the Paris Air Show. Routing to Le Bourget was via

Sofia, the flight time from Moscow lasting no more than one hour. It is highly ironic that, as both the Tu-144 and Concorde were making their world debuts, American politicians were effectively killing off their own SST programme. After Paris, the Tu-144 returned to the USSR and would not appear in public again until 1978, when the first production aircraft was rolled out from the manufacturing facility at the Venyukovsky fittings plant. The first flight by this machine was on 27 April, after which extensive flying trials took place. This progress came to an abrupt halt on 23 May when a pipe in one of the engine compartments split, allowing fuel to ignite on the hot surfaces of the engine. Fortunately, the experienced test crew of V. Popov and Elyan were able to bring the damaged Tu-144 in for a belly landing because the undercarriage

could not be lowered. This was not without casualties as Elyan was injured and two of the flight test engineers were killed. It would be left to the final three completed production aircraft to finish flight testing before the Tu-144 was cleared for Aeroflot service.

Design Changes

By this time the airframe had undergone some radical changes. The most obvious was in the double-delta wing and the fitting of retractable canard foreplanes just aft of the flight deck. The reworking of the wings increased the span and changed the leading-edge camber, while the use of more advanced materials reduced the weight of the airframe at the same time increasing its structural strength. The

ABOVE: **Wearing its Paris Air Show number 345, Tu-144 CCCP-77102 crashed at the show on 6 June 1973, killing all on board.** BBA Collection

RIGHT: **This photo reveals the height of the Tu-144 undercarriage as it dwarves the people around it at the Paris Air Show.** Real Wings Photographs

75.5ft (23m) long engine nacelles also underwent a complete reworking under the aegis of the Institute of Aerodynamics, becoming similar in design and layout to those fitted to Concorde. They too featured variable intake ramps and dump doors to control the airflow to the compressors, at the same time a more efficient anti-icing system was fitted. At the other end of the nacelle boxes the engine exhausts had also undergone some redesign work, being much improved in functionality, although no thrust reversers were fitted. Originally there had been a requirement to fit thrust reversers to the two outboard engines, although, due to their complexity and the efficiency of the tail brake chute as shown by the prototypes, this was rejected. Alterations were also made to the undercarriage: the nose leg had been extended in length and been brought forward in the bay, and the main undercarriage units had been completely redesigned. Replacing the multiple wheels on each axle, as fitted to the prototype bogies, those on the reworked aircraft had the wheels reduced to eight and the legs retracted into bays located between the engine intakes. Each mainwheel had a diameter of 37.4 inches (950 mm) and was pressurized to 297psi (21kg/sq cm).

The fuselage had also been increased in length by over 20ft (6m), which in turn led to an increase in the number of cabin windows to thirty-four. These then served an increased number of passengers, the complement growing to 140. There were three separate compartments, the forward one for first-class passenger, with a seat layout set at two plus one at a spacing of 40.2in (102cm), while the other compartments had a seat layout of two plus three with a spacing of 34.25in (87cm). Entrance to the aircraft was by a hydraulically-driven door on the forward left-hand side of the fuselage, as

This diagram illustrates well the complicated method used to retract the main undercarriage units into their engine nacelle bays. BBA Collection

well as further mechanically-operated doors for cabin access. Much of the passenger cabin interior decor was provided by organizations in East Germany. To give the passengers more confidence, the ejection seats for the flight crew were removed and replaced by more conventional seating. Other improvements had been undertaken to the nose-cone and its associated visor, the latter having glazing panels of increased size. Extra fuel tankage had also been included to increase the available on-board total to 26,100gal (118,750ltr). The fuel was contained in the wings, which was also the location for the forward c.g. balance tank. Other changes were made to the trim system, with the introduction of a fore and aft rapid transfer capability to augment the already installed fuel balance system; its introduction had been deemed necessary to counteract any possible imbalances experienced during take-off and landing.

Although the changes to the wings and the fuselage were fairly obvious, the greatest area of modification to the production Tu-144s was to the retractable canard foreplanes. Each of these spanned 20ft (6m), and were almost rectangular in shape. At the forward edge of each canard were leading edge slats and the trailing edge was equipped with flaps. When deployed, each canard showed a marked anhedral and

stood out from the fuselage at an angle of 90 degrees; upon retraction the canards folded back into fairings at the rear of the flight deck. The purpose for fitting these extras to production aircraft was to improve the handling during take-off and landing, their deployment meant that the elevons would act more like elevators than flaps during these phases. They also assisted in reducing the runway length requirements and improved handling in the low and slow area of the flight envelope.

Disaster in Paris

The first production aircraft made its maiden flight in August 1972; its first supersonic flight was on 20 September while flying between Moscow and Tashkent. The improved Tupolev Tu-144 made its first appearance in the West at the Paris Air Show in June 1973, although this aircraft, CCCP-77102, and its six occupants were lost in a crash following some violent manoeuvres and another eight were killed due to falling wreckage. Several claims were made about the crash, the most popular in the USSR being that a French Air Force Mirage IIIB on a photographic and filming sortie alongside the SST had caused it to undertake evasive manoeuvres to avoid a

collision. Before this the chief pilot Kozlov had tried to outperform the previous slot aircraft, Concorde. At the opening of the display the Tu-144 had made a slow flyby along runway 060 – so slow was it that watching journalists commented that they were worried about its reducing airspeed. Close to the end of the runway the afterburners were fully engaged and the Soviet SST made an almost vertical climb. Clearly this was beyond the stress design limitations as the left retractable canard was torn clear of its mounts and smashed into the wing root. The impact ruptured the adjacent wing tank and caused an explosion that resulted in the aircraft's crashing. Other investigations centred on the captain's misidentifying the designated flyby runway. The subsequent attempt to reposition the Tu-144 threw the co-pilot, who had been filming the show from the air, into the flying controls. This required a swift reaction from both pilots to recover control. Unfortunately, their efforts were far too enthusiastic and a main access panel came adrift and caused the aircraft to come apart through over-stressing.

In spite of the accident and its subsequent investigation, production of the Tu-144 continued for the only operator, Aeroflot. Grandiose plans were laid for commercial flights around the world, although the burgeoning reality was different since this

ABOVE: **Captured during a flyby at Le Bourget in May 1973 is the preproduction Tu-144, CCCP-77102. Although the wing planform was double delta in layout, there was some subtle blending of the harsher angles in an effort to improve aerodynamic behaviour.** C.P. Russell Smith Collection

RIGHT: **When Tu-144 CCCP-77102 crashed at Paris much of the debris was scattered outside the air-field boundary. This is part of the wing assembly with part of the conditioning pipework.** Real Wings Photographs

BELOW: **The retractable visor assembly fitted to the Tu-144 was far less subtle in construction, being likened to a greenhouse by many. Behind the cabin side windows were the fairings for the retractable canard.** C.P. Russell Smith Collection

Taxiing out at Paris in May 1973, this Tu-144 had its nose fully drooped and the visor retracted for better pilot vision. Note the prominent PFCU covers on the fin and rudder sections. C.P. Russell Smith Collection

fuel-hungry aircraft began to enter revenue-earning service during the 1973 oil crisis. The escalating price of fuel would be one of the reasons why the Tu-144 was removed from service far earlier than had been originally planned. However, having launched the first supersonic transport upon the world, the Russians and Tupolev were determined to put the technology to good use and therefore an intensive development programme was put in place to improve the aircraft yet further both in the air and on the ground.

Into and Out of Service

The result of this was the Tu-144D, which entered Aeroflot service on 1 November 1977. Although numerous commercial flights were carried out between Moscow and Alma Alta, Khazakhstan, the impression gained by most observers who travelled on the aircraft was that it was cramped, very noisy and subject to numerous in-flight emergencies. In total, 102 passenger flights were made before the service was cancelled as uneconomic. The final airframe was never fully competed, and was retained at the Voronezh manufacturing plant for spares use. During this period the passenger load was restricted to 100, as an increase to the maximum of 140

would have reduced the available range. Then came the crash of a Tu-144D on 23 May 1978 while on a test flight. This would turn out to be the last flight of a Tu-144 to carry passengers, although freight flights continued to the more distant parts of the Soviet empire.

During the late 1970s the Tu-144Ds undertook numerous flights, at the end of which a limited Certificate of Airworthiness was issued restricting the aircraft to service within the Russian sphere of influence. During a subsequent series of test flights the Tu-144 was subjected to a series of range–payload trials, the upshot of which was that with a 15-ton (15.3 tonnes) payload the aircraft could fly supersonically over a distance of 3,312 miles (5,330km) and with a load 2 tons lighter the range increased to 3,417–3,541 miles (5,500–5,700km). With the payload reduced to just 7 tons, the range increased to 3,852 miles (6,200km). During the 1980s the Tu-144s continued to be used for flight trials, mainly concerned with developing a second-generation heavy SST. Yet other trials included upper atmosphere tests, ozone-layer depletion studies, sonic boom effects, the thermal effects on materials and structures, aerodynamic studies, flight performance and behaviour, the observation of the boundary layer and the study of anomalous phenomena in the atmosphere. In

July 1983 one the Tu-144Ds crewed by chief test pilot S. Agapov and co-pilot B. Veremey established a sequence of world records, including an average speed around a closed loop of 621.4 miles (1,000km) of 1,262.4mph (2,032km/hr) with a load of 30 tons and a maximum altitude of 59,710ft (18,200m).

While the production aircraft were undertaking such trials and attempting to establish the type as adequate for passenger and freight use, discussions were being held on improving and developing the aircraft further. The first projected upgrade, designated the Tu-144DA, required the redesigning of the wing, which would be increased in area, while the engines would be uprated and matched to reworked variable intakes to improve both sub- and supersonic performance. As the wing had an increased area and volume, it was intended that 125 tons (127.5 tonnes) of extra fuel should be added. This in turn would see an improvement in the load-carrying capability as well as an increased range. The number of passengers would also be increased to a maximum of 160 and the maximum range was set at 4,660 miles (7,500km). This project was, in the event, stillborn, as were many others that followed. These included the Tu-244, also known as the SST-2, and several military versions. The first of these was the

The expanse of the elevons and the rudder fitted to the Tu-144 are clearly shown here, as is the careful blending of the wing leading edge. This aircraft is a production Tu-144S, CCCP-77110, with the Paris display code 345. After service with Aeroflot the aircraft was preserved at the Museum of Civil Aviation, Ulyanovsk. C.P. Russell Smith Collection

Tu-144 CCCP-77144 at Le Bourget in June 1975, wearing Aeroflot titling. After a limited flying career the aircraft had a second life as a NASA testbed. C.P. Russell Smith Collection

Tu-144PR, intended for use as a long-range interceptor; the Tu-144P, intended for electronic countermeasures; and two contemplated strategic versions, the Tu-144K and the Tu-144KP. The former was intended to launch stand-off missile attacks against ground targets and the latter was to attack naval vessels. The nascent Tu-244 would also have a handful of military derivatives envisaged for it; however, these, like those of the Tu-144, remained no more than paper prospects as

the less than successful Tu-160 swing-wing strategic bomber was designed instead. The Russian space programme also benefitted from the Tu-144 since at least one aircraft would be used to simulate the 'Buran' reusable spacecraft.

While the Tu-144 was being used as a test bed for various projects, strenuous attempts were being made to create an economically viable aircraft, not one heavily dependent upon state subsidies. A benefit not available to Aeroflot was the

succession of wealthy businessmen and celebrities who used Concorde as the fastest means to cross the Atlantic. This type of disposable capital was not available within the Warsaw Pact until after its collapse, by which time most of the surviving Russian SSTs were grounded or in museums. Also working against the Tu-144 near the end of its career was a growing official indifference which gradually saw support being withdrawn. Although the Tu-144 project had garnered the

The Tupolev Tu-244 was intended to be the version that would correct the numerous failings of the Tu-144. By the time it was schemed enthusiasm for the Russian SST was on the wane. BBA Collection

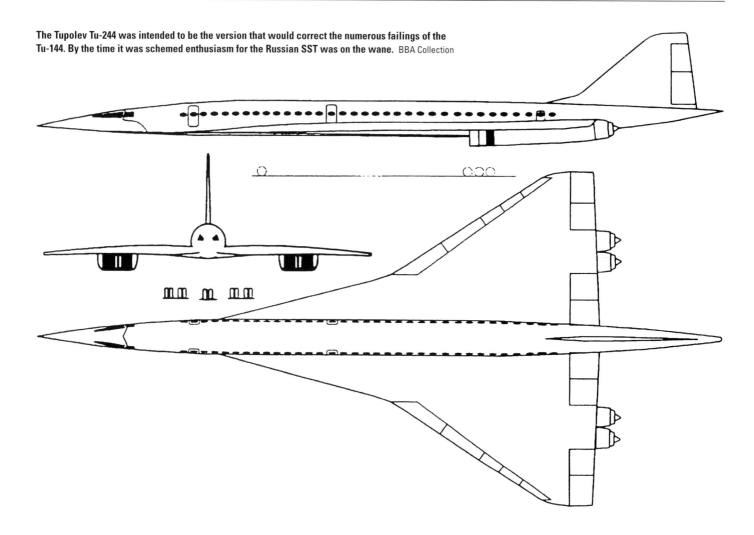

designation of a prestige programme, the increasing support being given to the selling of military aircraft such as the MiG-29 overseas soon outstripped it. The harsh economic reality of the overseas market was that fighters, not SSTs, made better sales and would, in effect, sound the beginning of the end.

The loss of a Tu-144 marked the end of any attempt to use the type for revenue service within and beyond the Soviet Union, and therefore other uses had to be found for the aircraft. Most of these concentrated upon the study of and trials concerning aerodynamic behaviour, engine performance improvements and the earth's ozone layer and its reported breakdown. The eventual collapse of the Warsaw Pact in 1989 seemed to many observers to be the death knell of the entire Tu-144 programme since a lack of general and specific finance threatened to lead to the permanent grounding of the entire airworthy fleet, which by then consisted of just three aircraft.

Resurrection

Fortunately, this would not be the case since NASA, plus interested parties from the American and the Russian aircraft industry, were in the market for a supersonic test bed for NASA's High Speed Research Program, which continued its activities for both civilian and military needs. The American companies included Boeing, McDonnell Douglas, Rockwell, Pratt & Whitney and General Electric. Pushing this forward politically was Vice President Gore, who countersigned the agreement with the Russian Prime Minister Victor Chernomyrdin. This programme had begun in the early 1990s and culminated in a series of test flights with the purpose of collecting data for in-depth comparisons with that garnered previously from theoretical and wind-tunnel experiments. Since the airframe had been constructed by Tupolev ANT, it was decided to nominate this organization to upgrade their own product. To this end

one of the remaining airframes was reworked as the Tu-144LL laboratory, which began test flying around 17 March 1996, soon after its roll-out and ground testing. The airframe chosen for this was the Tu-144D, 77114, one of the last to be built and which had flown only some 83hr, most of which involved flight testing. The modifications embodied in the Tu-144LL flying laboratory included the removal of the original NK-144 engines and their replacement by uprated NK-321 augmented turbofan powerplants, originally developed for the Tu-160 *Blackjack* swing-wing strategic bomber. To this end the engine nacelles and their systems were modified to allow these more powerful engines to be safely fitted. These engines were capable of generating 55,000lb (245kN) of thrust each, pushing the aircraft's top speed above Mach 2.3 quite comfortably and increasing the range to 4,040 miles (6,500km).

The maximum take-off weight for the Tu-144LL was 410,000lb (186,400kg), of

The Tu-144LL was a multi-agency/ company venture designed to investigate the NASA-sponsored Hi-Speed Flight programme. Although deemed successful, only one more flight was made, to the USA where a private buyer had purchased it for display. Courtesy NASA

BELOW: Seen from underneath, this shot of the Tu-144LL flying laboratory shows that the Tupolev OKB were close to achieving the correct configuration for a viable SST; the missing ingredient during the Aeroflot days was reliability. Courtesy NASA

Tu-144LL NASA Handling Report

Four handling test flights were conducted with the Tu-144LL SST with the object of collecting quantitative data and qualitative pilots' reports. The data was then compared with previous values and covered 'Neal-Smith' short-period damping, time delay, control anticipation parameters, phase delay, pitch bandwidth as a function of time delay, and the flight path as a function of pitch bandwidth. The baseline used to compare the data from the Tu-144LL was that generated by the Lockheed YF-12 and SR-71 and the North American XB-70, all of which had already been operated by NASA. The Tu-144LL was controlled by a conventional column and rudder pedals and rate feedbacks were added to aid damping. Turn co-ordination was aided at speeds between Mach 0.9 and 1.6 by an aileron–rudder circuit interconnect. At speeds higher than Mach 1.6 sideslip feedback was added for stability augmentation. The two primary instruments used during these phases were the vertical rate indicator (which displayed the aircraft's altitude and airspeed with the profiles for the climb to and descent from cruise flight) and the attitude ladder (which gave its display in 0.5 degree increments). The Tu-144LL was also fitted with an autopilot and an autothrottle, used only in the landing pattern.

The first handling flight test was carried out by a Russian crew who undertook a shake-down flight, Flight 20, since the aircraft had not flown for an extended period. After this flight and its subsequent rectification, the Tu-144LL was handed to an American crew of two pilots and three engineers. Flight 21 was dedicated to investigating the subsonic handling envelope and concentrated on take-off and landing characteristics and aircraft behaviour in subsonic cruise flight at Mach 0.9. Flights 22 and 23 covered flying at Mach 2, although the total time allotted was only 40min. During these flights specifically defined manoeuvres were carried out. Known as the integrated test block, these manoeuvres included pitch attitude, bank-angle, heading captures, steady heading sideslips and a deceleration and acceleration manoeuvre. A slow flight manoeuvre was also carried out, involving the pulling back of the control column to achieve a specified deceleration to capture the minimum speed before the stall. This was carried out in both level and banked flight. A simulated engine-out manoeuvre involved throttling back of an outboard engine to its power minimum, after which flight was stabilized and the crew performed a heading capture. Each of the take-offs was made with the nose canards extended and the nose set at 11 degrees droop. The nominal approach and landing was a visual one, with the canards extended, gear deployed, the nose at 17 degree droop, and autothrottle engaged. Approaches and landings were also carried out beyond the normal parameters, such as lateral offsets, retracted canards and with the nose up. Flights with the throttles set to manual and using the instrument landing system localizer were also undertaken. Other investigations in these flights included levelling off and maintaining subsonic and supersonic cruise altitude, making level turns under supersonic cruise conditions at Mach 2, and climbing to and descending from supersonic cruise flight.

The pilots' comments concerning the lateral directional characteristics pointed out the heavy control wheel and rudder forces. Although it was possible to roll the aircraft without too much trouble, they did comment that, with modification, the aircraft could be made to handle better, but even so the Tu-144LL was assessed as adequate. The full range of manoeuvres was carried out in the lateral axis, although the pilots thought that the steady heading sideslips required large pedal forces. Yaw damping was considered satisfactory, the pilots commenting that heading captures were easy to perform. Around the pitch axis the pilots noted that the controls were moderate to heavy, although they were not as deficient as the lateral axis. During pitch up, both pilots noticed that the aircraft had a tendency to bobble during the pitch attitude capture task in Flight 21. This in turn presented the pilots with few cues which led to some over-control of the aircraft. They also indicated that to control the pitch axis was a high workload task, especially during climb to and descent from the Mach 2 cruise condition.

Some of these behaviours were identified as due to the pilots' aggressive handling of the aircraft. During Flight 23 a smoother style of handling was tried; this resulted in a strong reduction in pitch bobbling and a gentler transition between manoeuvres. On this final flight both pilots commented that changing their handling of the Tu-144 reduced the workload considerably and made the aircraft easier to fly.

The flight-path dynamics of the Tu-144LL were investigated in both the subsonic and the supersonic cruise conditions. Difficulty was experienced in keeping vertical speed and flight-path control when following the VRI during the climb because of two effects: pitch attitude sensitivity and a perceived lag between pitch attitude and the flight path responses. As the total length of the flights was short, it was not possible to determine whether the lag was caused by instrumentation lag or the aircraft's dynamics. Further discrepancies were experienced between the power settings and pitch attitude when cruise altitudes were captured at speeds between Mach 0.9 and 2, although, once set, the aircraft was easy to control. Once at Mach 2 the Tu-144LL was found to handle well in turns, although the pilot had to maintain an attitude within the 3–3.5 degrees arc to maintain a steady turn. During these flights the pilots both commented on the fact that, during c.g. fuel transfer, their workloads increased dramatically.

Overall, the NASA pilots felt that there was adverse harmony between the controls caused by heavy forces during the roll; it was discovered that inputting a roll command caused an inadvertent pitch command input, which, in turn, produced relatively large pitch control transients leading to cross coupling between the axes. Other areas that gave rise to comment were that of throttle adjustments since their friction damping was so stiff as to restrict movement to two at a time. Such behaviour led the pilots to over-control power during acceleration and deceleration, which caused some problems during approaches and landings. However, some finesse of control could be achieved by adjusting the pitch of the aircraft, otherwise the engines behaved as advertised in normal cruise flight.

One of the most detailed parts of the analysis concerned the interestingly named Neal-Smith pitch bandwidth criterion trials. To ensure that this data was collected correctly, a lead lag compensator and pure time delay module were put into the control loop to represent a simple pilot model, thus the loop between pitch attitude and stick deflection transfer functions was closed. The compensator could be adjusted to meet specific closed loop characteristics and reacted to meet the preset characteristics and maximum amplitude of the frequency response of the closed loop. The data gathered during the flight trials indicated that the pilots were correct in their observation that the aircraft bobbled, and this increased depending on the severity of the manoeuvre. The data retrieved from these flights was carefully compared and revealed that the most sensitive area in handling was around the pitch axis, where both pilots commented on the tendency to overcorrect an over-pitch, while trying to capture a pitch attitude change. Much of this was experienced during Flight 21; by the time the data from Flight 23 was analysed the pilots had learned not to overcorrect the pitch-up, thus the aircraft would capture the pitch attitude change quite easily. However, in the supersonic regime the pitch-up tendency was reduced considerably and thus the pilots learned that reducing their pitch axis urgency would create a stable closed loop pitch response.

The conclusions drawn by the NASA pilots report centred around the use of the Neal-Smith data analysis as applied to the Tu-144LL flights. They held that more accurate flying was possible by using an inertially-derived vertical speed feedback, as opposed to pitch attitude as required by the analysis loop. Overall, however, the pilots commented that the Tu-144 could have been developed into a better aircraft had the time and funds been available; had the Tu-244 been developed many of the faults with the Tu-144 might have been successfully eradicated.

which 224,000lb (101,800kg) was fuel. The total cost of these modifications and upgrades, including the installation of a Damien PCM digital data system, was finally $350 million. Further installed equipment included thermocouples, pressure sensors, microphones and skin-friction gauges to measure the heat and noise generated when the aircraft was travelling at speed. The first sequence of nineteen flights began in June 1996 and included six flight and two ground experiments in the maiden flight schedule, which were concluded in February 1998. The experiments, which originally totalled fifty, covered the behaviour of the aircraft's exterior surface under various temperature and pressure loads, the internal structure and engine temperature, boundary layer airflow behaviour, the wings' ground-effect characteristics, interior and exterior noise profiles, handling qualities in several parts of the flight envelope, and the flexibility of the structure in flight.

NASA hired a late-production Tu-144 for use as a flying testbed; some of the changes made included replacing the original powerplants with those from a Tu-160 bomber. BBA Collection

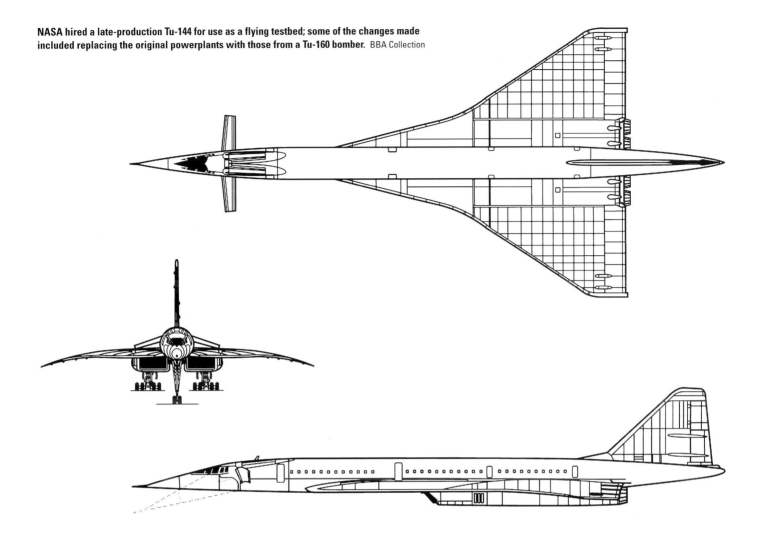

Experiments carried out on the ground included the effects of the airflow as it entered air-inlet structures and the effects on engine performance when supersonic shock waves rapidly changed position in the engine air inlet. During the second series of test flights the crews concentrated on further investigations into six of the airborne experiments from the first sequence. For this, further instrumentation was installed by Tupolev technicians to assist in the acquisition of data. The primary purpose of these flights and the extra equipment was to monitor the deflection of the wing. Most of the equipment was American and included transducers and sensors, their purpose being to measure sonic boom pressures, angle of attack and sideslip angles with improved accuracy. The crew selected to fly this programme were Robert Rivers from NASA Langley and Gordon Fullerton of NASA Dryden, who eventually collaborated on an extensive report on the handling of the

This head-on view of the Tu-144LL shows that, from certain angles, its looks rivalled Concorde's. Courtesy NASA

NASA Experiments with the Tu-144LL

Surface/structure equilibrium temperature verification: this required the installation of 248 thermocouples. Its purpose was to determine the types of material needed to build an aircraft capable of carrying 300 passengers at supersonic speeds.

Propulsion system thermal environment database: this required the installation of a further ninety-six thermocouples. Its purpose was to determine the detrimental effects heat had upon engines driving an aircraft at supersonic speeds and, as a side experiment, the best way to control the flow of air into the engine's compressor face.

Slender wing ground effects: the influence of ground effect on more conventional airliners was fully understood; however, the behaviour of a supersonic aircraft was not, and thus the amount of 'push back' by the air under the wings and the pilot's reaction to it needed investigation.

Structure/cabin noise: this required twenty-five flush-mounted pressure sensors, eight microphones and six accelerometers. High speed travel through air generates a substantial amount of noise, thus these experiments were needed to measure the noise coefficient, which would guide the development of adequate sound proofing.

Handling qualities assessment: a supersonic aircraft has different handling characteristics from other types, thus an in-depth investigation was thought necessary to determine the behaviour of a next-generation SST.

Coefficient of pressure, coefficient of friction and boundary-layer measurements: these required the taking of seventy-five wing static pressures. These experiments concentrated on the aerodynamic drag generated by a supersonic airframe and would give a better understanding of design criteria.

In-flight wing deflection measurements: these experiments were undertaken so that the safest coefficient of elasticity could be engineered into the wing structure.

Tu-144LL. The first three flights of the second series included handling at both subsonic and supersonic speeds, while the final four covered purely data collection. After the analysis of the generated data, seven more flights were carried out between September 1998 and April 1999. All the flights were carried out from the Tupolev airfield at the Zhukovsky Development Centre. Once they had been completed, the Tu-144LL was again grounded since NASA and its commercial partners had lost government funding to continue the further development of an American SST. The purpose of the flights was essentially to investigate the technology base for a second-generation American SST. The goals set for this next generation included environmental friendliness and economic performance. This second grounding would mean that yet again Concorde would remain as the only commercial SST in the world, the others being but dreams.

Tu-144D CCCP-77112 was originally on display at the Tupolev OKB, Zhukovsky, before being sold to Sinsheim Museum in Germany. Here cranes unload the airframe from its special barge. A similar procedure was required with the retired Air France Concorde sold to the same museum. Real Wings Photographs

CHAPTER EIGHT

Death and Disaster

As It Happened

'Concorde, Concorde zero 4590 you have flames, you have flames behind you!' The controller's voice was tinged with fear and disbelief – this was the flagship aircraft of Air France and it was on fire. This short phrase marked the end of Air France Concorde F-BTSC, and of one of the most impressive safety records in aviation history. And yet the warning signs had already been flagged up in the type's incident logs, which carried reports of tyre damage and failures, engine failures and punctures to the wing lower skinning.

On the morning of 25 July 2000 Air France Concorde Sierra Charlie was on the stand at Paris Charles de Gaulle Airport, scheduled to depart with a group of passengers, with the flight designation AF4590. It was under charter to a German tour operator who had sponsored a combined trip involving a flight to New York, to be followed by a cruise aboard the luxury liner MS *Deutschland* around Latin America. The scheduled departure time had been pushed back by the late arrival of the main luggage collection from Germany and its subsequent delayed loading. Adding to the delay was the need to rectify a No.2 engine thrust reverser problem, which had required the replacement of the Goodyear pneumatic actuator. Eventually the passenger complement of ninety-six Germans, two Danes, one American and one Austrian, plus the flight and cabin crew were aboard. The external walk around had been completed, the engines started, the tug hooked up and the Air France Concorde was pushed back. With the tug disconnected, the throttles were advanced to give taxi speed, the aircraft proceeding under ground control to the runway threshold. Cleared for take-off, Concorde was throttled up and swung round to point down the runway centreline. With brakes applied, the throttles were advanced, after which the afterburner ganged switch was lifted up to engage the augmentation. The brakes were released and the blended delta airframe began to rush down the tarmac strip at an ever increasing speed with the wind to her back. The recorded departure time was 14:42 local time; within 2min the flight was over.

13hr 58min *Crew*: 'Concorde for New York on Echo 26 we need the whole length of 26 right'

14hr 07min *Controller*: 'plan for 26 right' [Crew confirm and read back]

14hr 13min 13sec 'So total fuel gauge I've got ninety-six four with ninety-six three for ninety-five on board'

14hr 13min 46sec *First Officer*: 'Fire protection'; *Flight Engineer*: 'Tested'

14hr 14min 17sec *Captain*: 'The reference speeds are V1, 150 knots, VR 180, V2 220, 240, 280, it's displayed on the left'

14hr 14min 28sec *First Officer*: 'Trim'; *Captain*: 'It's thirteen degrees'

On a happier occasion, F-BTSC (the aircraft lost in the crash on 25 July 2000) touches down at Paris Charles de Gaulle. Bernard Charles

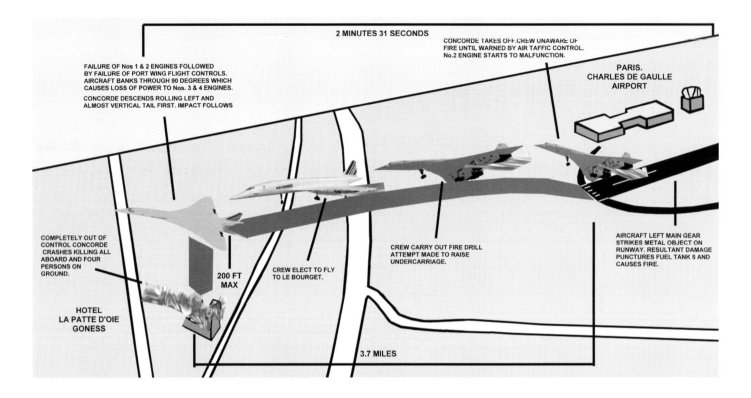

2 MINUTES 31 SECONDS

CONCORDE TAKES OFF. CREW UNAWARE OF
FIRE UNTIL WARNED BY AIR TAFFIC CONTROL.
No.2 ENGINE STARTS TO MALFUNCTION.

FAILURE OF Nos 1 & 2 ENGINES FOLLOWED
BY FAILURE OF PORT WING FLIGHT CONTROLS.
AIRCRAFT BANKS THROUGH 90 DEGREES WHICH
CAUSES LOSS OF POWER TO Nos. 3 & 4 ENGINES.

CONCORDE DESCENDS ROLLING LEFT AND
ALMOST VERTICAL TAIL FIRST. IMPACT FOLLOWS

PARIS.
CHARLES DE GAULLE
AIRPORT

COMPLETELY OUT OF
CONTROL CONCORDE
CRASHES KILLING ALL
ABOARD AND FOUR
PERSONS ON
GROUND.

200 FT
MAX

CREW ELECT TO FLY
TO LE BOURGET.

CREW CARRY OUT FIRE DRILL
ATTEMPT MADE TO RAISE
UNDERCARRIAGE.

AIRCRAFT LEFT MAIN GEAR
STRIKES METAL OBJECT ON
RUNWAY. RESULTANT DAMAGE
PUNCTURES FUEL TANK 5 AND
CAUSES FIRE.

HOTEL
LA PATTE D'OIE
GONESS

3.7 MILES

The last flight of Concorde Sierra Charlie was tragically short when, after struggling to maintain height and speed, the aircraft crashed on to a hotel. BBA Collection

14hr 14min 53sec *Captain*: 'Next the control lever is at fourteen and you'll have N2 of ninety-seven and a bit'; *Flight Engineer*: 'Ninety-seven'

14hr 34min *Controller*: 'Air France 4590, good morning, taxi to holding point 26 right via Romeo'; crew confirm need for the whole runway

14hr 37min 51sec *First Officer*: 'Hey – you've got the indicators going into green all the time'

14hr 38min 55sec *Flight Engineer*: 'you're right, we'll stay in yell-, in green'

14hr 38min 59sec *First Officer*: 'We'll stay in green, eh?'

14hr 39min 04sec *Captain*: 'So the take off is – at maximum take-off weight, one hundred eighty tons one hundred, which means four reheats with a minimum failure N2 of ninety-eight. Between zero and one hundred I stop for any aural warning – the tyre flash. The tyre flash and failure call-out from you right. Between 100 knots and V1 I ignore the gong I stop for and engine fire, a tyre flash and the failure call-out. After V1 we continue on the SID we just

talked about, we land back on runway 26 right'

14hr 40min 19sec *Captain*: 'How much fuel have we used?'; *Flight Engineer*: 'We've got 800 kilos there'

14hr 41min 09sec *Flight Engineer*: 'Brake temperatures checked one hundred fifty'; *Captain*: 'Is it hotter on the left or the right there?' *Flight Engineer*: 'It's about the same'

14hr 40min 02sec *Controller*: '4590 line up 26 right'; *Crew*: 'We line up and hold on 26 right 4590'

14hr 42min 17sec *Controller*: 'Air France 4590, runway 26 right, wind 90 degrees, 8 knots, take-off authorized'

14hr 42min 17sec *Co-pilot*: '4590 taking off 26 right'

14hr 42min 20sec *Pilot*: 'Is everybody ready?'

14hr 42min 22sec *Co-pilot*: 'Yes'

14hr 42min 24sec *Engineer*: 'Yes'

14hr 42min 31sec *Pilot*: 'Up to 100, 150, top'

14hr 42min 40sec *Engineer*: ' We have four heated up'

14hr 42min 54.6sec *Co-pilot*: '100 knots'

14hr 42min 55sec *Pilot*: 'Confirmed'

14hr 42min 57sec *Engineer*: 'Four green'

14hr 43min 03.7sec *Co-pilot*: 'V one'

14hr 43min 5sec *Pilot*: 'Confirmed'

14hr 43min 10.1sec [Noise recorded on CVR over the next few seconds to 14hr 43min 13.8sec]

14hr 43min 11.9sec *Co-pilot*: 'Watch out'

14hr 43min 13.4sec *Controller*: 'Concorde zero 4590! You have flames, you have flames behind you!'

14hr 43min 14sec *Flightdeck (voice not identified)*: 'Right'

14hr 43min 16.4sec *Engineer*: 'Stop'

14hr 43min 17sec *Co-pilot*: 'Well received'

14hr 43min 20.4sec *Engineer*: 'Breakdown eng–, breakdown engine number two'

14hr 43min 22.8sec [Fire alarm sounds]

14hr 43min 24.8sec *Flight Engineer*: 'Shut down engine number two'; *Flightdeck (voice not identified)*: 'It's burning badly – huh'

14hr 43min 25.8sec *Pilot*: 'Engine fire procedure'

14hr 43min 27.2sec *Co-pilot*: 'Watch, the airspeed, the airspeed, the airspeed'

14hr 43min 28sec *Controller*: 'It's burning badly and I'm not sure it's coming from the engine'

14hr 43min 29.3sec [Fire handle pulled]

14hr 43min 30sec *Pilot*: 'Gear on retract'

14hr 43min 31sec *Controller*: '4590, you have strong flame behind you – as you wish, you have priority for a return to the field'

14hr 43min 31.5sec *Engineer*: 'The gear'

14hr 43min 32sec *Controller*: 'Beginning reception of middle marker'

14hr 43min 40sec *Co-pilot*: 'Yes, well received'

14hr 43min 41sec *Engineer*: 'The gear – No!'

14hr 43min 42sec *Controller*: 'So, at your convenience, you have priority to land'

14hr 43min 42.3sec [Second fire alarm sounds]

14hr 43min 44.6sec *Co-pilot*: 'I'm trying'

14hr 43min 45.6sec *Engineer*: 'I'm firing it'

14hr 43min 48.2sec *Pilot*: 'Are you shutting down engine number two?'

14hr 43min 48.2sec *Engineer*: 'I've shut it down'

14hr 43min 49sec *Controller*: 'End reception middle marker'

14hr 43min 49.9sec *Co-pilot*: 'The airspeed'

14hr 43min 57sec *Co-pilot*: 'The gear won't come up'

14hr 43min 58.6sec [Third fire alarm sounds]

14hr 43min 59sec–44min 03sec *GPWS alarm*: 'Whoop whoop whoop, pull up … whoop whoop whoop, pull up'

14hr 43min 59sec *Co-pilot*: 'The airspeed'; *GPWS alarm*: 'Whoop whoop whoop, pull up'

14hr 44min 05sec *Fire Service Leader*: 'De Gaulle tower from Fire Service Leader, authorization to enter twenty-six right'; *Controller*: 'Fire Service Leader – the Concorde I don't know his intentions, get into position near the southern parallel runway, Fire Service Leader correction: the Concorde is returning on runway 09 in the opposite direction'

14hr 44min 14.6sec *Co-pilot*: 'Le Bourget, Le Bourget, Le Bourget'

14hr 44min 17sec *Pilot*: 'Too late, too late'

14hr 44min 18sec *Pilot*: 'No time, no time'

14hr 44min 18.5sec *Co-pilot*: 'Negative, we're trying Le Bourget'

14hr 44min 20sec *Co-pilot*: 'No'

14hr 44min 21sec *Fire Service Leader*: 'De Gaulle tower from Fire Service Leader: can you give me the situation of Concorde?'

[Pilot noises – sounds of exertion]

[Pilot noises – sounds of exertion]

[Pilot noises – sounds of exertion]

[The cockpit voice recorder made its last recording at 4:44:30pm; the recording ended at 4:44:31.6pm]

14hr 45min 10sec *Controller to Fire Service Leader*: 'The Concorde has crashed near Le Bourget, Fire Service Leader'

The wreckage still smoulders as the fire services turned up to douse the remains of Concorde and the hotel it hit. Real Wings Photographs

Engine Performance and Warning Data for F-BTSC	
14h 43m 11.7–12.3s: all four engines operating correctly	14h 43m 23.7–25.3s: No.1 engine at 4 per cent thrust; No.2 engine at 12 per cent thrust
14h 43m 12.7–13.3s: deviations in N1/N1 parameters engine No.2	14h 43m 26.2–28.4s: No.1 engine thrust falls to 45 per cent; No.2 engine throttle to fully retarded position
14h 43m 12–13s: engine surging Nos 1 and 2 engines	14h 43m 28.7–29.3s: No.2 engine shutting down
14h 43m 12.1–14.1s: the GO lamps go out, No.1 engine	14h 43m 28.3s: Nos 3 and 4 engines operating in contingency mode at full power
14h 43m 15.7–16.3s: confirmation of surge No.1 engine	
14h 43m 16.1–18.1s: No.1 engine GO light illuminates	14h 43m 35.5s: No.1 engine operating in contingency mode, although thrust no more than 5 per cent
14h 43m 16.7–17.3s: No.2 engine thrust drops to idle	
14h 43m 18.1–20s: No.1 engine GO light goes out; Nos 3 and 4 engine GO lights go out	14h 43m 59.5–44m 11.5s: No.1 engine underspeeding and suffers final surge
14h 43m 19.7–20.3s: No.1 engine thrust drops to 80 per cent	14h 44m 24.7–27s: Nos 3 and 4 engine levers retarded possibly by crew attempting to equalize asymmetric condition of aircraft
14h 43m 20.7–21.3s: No.2 engine recovers thrust to 15 per cent	

The statements may sound stark in nature, but they are taken from the cockpit recorder tape and the air traffic control tapes. Their accuracy is without doubt, unlike the media accounts, mostly hysterical and inaccurate, that followed this most tragic event. The baldness of the taped conversations exhibit an icy calmness which is remarkable considering the clamour of gongs, alarms and recorded warnings that were surrounding the crew as they struggled to bring their stricken Concorde under control and return it and its occupants safely to the ground. Eyewitness reports garnered just after the event stated that Concorde began its take-off run without any trace of a problem. At the point of rotation a flash of fire was observed in the vicinity of no.2 engine, this would quickly grow into a long streak of fire, estimated at 180–275yd (200–300m) in length, that did not appear to be subsiding. Although the aircraft managed to take-off, it was seen to be struggling to maintain height and forward airspeed. The direction of flight was seen to waver slightly before Concorde reared up, obviously out of control. As it continued its climb, it rolled 90 degrees to the ground, totally out of control, before falling out of the sky in a side slip and landing on the Hotelissimo, La Patte d'Oie, in Gonesse 3.7 miles (5.8km) from the airport. In the resulting impact and fireball, all 100 passengers, the crew of nine and four hotel employees were killed and the aircraft and the hotel annexe were destroyed. At the time of the crash F-BTSC had completed 11,989 flying hours and 3,978 cycles.

Seeking an Explanation

Once the smoke, dust and media feeding-frenzy had subsided, the crash investigators began their intensive search for the cause of the tragedy. To this end all the wreckage and debris were carefully noted and collected for further examination and reconstruction in a hangar at Toulouse. In the meantime, the British Airways Concorde fleet continued to fly, albeit after in-depth special checks; those of Air France were immediately grounded. Initially, the investigators looked at the possibilities of a terrorist bomb and engine failure as the prime causes. These were quickly discounted since the flight characteristics and the debris pattern did not fit any of the known crash profiles. By this time, the French accident investigation organization,

the Bureau Enquêtes-Accidents (BEA), with some assistance from the British Air Accident Investigation Branch, felt that enough evidence had been gathered and processed to allow them to issue a preliminary report, which duly appeared on 27 July. In it the BEA stated:

During take-off the aircraft had exceeded V One when the control tower warned the crew that flames were streaming from the rear of the aircraft. The cockpit voice recorder revealed that, upon rotation, the crew announced a failure in No.2 engine, adding shortly afterwards that the undercarriage would not retract. Analysis of the flight data recorder showed that during rotation there a loss of power in engine No.2, followed by a temporary loss of performance from No.1 engine. During its brief flight, the flight data recorder revealed that the aircraft's forward speed had barely increased and that its altitude had changed little. Although No.1 engine had regained full power after one minute, the power-plant started to malfunction again. Shortly after this, the Concorde banked sharply to the left and crashed. The resultant wreckage was concentrated in a limited area; although a certain amount of debris was spread along the aircraft's flightpath, there was also some debris found on the runway at Charles de Gaulle airport.

A follow-up report was issued by the BEA in August, that recommended that the Certificate of Airworthiness be withdrawn from the remaining Concorde fleet. In this the French investigators were fully supported by the Air Accident Investigation Branch in Britain. Other conclusions drawn in the same document involved some of the causes of the accident. This had been pinned down to a wing fuel tank having been punctured by sections of wheel after a tyre had suffered catastrophic explosive failure. Due to the lack of warning systems in that section of the wing, the crew would have been unaware of the source of the fire and therefore their first, obvious conclusion would be to contend that there was a problem with either No.1 or No.2 engine, or both. Further investigations were being undertaken to pin down the cause and thus the grounding order was strongly recommended to continue. To this end, the Certificate of Airworthiness paperwork was removed from each flightdeck, with those parked away from home being sealed to prevent removal. In December 2000 the BEA issued another and more detailed report that expanded further upon the investigators previous efforts. The document revealed that Concorde F-

Summary of the French Accident Report

main gear bogie which had been done in order to correct an acceptable deferred defect which related to the under-inflation detection system. Since the A01 check and rectification the aircraft had flown on service between 21 and 24 July.

Defects requiring rectification before the final flight included slight thrust surges in cruise at Mach 2, with illumination of a start-pump warning light. Rectification included in-depth checks of the thrust control units and replacement of the N1 limit amplifier. Further checks were carried out on the EGT sensing line. The brake overload warning light for wheel No.4 had illuminated, requiring the replacement of a cable and a slow leak had been detected in the blue hydraulic system that had required the replacement of the connecting joint on the artificial feel cylinder. The final item requiring attention was the tyre on wheel No.5, the whole assembly being replaced.

Before its final flight 'SC' had been placed on standby for F-BVFA, which had been the planned aircraft for AF 002 to New York, while F-BVFC had been allocated to flight AF 4590. Due a maintenance requirement, F-BVFA had been replaced by F-BVFC since the former had become unserviceable. This meant that F-BTSC was the only aircraft available for flight 4590. Before being allocated to this flight Sierra Charlie had been confirmed to have no acceptable deferred defects in its log, although the Garrett pneumatic motor driving the No.2 engine secondary exhaust nozzle bucket had been replaced, after which it was declared fit for flight.

Having confirmed the last known defects to afflict Sierra Charlie and the circumstances surrounding its allocation to flight 4590, the report concentrated upon the systems deemed to have played a significant part in the crash. The first to be defined was the undercarriage and its detectors, in particular the under-inflation warning system. This system lights two red tyre-warning lights on each of the pilots' instrument panels, while there was an amber warning on the second pilot's panel which illuminated a wheel light. There was also an amber tyre warning light on the engineer's panel. This detection system was inhibited when the speed of the wheels was below 10kt or the steering angle of the nose wheels exceeded 3 degrees and none of the throttle levers was in the fully forward position. The red tyre-warning lights would not illuminate if the indicated air speed exceeded 135kt. This system was self-monitoring and would illuminate a yellow system warning light that was situated on the engineer's panel and would light up should a fault be found in the under-pressure detection system. Retraction of the undercarriage was controlled by a lever with three positions: up, neutral and down. To retract the undercarriage electrical power needed to be available, although 'up' could not be selected until the left gear weight-off microswitch indicated that the shock absorber was fully uncompressed. During the retraction sequence the gear was fully up and locked after 12sec.

Other undercarriage items defined in the report included the way in which the braking system operated and was indicated, while the main-gear deflectors were covered in detail. Located to the front of each main-wheel bogie the role of the deflector was to shift water lifted by the tyres from entering the intakes. These weighed approximately 9lb (4kg) and were made from composite materials, except for the fasteners. In 1995 the deflectors were subjected to an optional Service Bulletin, SST 32-103, dated 12 January 1995, which proposed that two cables be inserted in the leading edge of the deflectors to reinforce them in case of failure. Although British Airways did this, Air France declined to do so. The wheels and tyres installed on F-BTSC were manufactured by Dunlop and Goodyear, respectively. All had been fitted during the previous two months. It was also noted that the use of retread tyres had ceased on Concorde during 1996.

The report then moved on to cover the fuel and the engines, it being noted that the aircraft had received a final top-up of Jet A1 fuel at 13.55hr, when an extra 66gal (300ltr) had dispensed to tanks 1, 2, 3 and 4. At this point the total fuel load was 208,000lb (94,470kg). The engines were notated next, the included data covering the individual serial number, number of cycles and of flying hours since installation, and the date of installation. The longest serving powerplant was in the No.2 position, having been installed on 1 August 1999. Given the fact that Concorde was the only airliner that used thrust augmentation or reheat during take-off, it was no surprise that there was a back-up system in place should an engine fail on take-off. Known as the contingency mode, it could be activated either by manual or automatic means. In either case, the following criterion needed to be satisfied: reheat needed to be activated on any engine, the take-off monitor was armed and that the N2 reading of any engine had to fall below 58.6 per cent indicated. When contingency mode was activated, the remaining three engines could increase thrust automatically to reach a theoretical maximum of 105 per cent. There is also a reheat cut-out which engaged

should the engine output fall below 75 per cent, although the function was restored when output reached 81 per cent thrust.

As the fire detection and sensing systems played a crucial part in the circumstances surrounding the crash, their functions were defined in depth. The detection system consisted of two loops, one of which detected fire around the engine and the other detected a torching flame in the vicinity of the combustion chamber. For an engine fire warning caption to illuminate, both loops had to detect a fault. Once this happened, an aural warning sounded to reinforce the illuminated light and the red flashing light on the individual engine-fire handle. Operation of this handle had the following results: the air conditioning bleed valve closed, the hydraulic shut-off valve did the same, as did the HP and the LP fuel valves, the reheat fuel valves and the secondary air inlets. The final effect of the pulling of the fire handle was the closing of the the auxiliary ground running flap. When tests were carried out on a serviceable Concorde it was discovered that these actions were completed in between 5 and 7sec, against a regulatory requirement of 30sec.

Each Olympus engine consisted of twelve modules, the maintenance of which was undertaken by Air France, SNECMA services or by GEAES, depending on the depth of engineering required, with the final assembly being carried out by General Electric Aircraft Engine Services. The maintenance covered included visual inspection, partial refurbishment and complete major overhauls, all based on the Olympus maintenance manual. Supporting the maintenance effort were readings taken by the flight engineer during supersonic flight; these included EGT and fuel flows.

Weights and balances were computer generated and based on three sets of parameters. The first was the Phase 1 forecast that was determined by entering known average weights for passengers, baggage and any intended freight. For Sierra Charlie this first total was 411,100lb (186,864kg). After correction the final taxi weight was calculated at 411,952lb (187,251kg), down to 409,752lb (186,251kg) at the point of turning on to the runway for take-off. The items noted aboard F-BTSC included 122 pieces of baggage, calculated to have an average weight of 45.5lb (20.7kg) giving a total of 5,555lb (2,525kg), although only 103 were noted on the manifest. Each passenger was given an average weight of 149lb (84kg) per adult and 77lb (35kg) for each child, plus 132lb (60kg) of newspapers. Given these calculations Concorde Sierra Charlie was slightly overloaded at 407,154lb (185,070kg) for its projected journey. C.g. percentages were the next area covered, these being predicted at 52.3 per cent at zero fuel weight, increasing to 54.2 per cent for taxiing with fuel. For a take-off weight of 406,736lb (184,880kg) the c.g. had to be at 54 per cent, thus to change the original percentage it was noted that at least 1,540lb (700kg) of fuel would need to be transferred forward from tank 11. In fact, the investigation discovered that the actual c.g. was 54.25 per cent, which would need at least 1,760lb (800kg) of fuel to be transferred forward from tank 11 to give a correct c.g. Should Concorde's weight and balance be outside the parameters, there was an alarm fitted to warn the crew to carry out corrective action.

Having determined the weights and balances, the other information requiring attention were the speed ranges covering the handling of the aircraft with either one or two engines shut down. In the flight manual the zero-rate climb speed with undercarriage retracted and three engines was 193kt, which increased to 262kt with only two engines running. With the undercarriage extended, the figures changed to 205kt and less than 300kt. These figures were vitally important in the operation of Concorde since falling below them would result in the aircraft's becoming unstable, thus leading to a stall. The figures generated for the distance needed for a three-engine take-off were 3,685yd (3,370m), the entire take-off run covering 4,046yd (3,700m). The tailwind of 8kt and the extra ton of cargo were determined to be negligible in causing the accident.

The behaviour of the flight control surfaces and systems were the next area to be investigated. An explanation of the hydraulic systems required to operate the flight control system followed, the noted point being that power to the PFCU synchro valves was derived from common sources. The avionics were also investigated in depth, the first being the Sundstrand Mk.1 ground proximity warning system, which had five function modes. The alarm noise identified on the cockpit voice recorder tape revealed that the GPWS was selected to Mode 3, which indicated that the nose was at 12.5 degrees, the radio altimeter height was greater than 50ft (15m), although the loss in altitude held previously was greater than that allowed. Having covered the major areas of the crew and the aircraft, the investigators turned their attention to the meteorological conditions. Over Europe at the time there was a succession of low pressure areas, while in the vicinity of Charles de Gaulle the wind speed over runway 26 was 4kt, although this increased to 8, gusting to 9 intermittently.

Concorde Sierra Charlie Wreckage Disposition

The debris trail for Concorde F-BTSC began on the runway where parts of the left under-carriage water deflector assembly were discovered 5,384ft (1,642m) from the end of runway 26R. Close by this point some sections of No.2 tyre were also discovered, including the cut section. The strip of metal about 17in (43cm) long was found in the same area on the runway shoulder. It still held some of its Cherrylok rivets. Also found in the vicinity was part of the lower skin surface from fuel tank No.5. Slightly further along the runway a brake servo valve cover showing overheating and deformation was discovered. From this point, further along the runway, signs of an explosion and dam-aged concrete were found. Indications that Concorde had begun to slew off the runway were revealed by the discovery of a broken light cover at the edge of the runway; it had been hit by Concorde's left undercarriage. At the 5,925ft (1,807m) point, marks made by a deflated tyre were noted; these lasted until the 7,672ft (2,340m) point and were con-sistent with that of the No.2 wheel. Further tyre tracks continue intermittently up to the 9,279ft (2,830m) point. Fuel and soot marks were found to start at a distance of 5,967ft (1,820m) from the threshold. These continued up to 9,082ft (2,770m) from the thresh-old, after which the burn evidence continued over the grass to the 10,377ft (3,165m) mark. From the end of the runway to the crash site further wreckage was located: at the 3,280ft (1,000m) mark a section of elevon was found, as was the tail-cone anti-collision light, a severely fire-damaged inspection panel from the left wing lower sur-face, plus seven inspection panels without fire damage evidence that had originally been fitted to the left wing upper surface dry bay. From the 3,280 to the 8,200ft (1,000–2,500m) point further wreckage consisting of another dry bay upper inspection panel, a fire-damaged duct section and fire-damaged sections from the tail-cone were discovered. As some of these items were burning when they hit the ground, there was supplementary fire damage. Further small items were discovered slightly further on, many of which were fire-damaged; there was also a trail of fire-damaged structural items, including rivets, honeycomb panels and sections from the rear fuselage.

At the crash site the team surmised that the aircraft had been heading along 120 degrees with little forward speed. On impact it broke up, distributing the wreckage mainly to the south. Due to its low speed, most of the wreckage was concentrated with-in a strip some 330 by 165ft (100 by 50m), except for the cockpit section which was out-side this zone. Inside this area, the wreckage was severely fire damaged; however, the front fuselage section had largely escaped. Other items were found outside the prima-ry zone, many being buried through the force of the impact. Complicating matters was the wreckage of the destroyed hotel, although, perversely, some of the important debris hit parts of the building, thus Nos 1 and 2 engines were found resting on a water tank. Inspection of the undercarriage units revealed that the legs remained in the locked-down position, even though the crew had attempted a retraction.

Inspection of the cockpit instrument panels revealed much pertinent data to the inves-tigators. Thus the engine gauges revealed that the thrust levels of the engines were at 28, 4, 80 and 85 per cent for Nos 1 to 4, respectively; however, the fuel flow indicators were mainly burnt beyond recognition. The indicators for the brake system showed a discrepancy between the left and the right side, that to the left being no more than 400psi (28kg/sq cm) while that to the right displayed 1,500psi (105kg/sq cm).

Both pilot's panels were successfully recovered and notes were made regarding the positions of the gauges, levers and switches. The first officer's panel revealed that the nose visor selector was in the down position, the undercarriage selector was between the down and the mid-selection position, the rudder indicator revealed that the upper section was deflected left by 20 degrees, while the lower section had deflected 12 degrees to the right, both were operating from the green hydraulic system. There was no evidence concerning the elevons since they were in mechanical mode. Observation of the airspeed indicator showed that the forward speed was 90kt while the 'STBY' flag was showing, the V2 bug was set at 230kt. Navigation instrument readings showed the HSI at 105 degrees, the ADI showed a 30-degree roll to the left, with the nose set at 32 degrees down; some other instruments were unreadable although the altimeter was indicating 240ft (73m). The panel clock was reading 14h 45m UTC.

The captain's instrument panel showed an HSI heading of 105 degrees, the ADI was at 15 degrees of roll to the left, the nose was indicating 75 degrees down, the standby horizon was at 90 degrees roll to the left, with 18 degrees nose up. Trim indication was at 54.3 per cent. The coaming instrumentation revealed that the autothrottles Nos 1 and 2 were selected to 'OFF', as were autopilot channels 1 and 2 and the flight directors Nos 1 and 2 were also in the 'OFF' position. Autothrottle speed was selected to 285kt, the altitude selection was 9,500ft (2,900m), the left display was reading a heading of 329 degrees and course 285 degrees, while the right display showed 338 degrees with a course of 287 degrees. The overhead panel displays revealed that the servo control hydraulic selectors were at normal, the auto ignition switches for Nos 1, 2 and 3 were set to 'ON', while No.4 had melted. The engine rating mode switches for Nos 1, 2, 3 and 4 were at 'TAKE OFF', and while the HP selector switches were damaged the select-ed positions were still visible and read No.1 'OPEN', No.2 was broken, No 3 was shut and No.4 was at 'TAKE OFF'. The No.2 engine shutdown/fire handle was pulled and pointing upwards added to which the fire extinguisher fired indicators were unread-able.

The investigators were fortunate to find the flying control indicator panel: thus the auto stab was unreadable on Channel 1, while No.2 displayed pitch axis to 'OFF', the roll axis was unreadable and the yaw axis was at 'OFF'. The artificial feel system showed that Channel No.1 was using the blue hydraulic circuit, the pitch axis was 'OFF', the roll axis was unreadable and the yaw axis was 'UP'. Channel No.2 was operating from the green circuit, while the pitch, roll and yaw axis were all selected to 'OFF'. By contrast, the inverter control was difficult to read; however, the investigators surmised that both the blue and the green channels were set to 'OFF'. The flight control mode selectors were damaged, although there was a strong supposition that the outer and middle elevons were in mechanical mode, the inner elevons were using the green hydraulic system, and the selected rudder circuit was blue. The anti-stall selectors Nos 1 and 2 were unreadable. It was not possible to read the central warning panel since most of the bulbs and covers were missing.

The flight engineer's panel sections were recovered, the first section reported on being the fire panel, which showed that the fire loop selectors indicated No.1 at 'BOTH', No.2 at 'LOOP A', No.3 'LOOP B', and No.4 at neutral. Engine system pressures for P7 showed that Nos 1, 2, 3 and 4 engines displayed readings of 18, 12, 18 and 18psi (1.27, 0.84, 1.27 and 1.27kg/sq cm), respectively. Further system readings showed the brake hydraulic pressure was reading 6,000psi (422kg/sq cm) with an indicator flag, the brake fan switch was at 'ON', and the brake temperature reading was 170°C. The panel clock stopped at 14h 45m UTC. The engine secondary nozzle indicators were shown to be at 0, 15 and 5 degrees and unreadable for Nos 1, 2, 3 and 4 engine, respectively.

BTSC had taken off from runway 26R, achieving a take-off speed upon rotation of 175kt. During the take-off run, the left-hand main gear had run over a strip of metal that had fallen off a Continental DC-10 that had left a short time earlier. It was later discovered that one of the engine rubbing strips had become detached during take-off. When the investigators followed this lead, they found that at an earlier stop the DC-10 had been found to be missing a rubbing strip and that therefore a replacement had been locally manufactured by the inspecting mechanic and fitted. Unfortunately, the material was of the incorrect specification, being too soft to be held in place by the few retaining rivets. Such were the stresses induced during the take-off run that the strip was pulled over the rivets and fell on to the runway. This innocuous piece of metal landed at such an angle as to force its upwards edge into No.2 tyre on the left-hand main undercarriage of the Concorde. This in turn caused explosive decompres-sion of the tyre and some damage to the hub. The force generated by the tyre failure converted sections of the tyre into high speed projectiles. These then hit the under-surface of the wing, puncturing No.5 fuel tank. The shock of the penetration appears to have deformed the fuel tank wall and sent a severe shockwave through the fuel. The result caused fuel to leak under pressure from the rupture and the venting fuel swirled about like an aerosol around the undercarriage bay before igniting. The resulting fire then caused malfunctions in both left-hand engines, the final cause of which still needed to be determined. Still

The flight engineer's central fuel and air-conditioning panel was recovered but damaged and therefore the investigators were able to determine the state of the fuel tanks and their contents:

tank no.9: fuel quantity indicated: 11 tons; left pump to 'AUTO', right pump to 'ON'

tank no.10: fuel quantity indicated 12 tons; left pump to 'OFF', right pump to 'AUTO'

tank no.5A: fuel quantity indicated 2.4 tons; both pumps to 'ON'

tank no.7A: fuel quantity indicated 2.2 tons; both pumps to 'ON'

tank no.5: fuel quantity indicated 2 tons; both pumps unreadable

tank no.6: fuel quantity indicated 4.6 tons; left-hand pump unreadable, right-hand pump to 'ON'

tank no.1: fuel quantity indicated 4.2 tons; both standby pumps to 'ON', main pump to 'ON'

tank no.2: fuel quantity indicated 0.11 tons; all three pumps to 'ON'

tank no.7: fuel quantity indicated 6.6 tons; pump switches unreadable

tank no.8: fuel quantity indicated 12.8 tons; both pumps to 'ON'

tank no.3: fuel quantity indicated 4.3 tons; pump switches unreadable

tank no.4: fuel quantity indicated 4.3 tons; pump switches unreadable

tank no.11: fuel quantity indicated 10 tons; left-hand hydraulic pump to 'AUTO', right-hand to 'OFF'; electric pump indicators unreadable; main left in valve 'SHUT'; override not readable; main right inlet valve and override unreadable.

The standby inlet valves Nos 5, 6 and 1 were selected 'OPEN', while No.2 was at 'SHUT'. Standby inlet valves Nos 3, 4, 10 and 7 were at 'SHUT' and No.8 was at 'OPEN'. Fuel jettison switches No.1 and 3 were in the intermediate position; No.4 was 'OPEN' and No.2 was 'SHUT'. The master jettison and trim pipe drains were unreadable. Other fuel readings include a zero fuel weight of 91.9 tons with a c.g. of 52.29 per cent and the total contents indicator was at 78.8 tons with a warning flag showing.

The hydraulic indicators on the flight engineer's panel showed that the green circuit had a level below zero with a warning flag; Nos 1 and 2 pump shut-off valves showed indicator flags and their switches and indicators were at 'ON'. Hydraulic pressure showed 2,000psi (141kg/sq cm) with an indicator flag. The yellow circuit indicated a total contents of '6 US gal' (23ltr) with a warning flag; pumps Nos 2 and 4 shut-off valve showed warning flags and the pumps and indicators were set to 'ON'. System pressures were unreadable. The blue circuit showed a total contents level of '2.7 US gal' (10ltr) and the shut-off valves for Nos 3 and 4 were showing warning flags. Nos 3 and 4 hydraulic pumps were at 'ON' and the selector for No.3 pump was at 'OFF'; No.4 was at 'OFF'. Hydraulic pressure was at 6,000psi (422kg/sq cm) with a warning flag. All alternator switches were at 'ON', although outputs for Nos 1, 2 and 3 had unreadable outputs, that of No.4 showed an output of '60kW'.

The flight engineer's electrical control panel did not reveal many details through being badly burnt, however, some information was retrievable as to the state of the electrical system at the time of the crash. Data from this panel showed that the transformer rectifier units were outputting, thus No.1 was burnt beyond use, No.2 was broken, No.3 30A and No.4 70A. The TRU selectors were: TR1 unreadable, TR2 'NORMAL', TR3 'ISOL', and TR4 was missing. All four engine nozzle indicators were at 'NORMAL' but damaged and the fuel tank pressure was at zero. Other data recovered from the panel included the passenger oxygen pressure at 40psi (2.8kg/sq cm), the crew oxygen at zero, the selector was missing, and the four fire-extinguisher cartridge indicators were at 'FULL', although the check selectors were unreadable.

When the investigators began to interrogate the recovered wreckage the first observation they made was that the upper secondary exhaust nozzles for Nos 1, 2 and 4 engines were in place but No.3 had separated. A similar situation was discovered with regard to the primary exhaust nozzles. No nozzle sections showed signs of overheating nor were any signs of an uncontained engine burst found. Observation of the engines showed that nozzles Nos 1 and 2 were at 21 degrees conversant with either the take-off or the shut down of the engines, and the positions of the other two were at zero. Investigation of No.2 compressor showed that the engine was barely turning at the time of impact and showed signs of FOD damage, as did the compressor of No.1 engine. By contrast, both Nos 3 and 4 engines showed indications of operating at a much higher thrust than the matching pair on the left-hand side. None of the engines showed signs of fire damage. Next on the investigators' list were the wheels. No.1 wheel was completely burnt; although there was no evidence of material separation, the hubs were complete while the brake unit had separated from the wheel and axle; all were besmirched by soot. No.2 wheel showed fire damage and the two beads were no longer linked by the tread. The outer bead of the tyre was complete but the inner was broken, with the reinforcing wires showing through. A section of the tyre was found to be missing. The wheel hub was found to be complete and still retained the brake unit. The other two wheels on the left-hand bogie, Nos 5 and 6, were found to be complete with some post-crash fire damage; both wheel hubs were still in place with brake units still mounted.

The reconstruction of the debris concentrated around the left-hand wing and nacelles. However, a full reconstruction was not possible since there had been destruction, especially in the vicinity of the main-gear well. Much of the material from No.5 fuel tank was not recovered. Another area of the aircraft for which little was found was the tail-cone, although No.11 fuel tank situated just forward revealed much material plus a certain amount of the vent system pipework. The fire spread to the tail-cone via the auxiliary tailwheel gear door.

The investigators also took time to ascertain the positions of the crew seats, which were found to be in the correct positions for take-off. As the undercarriage had caused problems during the crash, the positions were of serious interest to the BEA and the AAIB. Examination showed that both main legs were locked down but that the nose-gear lock had been broken and that the doors and the leg had started to move.

Having covered the wreckage from Concorde, the investigators turned their attentions to the DC-10 from which the metal strip had come. This was quickly identified as a rubbing strip from a CF6-50 engine thrust reverser cowl. A check of the departure records for Charles de Gaulle revealed that the strip had come from a DC-10 registered as N13067 and operated by Continental Airlines to Newark, NJ as flight COA 55. To confirm this, help was requested from, and granted by, the NTSB and the FAA. When the aircraft was located and grounded for investigation it was discovered that the lower left wear strip on the right engine was missing. It was also found that the replacement strip had been incorrectly fitted. Servicing had previously been carried out by Israeli Aircraft Industries and at Houston, where parts of the cowl rubbing strips had been replaced. Since it is difficult to see these strips when the thrust reverser cowl is in the normal position the fitting of an incorrect part was not easily determined.

ablaze, the aircraft took off with a stabilized flame plume streaming behind it. At this point the No.2 engine fire-warning light illuminated, to which the response of the crew was to announce their intention to shut the engine down. Although Concorde was airborne, the aircraft was unable to accelerate since the undercarriage legs were stuck in the down position and because of the behaviour of the port engines.

One matter that was quickly discounted from the investigation concerning the undercarriage was a bearing spacer found to be missing from the left-hand bogie gear mounting. Although some eyewitnesses had mentioned that Concorde appeared to be drifting slightly to the left during and after its take-off run, this was ruled out from causing the undercarriage malfunction. The intense fire in the wing was determined as the reason for the undercarriage staying down, either through failure of the electrical control or the hydraulic systems, or through a complete or partial failure of both. At this point the crew reported that the aircraft was stable even though its speed was not increasing; they also stated that they felt confident enough to fly the stricken airliner on to Le Bourget since this would enable them to make a virtually straight-in landing. Shortly after this report the port engines had virtually shut down due to a combination of hot air and fuel in the intake, which blocked off the air supply to the engines. Also added to the mix was a structural failure in the vicinity of the intake box assembly which caused distortion to the mounting. This imbalance in engine power and a follow-on failure of the flight control system caused

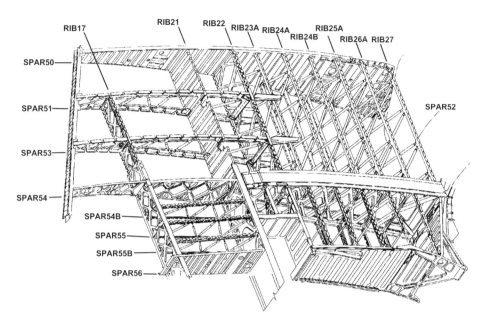

The structure surrounding No.5 fuel tank was quite closely spaced, imparting great strength in that region; however, it was unable to restrain the hydraulically ejected fuel from venting into the airflow. BBA Collection

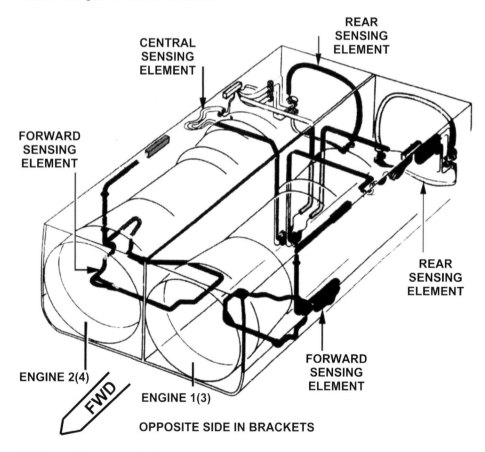

This diagram illustrates the fire-detection system fitted in the port engine nacelle (the starboard was similar). This system informed the crew about a spurious fire in No.2 engine, when, in reality, the fire was in the wing tank which had no detector system. BBA Collection

the aircraft angle of attack and bank to increase beyond the aircraft's flight envelope parameters. This then caused a thrust drag imbalance, which, coupled to the asymmetric thrust of the two remaining engines, pushed the aircraft right over so that it was travelling at right angles to the ground. Now totally outside the design parameters, the remaining two engines, Nos 3 and 4, then experienced uncommanded shut-downs due to slipstream distortion into the engine intakes. Now totally out of control, the airliner crashed.

The only area of investigation that the British and the French could not agree upon was the source of the fires. Three points of ignition were identified: electrical, hot engine contact or contact with the emissions from the air vent in the undercarriage bay. The last was thoroughly examined by a team from BAe Systems, who conclusively proved that the vent was not the source since the emissions were not hot enough to ignite any fuel whatever its then condition. This left the BEA investigators and their British counterparts to look more closely at the other two possibilities. They performed a simulation that would mimic as closely as possible the behaviour of a large object striking a large, flat surface and its subsequent after-effects. This simulation showed that the skin panel suffered a severe bending moment, which caused a hydraulic cycling effect inside the fuel tank. This then caused the motion of the fuel to split the inner tank skin open, followed by a rupture to the outer skin. Hydraulic pressure acting on the fuel forced it through the rupture where it swirled into a vaporous state. Further testing prove that the original source of ignition was electrical, this being supplemented by more fuel's igniting on a hot engine surface. Yet again the missing bogie bearing spacer was found to have had no effect on events.

Returning to Service

As each stage of the investigation report was released it was greeted by media speculation, most of which was ill-informed. Given Concorde's safety record in comparison with other civil airliners, it had always been the intention of Air France and British Airways to return their Concorde fleets to service. The first part of this process was to consult with the two air accident boards, plus senior representatives from the manufacturers. After a series of meetings running in parallel with the investigations, the interested

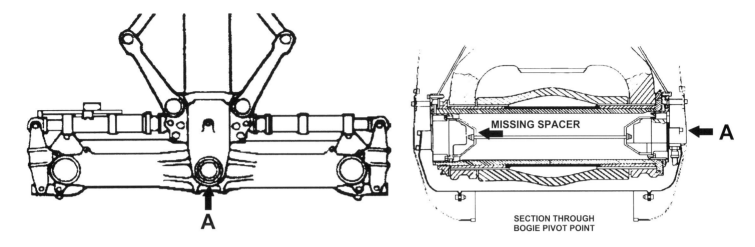

SECTION THROUGH
BOGIE PIVOT POINT

This general head-on view of the main undercarriage bogie mount shows the location of the missing spacer that was thought at first to have contributed to the events that overtook Sierra Charlie. Although not directly responsible, it did call into question some of the engineering practices applied to the French Concorde fleet. BBA Collection

The BEA Final Crash Report

At the time of the crash the aircraft possessed a valid Certificate of Airworthiness, and the captain's and the first engineer's documentation and certification were up to date; however, the first officer's licence became invalid after 18 July 2000. The spacer in the left-hand landing-gear bogie was not reinstalled during its replacement on 17 July 2000; however, its omission did not contribute to the crash. As regards the paperwork, the aircraft had no outstanding acceptable deferred defects and the Concorde was operating within limits. Although the all-up weight was over by 1 ton, the effect on take-off performance was negligible. During take-off, after reaching V1 tyre No.2 was cut by a metallic strip lying on the runway; this had come from a DC-10 which had departed 5min earlier. This strip had been replaced at Tel Aviv and later at Houston. In the latter case the manufacturer's instructions had not been heeded. Damaged sections of tyre and No.5 fuel tank were found on the runway; the piece of tyre had set up a hydrodynamic pressure surge in the fuel which had then forced fuel out on to the runway. The fuel was then ignited, probably by electrical sparks. The flames were reported to the crew by the air traffic controller; their response was to shut down No.2 engine. Further problems were experienced with both left-hand engines, which included surging. Although the Concorde was travelling forward slowly, its speed and height were diminishing as problems were being experienced with the retracting of the undercarriage. This had been traced to the incomplete opening of the left-hand main-gear door which stopped the gear cycling through. With the final loss of thrust to No.1 engine, the aircraft adopted a pronounced angle of attack and roll attitude. The loss of thrust to Nos 3 and 4 engines was traced to a deliberate retardation of the throttles and surging caused by excessive airflow disruption; however, its effect was to reduce the rate of roll. At the point of impact the aircraft was travelling forward, below safe speed, was losing altitude and had almost levelled out. On contact with the ground, a building was destroyed and the wreckage consumed in a violent fire. The investigators concluded that, even if the engines had been operating normally, the damage to the aircraft's structure and systems would have led to the eventual destruction of the Concorde.

The probable causes were determined as starting with the high-speed impact of No.2 tyre with a metal strip on the runway, which led to its destruction. This led to the puncturing of No.5 fuel tank which, in conjunction with the hydrodynamic forces imparted upon the fuel, caused a massive leak. This in turn was ignited by either an electrical arc from a damaged loom in the undercarriage bay or contact with the hot parts of the engine, or both. This led to a sheet of flame streaming behind the aircraft, which, in turn, caused massive damage to the structure and the systems in the wing plus a severe loss of thrust from Nos 1 and 2 engines. Although not a primary cause of the accident, the impossibility of retracting the undercarriage and its assistance in retaining and stabilizing of the flame stream played a significant part.

The recommendations specific to Concorde operation as recommended by the BEA and supported by AAIB included:

- That the manufacturers and airworthiness authorities should improve the analysis covering the functioning of the aircraft systems and improve the corrective action response.

- That Air France should improve the emergency procedures in the Concorde Operations Manual in dealing with emergencies.

- That Air France should install engine data recorders that monitored their parameters every second; this did not apply to British Airways Concordes which already had such a system installed.

- That the DGAC should undertake an audit of Air France Concorde operations and maintenance procedures.

- That the DGAC should carry out further investigations and regulation concerning aircraft tyres and their conformity to requirements.

- That the same organization should improve the sweeping and collection of debris on and from airfields within France either by regulation or by agreement with the relevant organizations.

- That the FAA should carry out a full audit on Continental Airlines and its subcontractors concerning the application and adherence to maintenance procedures.

- That the IACO should confirm dates for the installation of video recorders on board aircraft undertaking public transport flights.

- That the DGAC and other regulatory bodies should institute a programme to install external viewers so that crews could observe hidden parts of the airframe for damage or other problems.

- That the IACO in conjunction with manufacturers and other authorities should firm up the proposals and implement them to identify all known dangerous substances aboard each type of civil aircraft.

ABOVE: **During the modification process many of Concorde's main components, such as the engines and the majority of the wing access panels, were removed.** Courtesy British Airways

This view shows a BA engineer fitting one of the impregnated mats in the fuel tanks. This essential modification was required to allow a new Certificate of Airworthiness to be issued. Courtesy British Airways

parties produced a blueprint for action that allowed Concorde to resume revenue operations. The main areas highlighted for modification included the fuel tanks and the structure surrounding the undercarriage bays, plus the adding of further protection to any pipework and electrical looms. The primary form of protection chosen for the modification programme was Kevlar, a synthetic fibre developed by Dupont de Nemours, manufactured into specially shaped panels. Kevlar had been chosen since it has great resistance to high-speed impacts from hard objects and thus is difficult to penetrate. The hydraulic system pipelines would be further protected by fitting reinforced conduits over them and similar protection would be applied to the vulnerable wiring

ABOVE: **After the Concorde crash in July 2000 all others were grounded and impounded. This is F-BVFC, complete with impound stickers over the doors and windows.** Justin Cederholm

RIGHT: **As well as the impounding stickers, the airport authorities placed a tail support under the rear fuselage to protect the airframe from accidental damage.** Justin Cederholm

looms. The total modification cost was initially estimated at £17 million for each aircraft, added to which BA had decided to refurbish the interiors of their Concordes for a further £14 million. While the interested parties were discussing the modification programme and its requirements, one of the impounded Air France Concordes was flown home from JFK. This machine, F-BVFC, had completed a transatlantic flight to the USA and was waiting to return when Sierra Charlie crashed. To allow the aircraft to leave the USA a special licence was authorized to cover a single flight, although only the crew were allowed to travel, passengers were strictly forbidden. This would be the last flight for several months.

It would not be until 18 January 2001 that Air France Concorde, F-BVFB, left Charles de Gaulle airport for a short flight to Istres. Here the aircraft underwent fuel-flow and dispersion trials in advance of a return to service. While the French authorities were undertaking their checks, British Airways

and its engineers were beginning to modify Concorde G-BOAF Alpha Foxtrot. Although the modifications to the hydraulic and electrical systems went without a hitch, there were some problems with the installation of the Kevlar mats in the fuel tanks. These had been manufactured by using the original drawings; however, when the time came to install them they would not fit. After double-checking the drawings and then the given measurements against the internal structure of Alpha Foxtrot, the engineers found that there were discrepancies. The decision was taken to undertake similar checks with the remainder of the British Airways fleet. These too revealed that the internal structure of each tank floor was marginally different. A request to Air France to undertake similar checks showed a similar situation and thus it was decided that each of the remaining aircraft would need to be individually measured to ensure an accurate fit of the Kevlar mats. The conclusion drawn from these investigations was

that, although each airframe section was constructed on jigs, each Concorde was virtually hand-built. Modifications to the French Concordes were undertaken by the Air France maintenance division, who assigned a team of twenty-five to the job, who first looked after the stored aircraft before moving on to incorporating the modifications. When this programme was fully geared up, over a hundred engineers were assigned to it, augmented by thirty sheet-metal workers drawn from Orly, Le Bourget and Riossy who were specifically assigned to the fuel tanks. Three engine technicians were also seconded, as were teams from the avionics and mechanical workshops to undertake component overhauls. In the background the logistics branch also joined in, their role being to oversee purchasing and warehouse supplies. After the modifications were completed on each aircraft it was inspected by the Direction Générale de l'Aviation and the Civil Aviation Authority before being certified for return to service.

TOP: **After a successful post-modification test flight, F-BVFC lands at Charles de Gaulle airport.** Bernard Charles

ABOVE: **Foxtrot Bravo garners nearly the same number of admirers as it taxies, as met the prototype on its roll-out. After the full modification and flight-test programme had been completed Air France was granted a Certificate of Airworthiness to resume Concorde operations, which they did on 7 November 2001.**
Bernard Charles

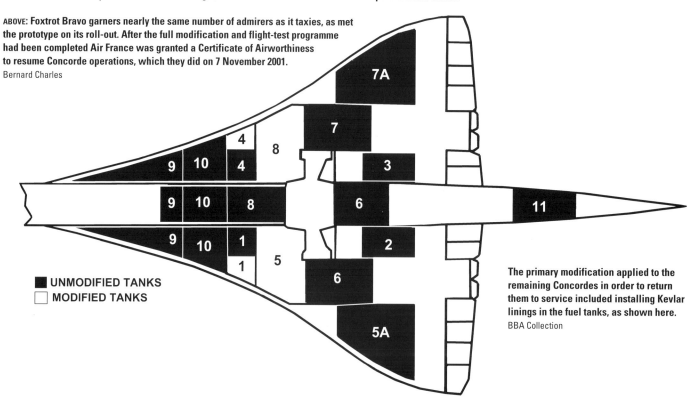

■ UNMODIFIED TANKS
□ MODIFIED TANKS

The primary modification applied to the remaining Concordes in order to return them to service included installing Kevlar linings in the fuel tanks, as shown here.
BBA Collection

After 633 flying hours, Concorde 101, G-AXDN, was retired to the Imperial War Museum at Duxford, Cambridgeshire on 20 August 1975. BBA Collection

A New Servicing Regime

Supporting the modification programme was an improved servicing schedule to be fully adopted by both Air France and British Airways. This started with a pre-flight check before every scheduled departure, followed by a daily check covering routine operations and inspections every 24hr, both of which could be carried out on the ramp. More thorough inspections and maintenance needed hangar space to carry out. These started with a Check A, carried out every 210hr and consisting of preset checks plus any special requirements; Check B was to be carried out every 420 flying hours and required a preset group of checks plus any special requirements; Check C was to be carried out every 1,680 flying hours and followed a similar pattern to the two previous inspections. After 6,000 flying hours Check IL was made which required greater in-depth inspections and maintenance, again plus any special requirements. The final maintenance requirement was Check D or a major overhaul. This required the aircraft to be grounded for about a year and was required after 12,000 flying hours. As part of this, the Concorde was stripped of most of its operational equipment which was then sent to the relevant contractors for a full rework. Once the airframe was, in effect, empty it was to be subjected to full inspections, repairs and modifications, plus extensive non-destructive testing for cracks and other defects. Once the airframe had been virtually rebuilt the systems components would be reinstalled and the aircraft subjected to extensive pre-flight testing. While the airframe was being overhauled the engines would be overhauled either by Rolls-Royce and SNECMA on behalf of British Airways, while the Air France ones were refurbished under the guidance of the Air France industrial logistics branch.

BA Concorde G-BOAA was one two airframes not subject to the modification programme; it thus remained in store at Heathrow. BBA Collection

BA Concorde Alpha Bravo is the other airframe not modified; it too remained at Heathrow. BBA Collection

Crew Training

One final aspect of returning Concorde to service concerned the training of the flight and cabin crews. For Air France this meant that twelve captains, eleven first officers and eleven flight engineers required continuation training while Concorde was grounded. Unlike British Airways, Air France crews were hired on a twice yearly basis from the general pool of the airline's crews. The training undertaken to keep up to date in relation to Concorde required each crew to fly 4hr of group simulator training, comprising three take-offs and landings. Further flight simulator missions were required to ensure crew type-rating currency. When Concorde was being cleared for service after modification, the crews undertook technical verification flights followed by non-commercial training flights. Supporting these flights were additional simulator missions and ground classroom training.

The Concorde cabin crews were seventy-six strong, rostered as required to cover each commercial flight. Each cabin crew member needed to have at least three years' experience and pursers needed at least three years' seniority in post before being considered for Concorde. All cabin staff wanting to fly on Concorde were required to have excellent English and a second foreign language. Once chosen for training they were cleared only when the deciding committee had interviewed them in depth. This committee comprised seven instructors, six female and nine male pursers, plus others drawn from twenty-six female and twenty-seven male flight attendants, all with an average age of 32 and either then serving or recently retired Concorde cabin crew. The

With a tug attached by a towing arm to the aircraft, Concorde G-BOAC is moved from the ramp. After the post-crash modifications had been made, the aircraft returned to service on 11 July 2002. BBA Collection

Pictured at Filton awaiting maintenance was BA Concorde G-BOAD, which underwent post-crash modification at Heathrow and returned to revenue service in September 2001. BBA Collection

training of the cabin crew involved two courses: a safety course followed by a three-day marketing course. The first consisted of an intensive theoretical section dealing with safety equipment, safety instruction presentation and features specific to Concorde. This was followed by a practical part covering evacuation procedures, the testing of equipment, such as fire extinguishers and oxygen masks, plus a familiarization briefing covering Concorde and its on-board equipment handling. The marketing course was held in the in-flight services school and was attended by those cabin crew who had passed the Concorde course. This course covered customer profiling, interaction with flight crews and ground staff, the Concorde lounge at Charles de Gaulle airport, briefing

preparation, product promotion, in-flight catering, plus, for the pursers, cabin management. After the Concorde crash, cabin staff undertook cabin simulator training to familiarize themselves with the situations that could be encountered in flight.

Maintenance and Modifications

When the Air France Concorde fleet was grounded after revocation of their Certificates of Airworthiness, the airline began a sequence of maintenance checks that included running the engines and systems every fifteen days. In parallel with the airframe modifications, the tyre manufacturers

Michelin were undertaking development work on a new tyre, known as the Near Zero Growth Tyre, that would be resistant to the kind of failure that had afflicted Sierra Charlie. The first two aircraft to return to services were sent to Istres for trials work; F-BVFB was used from 18 January to 3 February 2001 for aerodynamic checks on fuel leakage and dispersal and F-BTSD was used for Michelin tyre trials from 17 April to 5 May. An extensive series of taxi and flight tests were taken to prove the validity of the new type and to reinforce the data gained from the development programme in the laboratory. On 8 June the trials ended and were declared a success.

Modifications continued apace on Alpha Foxtrot with the aircraft beginning taxi

After it had flown nearly 13,000hr, Air France F-BTSD was delivered in June 2003 to the museum at Le Bourget. BBA Collection

This almost head-on view shows graphically the visor and its location when retracted. BA Concorde
G-BOAF would be the first post-crash modified aircraft to re-enter service in July 2001. BBA Collection

With its visor fully retracted, BA Concorde Alpha Echo taxies towards the runway at Heathrow. It re-entered
service in September 2001 alongside Alpha Delta. BBA Collection

trials at Heathrow on 4 July. On 17 July the same machine left on its much anticipated test flight. Aboard for this momentous flight were Capt 'Jock' Reid, acting as an observer on behalf of the Civil Aviation Authority, and Capt Mike Bannister, the senior Concorde pilot, for British Airways. The purpose of the flight was to simulate a complete transatlantic flight to see how the new liners and their weight would affect the aircraft's behaviour and trim. It was also important to see how well the fuel acted as a heat sink. Having flown out over the Atlantic at

both subsonic and supersonic speeds, the Concorde turned back and landed at RAF Brize Norton. A series of intensive post-flight inspections were concluded successfully. The aircraft left three days later for another verification flight, after which it landed back at Heathrow.

During the following August and September the final pieces of information needed to return Concorde to revenue-earning service were appearing. Both Air France and British Airways' crews were taking refresher courses in the simulator, while the CAA

and its French equivalent the DGAC undertook a thorough review of the modifications proposed by the manufacturers. On 5 September 2001 the authorities jointly issued a mandatory airworthiness directive that allowed each Concorde to return to service and regain its Certificate of Airworthiness as each completed the modification process, independent inspection and signing off. With the paperwork trail being completed, each airline made plans to restart supersonic commercial flying. Air France opted for a restart in November and British

Wearing the Chatham Dockyard flag on its fin, BA Concorde G-BOAC roars off from Heathrow, its undercarriage units retracting quickly. BBA Collection

Airways decided that its restart date would be slightly earlier in October.

The mandatory modifications required to allow Concorde back into the air included the fitting of the Kevlar linings, of Michelin Near Zero Growth Tyres instead of the normal type, and the protection and reinforcement of the hydraulic pipelines and electrical looms. Each of the mats was saturated with Viton, a waterproof sealant developed specifically for Kevlar. The new tyre was made from composite materials that deflate in such a manner as to protect other parts of the undercarriage. Secondary modifications also declared as mandatory included removal of the water-deflection retention cable from the undercarriage and the reprofiling of deflectors to accommodate the changed tyre profiles. A modification was also required to the anti-skid protocols to take note of the changed mainwheel tyres, and a flat-tyre detector system was also required. This detection system was defined as a 'NOGO' item should it fail in operation. One further change was insisted upon in the aircraft's operating procedures concerning the operation of the brake-cooling fans which were to be switched off during the take-off and the landing phase. While both Concorde fleets were safely in their hangars the opportunity was also taken to incorporate Mod Spar 72; applied to the rear spar, this modification was carried out on all the aircraft, whether cracks had been detected or not.

Optimism Restored

While the aircraft were undergoing modifications the public relations department of each airline was also limbering up to modify the public perception of the type as a safe and fast mode of transport, now even safer to fly in than before. To this end a massive worldwide consultation and marketing exercise was undertaken which would ask just one question: 'Do our normal

With its nose still drooped, Air France Concorde F-BVFA speeds past the camera; it has since been delivered to the Smithsonian Institute in Washington, DC. Bernard Charles.

AF Concorde F-BVFC flies past the camera on its way to the USA. Foxtrot Charlie subsequently went to its Toulouse birthplace for display. BBA Collection

---

French Cuisine in the Skies

To celebrate the return of the Air France Concorde fleet to service, the airline engaged a well-known chef plus Phillippe Faure-Brac, world sommelier champion of 1992, to create something extra special.

Their creation covered two distinct menus, one for AF002, the flight from New York, and one for AF001, the Paris departure. The New York menu began with champagne and caviar, this being followed by a choice of hors d'oeuvre consisting of lobster with baby vegetables or pâté de foie gras in port aspic, both being accompanied by fresh garden salad. The main courses offered included panned tenderloin steak served with celery purée, plus eggplant ratatouille with oyster mushrooms and olive oil; the alternative was turban of sole garnished with black olive purée with vegetable confit and cheese ravioli, both served with a medley of vegetables. Passengers were then offered a selection of fine cheeses and a fresh fruit platter of melons, mangoes and strawberries. Should there be a small spot requiring further nourishment, the cabin crew could offer chocolate eclairs, strawberry and coconut tartlet or a vanilla macaroon.

As the departure from Paris was scheduled to arrive at breakfast time in New York, the menu was adjusted accordingly. For openers, passengers were served petals of mango and kiwi fruit garnished with red fruits. This would be followed by a choice of hot or cold dishes which featured the chef's special; this comprised scrambled eggs with truffles and medallions of Maine lobster served with creamed white morels. To cater for vegetarians there was a hotpot of a timbale of polenta with a medley of spring vegetables. There was also a gourmet platter of foie gras marbled with truffles, garnished with Bordeaux-infused aspic. A final meal offered was a seafood platter consisting of layered monkfish, truffle and chanterelle fricassee, served with sautéed king prawns seasoned with paprika. Supporting the main meal were a selection of French regional cheeses and raspberry tart, ganache-filled gateau or vanilla macaroon.

As the menu was intended as a gourmet's delight, the wine list was intended to compliment it. Thus from November 2001 to January 2002 the list consisted of Champagne Cuvée Spéciale: Champagne Dom Perignon 1993, Bourgogne Blanc Meursault 1er Cru 1996 Laboure Roi, Bourgogne Rouge Nuits Saint Georges 'Les Porets' 1993 Antonin Rodet, Bordeaux Rouge Pomerol 1996 Château La Croix Du Casse and Bordeaux Blanc Liquoreux Sauternes 1er Grand Cru Classe 1994 Château Rieussec. The list from February 2002 to March 2002 consisted of Champagne Curvée Spéciale Krug Grande Cuvée, Bourgogne Blanc Chablis Grand Cru 'Les Clos' 1997 Simonnet-Febvre, Bourgogne Rouge Volnay 1er Cru 'Les Taillepieds' 1996 Bouchard Père et Fils, Bordeaux Rouge Pauillac Grand Cru Classe Château Batailley 1996, and Bordeaux Blanc Liquoreux Sauternes 1er Grand Cru Classe 1994 Château Rieussec. Subsequent wine lists consisted of a variety of these wines and continued until the Air France Concorde fleet was withdrawn from service.

Concorde passengers want the aircraft to return to service and, even more importantly, would they wish to fly in it?' Fortunately for the airlines the passengers voted yes, and so on 7 November 2001 the two despatched a Concorde each, ostensibly on a routine flight, from Charles de Gaulle and Heathrow. For Air France, getting Concorde back into the air and back as the acknowledged leader of the fleet was laid down in a press release running to fourteen A4 pages in October 2001; consisting of four sections, the press statement covered the plan to present Concorde to its passengers, the revised training given to the flight and the cabin crew, in-depth technical modification assessments, and several annexes covering related matters. Much of

the information covered the bare facts, although some were trumpeted more than others, such as pointing out that an AF Concorde was the first aircraft of the day from Europe to land in the USA. Flight departure from Charles de Gaulle on its scheduled service to New York would subsequently be at 10:30 instead of 11:00hr. This change enabled the aircraft to land at JFK Airport at 8:20hr local time and thus passengers would have more time to catch internal flight connections, plus there was the added advantage in the reduction of the previous long wait at customs and immigration. The return flight left New York at 8:00hr local time and was scheduled to land at Paris at 17:45hr local time; this allowed passengers to depart on

prebooked flights to at least sixty major cities within Europe.

Unlike other airline passengers, those boarding Concorde were allowed to choose their own seats, while other complimentary and preferential services were also offered, such as hotel booking, car rentals and office and conference space at several airports or centres. To speed the Concorde passenger through to his or her seat, there were dedicated check-in desks at the French and the American airports; this allowed the passenger to check in 45min before departure, instead of undergoing the normal, interminable wait. Added to this, experienced staff assisted the passenger in any way possible. Baggage was also given the special Concorde treatment; thus the items were covered in protective plastic coverings, each identified by the Concorde logo baggage tag. At each destination the baggage was pushed through customs to expedite formalities. As Concorde passengers had paid over the odds for their tickets they were granted yet other privileges. These included exclusive lounges at each destination airport, that at Charles de Gaulle being the airside l'Espace lounge in Terminal 2A, where passengers were granted a full-length view of their aircraft and direct access to it. Passenger transfer was also expedited at both Paris and New York; at the former a courtesy taxi service was offered and at the latter a limousine was provided.

Although the fares charged by Air France to its Concorde passengers might seem

between Paris and New York, although they had to travel together over both legs.

Before relaunching their Concorde service, Air France released some interesting statistics concerning their passenger breakdown: two-thirds travelled on business, of whom 80 per cent were male. The clientele by nation included 50 per cent from the USA, while of the remainder 48 per cent were French. Other facts released included the information that most Concorde passengers flew on the aircraft a minimum of four times a year, and a substantial number travelled almost monthly. Other benefits for Air France passengers include a frequent-flyer programme which allowed passengers to accrue credits for each supersonic flight; to gain a free round-trip Concorde ticket a passenger needed to amass 160,000 miles.

airframes through a complete rebuilding. During this period it was estimated that each Concorde would complete about 8,500 supersonic cycles. While taking part in the modification development process, British Airways would also undertake an investigation into extending their fleet's life to complete at least 10,500 cycles. Had this programme been done, the airline estimated that Concorde would retire between 2015 and 2018, by which time the airframes would be forty or more years old. Although these plans in the end came to naught, British Airways was hoping that a manufacturer or consortium would produce a Concorde replacement. But on 10 April 2003 Air France and British Airways issued a joint statement that they would discontinue Concorde operations during the year.

AF Concorde F-BVFF pictured just after take-off from Paris. This machine was not given the post-crash modifications and its fate is uncertain. BBA Collection

steep, the price did include the flight to Paris from airports within Europe. The fares charged at the Air France relaunch included a round trip Paris–New York–Paris for 8,000 euros/£5,509/$8,621, although this dropped to 6,600 euros/£4,545/$7,113 if the ticket were purchased four days before departure. Other fares included travelling one way in Concorde with a return in first-class subsonic for 9,280 euros/£6,390/$10,000, while a similar trip with a return in business class cost 8,274 euros/£5,697/$8,916. As a bonus, a companion fare of 50 per cent of the original, full fare was available for anyone accompanying a passenger travelling on a round-trip Concorde ticket

Optimism Dashed

In complete contrast to the receptions given to the aircraft in earlier years, the simultaneous landings in New York were greeted with tumultuous welcomes, both airlines deeming the flights successful. After returning to their normal flight schedule, the Concorde fleets settled back into their standard pattern of operation. Once the aircraft were flying again, the airlines issued a joint statement that, given steady usage, the fleets would remain in service until 2010, at which point it would be decided whether to replace Concorde with a completely new build type or put selected

The statement concentrated upon the reason for the aircraft's retirement: the reduction in passenger numbers since Concorde had returned to service accompanied by increasing costs, which meant that the type was no longer economically viable. Air France was the first to withdraw Concorde from revenue service in June.

Before then, however, British Airways flew the usual Barbados flights, beginning on 26 July and ending on 30 August, as well as the normal daily runs to New York. If this were not enough, a final trip to the Royal International Air Tattoo was undertaken during 19–20 July, where many said an emotional last farewell to the white

Disposal of the Air France and the British Airways Concorde Fleet

Air France announced the disposal details for its Concorde fleet before British Airways. On 12 June 2003 F-BVFA was flown to Washington for display in the Smithsonian Museum. F-BVFC was returned to its birthplace of Toulouse on 27 June, while F-BVFB was promised to the Auto und Technik Museum at Sinsheim, Germany, upon payment of a symbolic Euro. The final flyable aircraft, F-BTSD, was despatched to the museum at Le Bourget during June to join the prototype F-WTSS. The fate of the final aircraft, F-BVFF, is undecided, although as an unmodified airframe it is likely to be a candidate for scrapping.

The aircraft that faced the most complicated journey was F-BVFB, which landed at Karlsruhe-Baden Baden on 24 June 2003. However, this was not the end of its journey and a certain amount of dismantling was required so that the aircraft could continue, first by ship, then by road to Sinsheim. Even with the outer wing panels removed, the roads needed modification to road signs and the like to allow the aircraft through. The greatest difficulty that faced the museum was how to get the aircraft off its transportation ship. This was solved by the use of a pair of special cranes. Foxtrot Bravo finally arrived on 18 July 2003.

There is one further twist in the Air France Concorde tale concerning aircraft F-BVFC. It was impounded on the orders of Judge Christophe Regnard soon after landing at Toulouse. The reason was an attempt to disprove the thoroughly researched BEA crash report and attempt to blame the accident on the absence of the spacer in the left hand bogie. Findings of a different cause would possibly exonerate the tyre manufacturer Goodyear from legal responsibility.

Although Air France retired their Concorde fleet with little fanfare, British Airways decided that such a singular event should be marked with more ceremony. To this end a tour of Britain was organized that encompassed

the major cities. Thus on 20 October 2003 Birmingham saw the famous delta, G-BOAC, while the following day Belfast was the venue with G-BOAE visiting. On 22 October Manchester was visited by G-BOAG while Cardiff International followed the next day seeing G-BOAE touching down. The final visit was made to Edinburgh on 24 October by G-BOAG. Just prior to 16:00 hours that afternoon the final three Concorde flights were sighted inbound to London, Heathrow. In succession G-BOAF, G-BOAE and G-BOAG touched down. At 16:05 hours on 24 October 2003 British Airways became just another airline. The Americas were not ignored either as earlier that month Toronto, Boston and Washington, Dulles, were graced by the elegant delta.

Prior to the final flights of the BA Concorde fleet there was much speculation about its final disposal. There was talk about retaining one for special flights and air displays. However, financial realities meant that such a plan was soon scrapped and the dispersal plan was put into place. The first aircraft to leave Heathrow was G-BOAC, which landed at Manchester on 31 October, while G-BOAG was flown across the Atlantic to Seattle for display in the Museum of Flight on 5 November. On 10 November G-BOAD was flown into JFK Airport for eventual display on a barge alongside the retired carrier USS *Intrepid*. A week later G-BOAE was delivered by Captain Mike Bannister to Grantley Adams Airport in the Bahamas. The final remaining flyable Concorde, G-BOAF, landed at Filton on 26 November this being the last ever Concorde flight. Of the three remaining machines G-BOAA is due to go to the Museum of Flight, East Fortune, Scotland, in sections where it will be reassembled, while G-BOAB is slated for display at Heathrow. The one remaining aircraft, G-BBGD, is scheduled to leave Filton where it has been used as a spares source for eventual display at Brooklands Air Museum.

delta. Events planned for the BA Concorde fleet before retirement included a visit to Toronto, on 1 October, to be followed by visits to Boston on 8 October and Washington, Dulles on 14 October. Once the North American trip had been completed one aircraft was be used for a series of farewell flights around Britain during the period 20–24 October, taking in Birmingham, Cardiff, Manchester, Belfast and Edinburgh. On 24 October a British Airways Concorde landed at Heathrow after returning from New York, shut down its engines, and an era drew to a close.

In a not unsurprising move, Sir Richard Branson, founder of Virgin Atlantic, offered to purchase the five remaining BA aircraft for £5 million to continue operations, a massive increase from the original offer of just £5! However, his approaches were quickly rebuffed by the chairman of BA, Lord Marshall, who stated that Airbus Industries/EADS would be ending technical support – allegedly at the behest of British Airways – in late 2003, although Air France were cited as the more likely candidate for such a move. The withdrawal of technical aid and its attendant engineering authority support would require any new operator to reapply for type certification, with its massive expense and the possibility of failure; this difficulty would be compounded by the need to find an engineering authority and support organization. Although the chances of Virgin Atlantic taking over Concorde operations were looking increasingly slim, Branson had been in touch with the BA board concerning the formation of a charitable trust whose sole concern would be to keep one or two of these aircraft in semi-commercial service. To reinforce its commitment to Concorde, Virgin Atlantic promised to donate £1 million to start the ball rolling. There were still problems to be resolved with this plan, although British Airways had expressed an interest in keeping one airframe semi-active for special occasions. However, all this came to naught when BA decided to dispose of the entire fleet to selected museums around the world, thus ending any speculation about the future of Concorde.

A fitting closing photograph for this chapter is that of F-BTSC blasting away from the camera with all four 'burners' lit. BBA Collection

CHAPTER NINE

SST into the Future

Really the End?

Now that Concorde has finally retired from commercial service, will this be the end of supersonic flight for transporting passengers around the globe?

The first attempt to replace or extend Concorde was by the Anglo-French consortium. Having run the full gamut of prototypes, preproduction and production machines to deliver no more than twenty airframes, the next two scheduled production machines were identified as airframes 217 and 218.

These were destined to be designated as 'B' Concordes. Changes from the first production version included extended wingtip outer panels and leading-edge flaps for better handling at lower speeds. The flaps were designed to be selectable in three positions: in the fully-up position the airframe was cleared for supersonic flight; in the mid position the flaps catered for subsonic cruising and the initial approach to an airfield; in the fully-down position the flaps would be used only during take-off and landing. This version never entered production and thus No. 216 was the final airframe.

Although the majority of the airlines that had expressed interest later cancelled their options, leaving just British Airways and Air France to fly the Concorde flag, a further contract nearly came to fruition. This was the interest expressed by Federal Express for freight carrying. Three plus crews were required from BA; however, contract wrangles eventually killed the entire deal. This left the handful of remaining white-tail Concordes looking for useful employment before their final acquisition by BA and Air France. One idea was to use at least one as a supersonic flying test bed. The projected changes were regarded as minimal; the greatest change was the installation of canard wings on the forward fuselage for improved stability while an external load was being carried on a pylon under the fuselage. This was intended to carry either an engine or other stores.

AERODYNAMIC IMPROVEMENT CHART		C_L	LIFT/DRAG RATIO		CL/CD
			AIRCRAFT 'A'	AIRCRAFT 'B'	GAIN
TAKE OFF	ZERO CLIMB GRADIENT 0.77		3.94	4.24	7.6
	SECOND SEGMENT	0.614	4.97	5.58	12.3
	NOISE ABATEMENT PROCEDURE	0.480	6.00	7.38	23.0
APPROACH		0.600	4.35	4.75	9.2
HOLD AT 250 KTS 10,000 FT		0.280	9.27	13.1	41.3
SUBSONIC CRUISE AT M= 0.93		0.200	11.47	12.92	12.6
SUPERSONIC CRUISE **ISA + 5°C**	610 ENGINE	0.125	7.14	N/A	7.7%
	610 ENGINE + 25%	0.152	N/A	7.69	

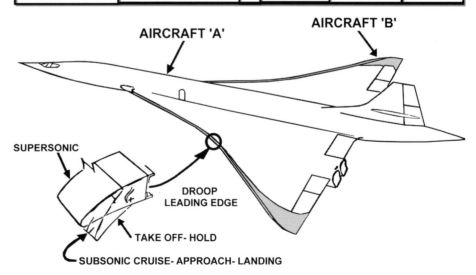

From airframe 217 the Concorde production standard was scheduled to switch over to the 'B' design shown here. Unfortunately, manufacture stopped at airframe 216.
BBA Collection

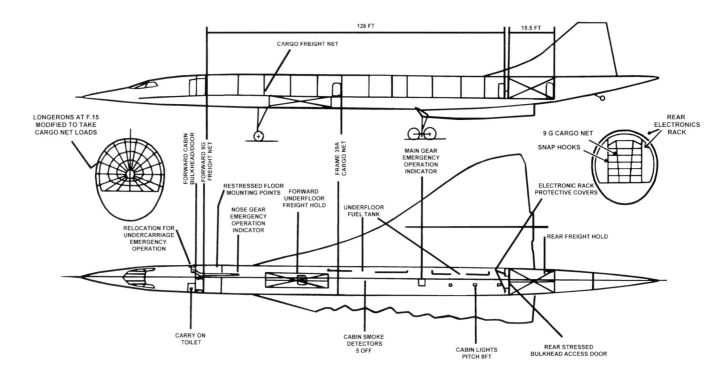

126 FT | 15.5 FT

CARGO FREIGHT NET

LONGERONS AT F.15 MODIFIED TO TAKE CARGO NET LOADS

REAR ELECTRONICS RACK

9 G CARGO NET

SNAP HOOKS

FORWARD CABIN BULKHEAD/DOOR
FORWARD 9G FREIGHT NET
RESTRESSED FLOOR MOUNTING POINTS
FORWARD UNDERFLOOR FREIGHT HOLD
NOSE GEAR EMERGENCY OPERATION INDICATOR
FRAME 39A CARGO NET
UNDERFLOOR FUEL TANK
MAIN GEAR EMERGENCY OPERATION INDICATOR
ELECTRONIC RACK PROTECTIVE COVERS
REAR FREIGHT HOLD

RELOCATION FOR UNDERCARRIAGE EMERGENCY OPERATION

CARRY ON TOILET
CABIN SMOKE DETECTORS 5 OFF
CABIN LIGHTS PITCH 8FT
REAR STRESSED BULKHEAD ACCESS DOOR

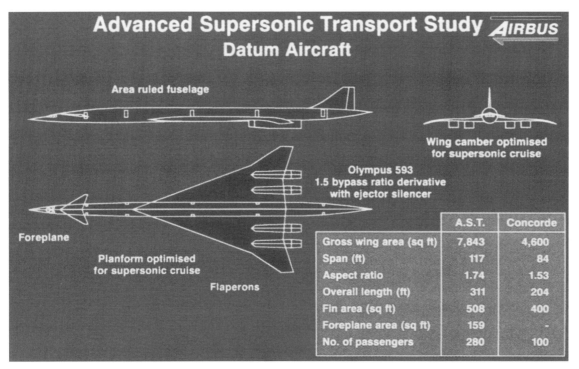

Advanced Supersonic Transport Study AIRBUS
Datum Aircraft

Area ruled fuselage

Wing camber optimised for supersonic cruise

Olympus 593
1.5 bypass ratio derivative with ejector silencer

Foreplane

Planform optimised for supersonic cruise

Flaperons

	A.S.T.	Concorde
Gross wing area (sq ft)	7,843	4,600
Span (ft)	117	84
Aspect ratio	1.74	1.53
Overall length (ft)	311	204
Fin area (sq ft)	508	400
Foreplane area (sq ft)	159	-
No. of passengers	280	100

ABOVE: **One of the first proposals suggested for Concorde included modifying some of the then spare white tails for use in the high-speed freight role on behalf of Federal Express.**
BBA Collection

LEFT: **This diagram illustrates the current thinking at Airbus Industrie concerning a replacement for Concorde. Whether this is feasible remains to be seen.**
BBA Collection

Taking the concept slightly further forward, there were slight rumblings from the Ministry of Defence concerning a heavily modified version of the Concorde as a replacement for the ageing Vulcan B.2 bomber; this would have been known, not unsurprisingly, as the Vulcan B.3.

None of these ever matured. But the popularity of Concorde meant that the concept of the supersonic transport was not completely dead. The situation in the USA was similar, while in Russia the indigenous aerospace industry managed to resurrect its SST programme, albeit only briefly, at the behest of NASA and its partners (see Chapter 7) since there was no funding available from the Russian government to continue any flying or development.

In the United Kingdom the British Aircraft Corporation became part of British Aerospace, later renamed British Aerospace Systems. In France Sud Aviation had evolved into Aérospatiale, before growing into Airbus Industrie. Both organizations were heavily involved in the design, manufacture and production of numerous versions of the Airbus range and thus it should

EVOLUTION DES CONFIGURATIONS ÉTUDIÉES À AEROSPATIALE ENTRE (1979-1989)

HISTORY OF CONFIGURATION STUDIES AT AEROSPATIALE (1979-1989)

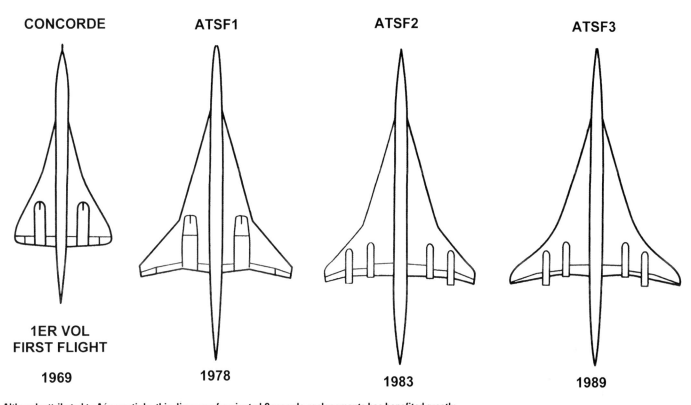

Although attributed to Aérospatiale, this diagram of projected Concorde replacements has benefited greatly from input by British Aerospace. BBA Collection

come as no surprise that both were heavily involved in the development of a replacement for Concorde. Although Concorde 'B' had seemed a distinct possibility, in reality it was no more than a minor upgrade of the original. Therefore Airbus began to design a new SST while drawing on the advances in the understanding of aerodynamic behaviour gained since Concorde was designed. Added to this was the ability to model by computer not only the aircraft designs themselves, but their behaviour in flight before either models or prototypes were built. All the designs were much larger than Concorde and featured engines mounted in a variety of positions. These studies ran until 1989 before the funding was scaled back and the project put on hold, although the studies continued. Before being scaled back, Airbus had prepared three designs known as the ATSF 1, 2 and 3. All were based around a double-delta

wing layout and mounted four engines. Only the ATSF 1 retained the concept of engines in nacelles in a similar manner to Concorde. The other two designs placed the engines in separate pods under the wings. Changes were also made to the engines themselves: gone would be the pollution-generating Olympus engines to be replaced by more efficient powerplants that not only burned fuel more efficiently but greatly reduced the pollution output.

Three distinct types of powerplant have been under investigation by the Anglo-French consortium and its counterparts in the USA, all substantially different from the preceding Rolls-Royce Olympus and its SNECMA thrust augmenter, as the studies concentrated on a turbine bypass turbojet, the double bypass turbofan and the tandem bypass, a proof-of-concept engine offering both a high and a low bypass mode.

New American Interest

In the USA, cancellation of the indigenous SST programme left the participating companies in a state of limbo. Having gained much data throughout the development programme and learned how not to apply it, interest in an American SST still lingered, even though no funds were available to pursue the concept further. It would fall to NASA to pick up the SST baton and take it further as part of the Supersonic Cruise Research Program, which had started life as the Advanced Supersonic Technology Program.

Note the abandonment of 'supersonic transport' in order to spare Congressional blushes. This project began in 1971 and ended in 1981 with an annual budget of between $12.5 and 17.2 million (£8–11.7 million). In this period NASA drew the conclusion that there would be an after-

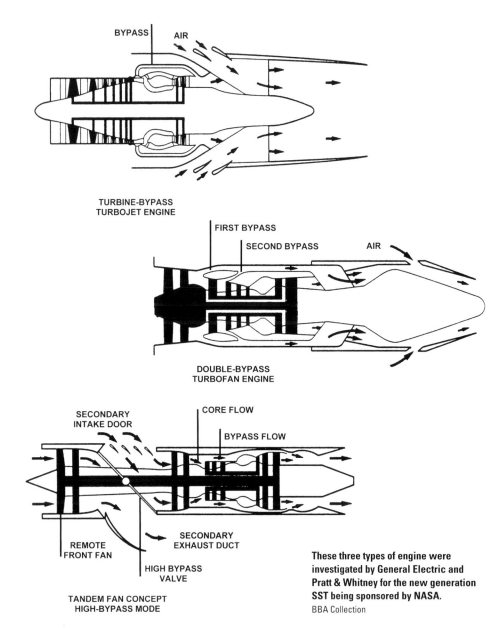

TURBINE-BYPASS
TURBOJET ENGINE

DOUBLE-BYPASS
TURBOFAN ENGINE

TANDEM FAN CONCEPT
HIGH-BYPASS MODE

These three types of engine were investigated by General Electric and Pratt & Whitney for the new generation SST being sponsored by NASA.
BBA Collection

reversed this decision and a recommended restoration of the technology budget was pushed through. Following this decision NASA felt that enough had been achieved for them to issue development contracts to Boeing and McDonnell Douglas for the design of a second-generation SST, to be called the High Speed Civil Transport (HSCT). Three years later NASA upgraded the programme and renamed it the High Speed Research Program. This was seen as an essential first building block in the subsequent development of a joint industry/government high-speed civil transport. The purpose of the exercise was aimed more towards environmental standards development, not to the furtherance of technology, much of which was already coming to fruition. The three key environmental areas undergoing assessment as part of the High Speed Research (HSR) programme included the depletion of the ozone layer by engine exhaust emissions, airport and surrounding community area noise, and the effects of sonic boom. This last point required further in-depth analysis since its compulsory confinement to the subsonic regime overland would reduce a new aircraft's economic viability. Within NASA four separate divisions were involved: the Langley Research Center in Virginia, the Lewis Flight Center in Ohio, the Dryden Flight Research Center at Edwards AFB and the Ames Research Center in California. Langley was charged with the management of the entire programme, as well as development work on aerodynamics, airframe materials and structures, flight deck ergonomics plus airframe/systems integration. The Lewis Center (later renamed Glenn) was responsible for engine and propulsion systems, and Ames and Dryden were responsible for covering any flight-test requirements. Joining the four NASA divisions were teams from Boeing Aircraft, McDonnell Douglas, Honeywell, General Electric and Pratt & Whitney.

NASA's Plans

To further the development aims of the HSR programme NASA issued contracts to cover specific areas of investigation. The most important of these went to General Electric and Pratt & Whitney, who acted in concert with the Lewis Center, under the title of the Enabling Propulsion Materials Program. Their expertise was needed in the fields of fibre analysis, fabrication of composites and structural analysis techniques,

Concorde market for at least 300 SSTs, especially if the US airlines could be persuaded to take at least half. While NASA was spearheading the SST concept on behalf of government, the aircraft manufacturers were also researching their own SST ideas. Boeing came up with a project based around a blended-wing/fuselage concept which derived its propulsion from variable cycle engines, and Douglas concentrated on an aircraft based around a delta wing, an idea that Lockheed were also studying closely, although in their case the engines were podded and mounted above and below the wing.

In the closing months of 1978 British Aerospace and McDonnell Douglas joined together to investigate a joint SST programme, with NASA entering during 1980 to further the development of all possible and potential technologies. All the partners eventually agreed that a viable second-generation SST could be in service by 1990. The joining together of McDonnell Douglas with British Aerospace was a continuation of an earlier collaboration that had involved Rolls-Royce in an investigation of noise-reducing engine exhausts. The addition of a government agency would end fairly quickly, since the administration of President Reagan felt that there would be few benefits forthcoming and that the funding could be better used elsewhere. As ever in American politics, persuasion and political muscle all of which would be needed for such exotic disciplines as ceramics, intermetallic and metal matrix composites, all needed to withstand the great temperatures at the core of any engine. Airframe contracts were handed out to Boeing, Lockheed and McDonnell Douglas, their role also being to investigate the development and application of new materials capable of withstanding high temperatures and their associated manufacturing techniques. The materials under investigation included intermediate temperature aluminium, aluminium/lithium alloys, high temperature titanium alloys, high temperature polymers and composites, higher temperature polymers, metal matrix composites and carbon/carbon composites. As high-power computers were now available to the development teams, they were also tasked with creating mathematical models of these materials in order to predict their useful service life and to plan mechanical trials of structural sections, which would simulate long-term flight conditions and effects of fatigue.

It was during this phase that Boeing suggested that the airline market was now

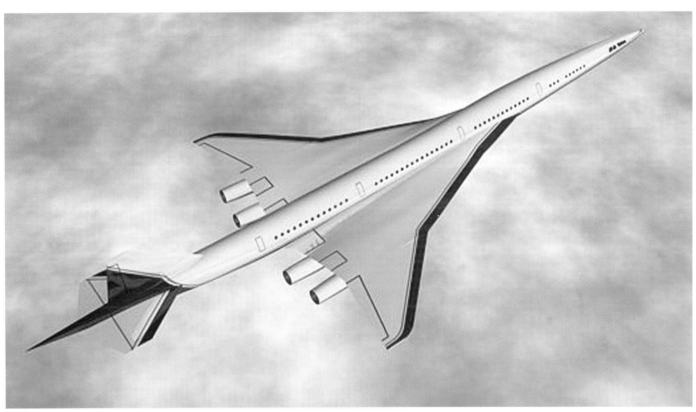

ABOVE: **This illustrates the second stab the USA made at creating its own SST. Much advanced development work on airframe structures and engines had been accomplished before the programme was cancelled.** BBA Collection

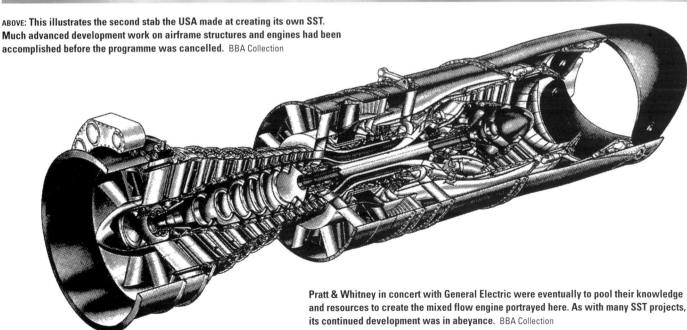

Pratt & Whitney in concert with General Electric were eventually to pool their knowledge and resources to create the mixed flow engine portrayed here. As with many SST projects, its continued development was in abeyance. BBA Collection

Although powerful computers can model much of a projected aircraft's behaviour, it is natural to want to see the results in reality. As current techniques now enable wind-tunnel models to be produced more cheaply, more quickly and more accurately, it is possible to produce changes within days. Courtesy NASA

capable of taking on an economically-viable and environmentally-acceptable, supersonic transport. However, getting these two aspects to gel in one airframe would be the difficult part, and therefore the manufacturers suggested a joint industry/NASA working party to push development further. The topics that could be dealt with most easily included low-emission engines, noise suppressors, variable cycle powerplants, high-temperature composites, high-lift devices and their AFCS systems, all of which were quickly achievable. Longer-term goals on which some research had been done included advance engine and airframe concepts, laminar flow control, improved high-temperature materials and a completely new idea – high thermal-stability fuels.

Since much of this technology was already well advanced, NASA decided to bring forward Phase 2 of the HSR programme, which had been pencilled in for 1996. But by 1993, the environment-based

Phase 1 had been completed and so the technology phase was begun. This was a joint venture and required that the wording needed to gain the appropriate Federal funding played more upon the positives than the negatives, thus much was made of the economic benefits, the number of highly-paid jobs that would be created and the improvement in the industrial strength of the nation. However, the slightly negative side was the cost, estimated at $4.5 billion, which would be needed before the aviation industry could even begin construction and certification. As this was an era of political and economic uncertainty, it was suggested that the government should cover most of the development costs since the manufacturers felt unable to contribute any funding until the HSCT was closer to reality. It was also stressed that as much of the proposed developments were high-risk, the manufacturers and their subcontractors would have to wait up to fifteen years before gaining any financial reward for their efforts.

Although Phase1 had been completed relatively easily, it was recognized that the three areas primarily involved in Phase 2 would involve great risk and difficulty. These were airframe technology, propulsion and the ergonomics of the flight deck. The airframe part was intended to build upon already available aerodynamic technologies, although the goals were stringent in their outline, these being a 33 per cent range increase coupled to a 50 per cent reduction in the noise footprint of any new aircraft. Allied to the aerodynamics was the desire to develop materials and construction methods that could reduce the aircraft's basic weight by up to 40 per cent, even though there was still a requirement for the structures to be able to withstand temperatures up to 180°C, with a fatigue life of 60,000 flying hours. The structure of an airframe built to these specifications would follow many earlier ideas, based around composite frames and ribs to which would be attached honeycomb composite panelling. At the points of great heat, such as the nose, intake lips and leading edges, the structure would be titanium honeycomb-based. In a change from previous concepts, only formed honeycomb panels would be used in the manufacture of the outer wing panels, fin tip and rudder.

Unlike Britain, which has only one primary engine builder, there are several in the USA and thus any collaboration between the major players was unusual. But both General Electric and Pratt & Whitney soon realized that to work together on such a project could only benefit both, even if the home-grown second-generation SST failed to move beyond the drawing board. During their collaboration the companies investigated materials capable of withstanding temperatures up to 3,000°C and the use of ceramic matrix and intermetallic composites in the hotter sections of the engine, including the exhaust nozzle.

During December 1995 a single design was chosen to be the focus of an intensive technology drive that would concentrate all those involved in the programme for the next three years. The chosen design intended for use as the Technology Concept Aircraft was based on a concept that had evolved from the earlier Boeing and Douglas HSCT designs. This would accommodate 300 passengers, seated in three separate compartments travelling at a speed of Mach 2.4 over a distance of 5,000 miles (8,000km). The initial design was carried out on computers using extensive

LEFT: This is an HSR test shape about to be run into the wind tunnel for testing. Note the use of tailplanes, although in this instance the engines are under the wings not under the tailplanes, as in the early Boeing model. Courtesy NASA

BELOW: The same aircraft model seen from underneath; note the engines mounted to the rear of the wing. Courtesy NASA

mathematical modelling, followed by the wind-tunnel testing of precision manufactured models. This kind of modelling, it was postulated, would enable the design team to create an aircraft of superior performance to satisfy the most stringent environmental requirements. Such concentration would also allow the developers to narrow their perspectives, thus as regards the engines, two designs based on a modified turbofan emerged: the mixed flow turbofan and the fan on blade. In each case the aim was to reduce engine noise on take-off and landing. This would be achieved by mixing ambient air with engine exhaust gases. This in turn would lead on to research into mixer ejector nozzles, which meant that the mixed flow turbofan was chosen as the preferred powerplant. The use of any engine in both the subsonic and the supersonic regime is always a source of conflict and so it is surprising that a mixed powerplant arrangement was not investigated; the Concorde designers had looked at this idea but had shelved it due to the projected airframe's size. As the American airframe would have been larger, it would have been possible to build efficient, subsonic turbofans into the rear of the fuselage for use during take-off, landing and overland cruising, while the turbojets mounted externally could have been used supersonically. The

In this instance the HSR model is being used to flight-test the wing and so the
tailplanes and fin have been removed. Courtesy NASA

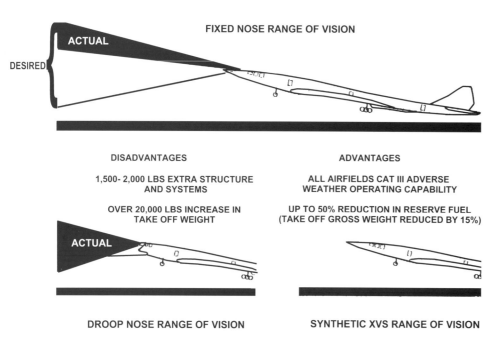

FIXED NOSE RANGE OF VISION

ACTUAL

DESIRED

DISADVANTAGES	ADVANTAGES
1,500- 2,000 LBS EXTRA STRUCTURE AND SYSTEMS	ALL AIRFIELDS CAT III ADVERSE WEATHER OPERATING CAPABILITY
OVER 20,000 LBS INCREASE IN TAKE OFF WEIGHT	UP TO 50% REDUCTION IN RESERVE FUEL (TAKE OFF GROSS WEIGHT REDUCED BY 15%)

ACTUAL

DROOP NOSE RANGE OF VISION   **SYNTHETIC XVS RANGE OF VISION**

NASA issued some diagrams to illustrate why any future SST should have XVS fitted
instead of having to rely on the normal visual cues for the pilots. Courtesy NASA

airframe designers were also looking at
new ways of doing things; one of the first
to gain their attention was that of the visual requirements of the pilots. Concorde,
from its outset, had been beset by restrictions when the visor was fully up, and even
with the bigger clear panels fitted to the
production aircraft the crew's vision was
restricted. By contrast, NASA and the
manufacturers had every intention of
eliminating windscreens entirely. In their
place would be computer-aided vision systems whose results would be displayed on
cockpit screens. Although it was accepted
that such developments would need extensive testing for accuracy, safety and
consistency, the saving in weight by deleting the nose-droop mechanism was
thought worthwhile. This would have
allowed for a slightly longer nose, which,
in turn, would have reduced the airframe's
drag coefficient.

To test this technology, test flying was
carried out during 1995–97 using a NASA
Boeing 737 and a Westinghouse-owned
BAC-111 test bed configured for avionics
test usage. The first trials involved external
sensors capable of detecting other aircraft
and major obstacles on the ground; these
were followed by flying approaches and
landings with a fully-enclosed cockpit
installed in the passenger cabin of the Boeing. The completion of these trials was followed by another sequence which also used
the Boeing, in which an external vision
system, XVS, was fitted into the main
pilot's panel. During these flights real-
world visual cues were compared in depth
with the display on the XVS panels.
Although a few problems were experienced, being rectified as they occurred, the
trials were deemed a complete success and
convinced all the design teams that the
windowless cockpit was more than feasible.

While the technical advances were coming thick and fast, scientific ones were also
happening apace. Specialists in environmental studies were gathered from all over
the world to develop computer models of
the earth's atmosphere and the effects of
engine exhausts on stratospheric ozone.
Although computer modelling could predict some results, real research was also
needed. This took the form of the NASA E-
2R high altitude research aircraft, based on
the Lockheed U-2R reconnaissance platform. This long-spanned airframe was ideal
for high altitude atmospheric sampling and
was also employed in sampling the atmosphere before and after Concorde had passed

through for purposes of comparison. Other potential hazards of flying above 35,000ft (10,700m), and rarely considered, are cosmic and solar radiation. As the HSCT was intended to operate at altitudes between 52,000 and 70,000ft (15,900–21,300m) the hazard from both types of radiation was measurably increased and thus the E-2R was used to gather data for analysis.

Also being examined in depth was the possibility of making laminar airflow a distinct reality. This version of the test aircraft employed microholes in wing skins in the areas most susceptible to airflow turbulence. Smoothing this turbulent air would reduce skin friction drag which in turn would reduce operating costs since less fuel would be needed. To test a laminar wing section in action, one of the NASA F-16XL development aircraft was fitted with a section of wing and flew trials from the NASA Dryden Flight Research Center at Edwards AFB, California.

While the more conventional SST, capable of operating in the Mach 2–3

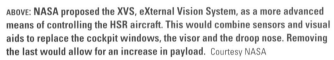

ABOVE: **NASA proposed the XVS, eXternal Vision System, as a more advanced means of controlling the HSR aircraft. This would combine sensors and visual aids to replace the cockpit windows, the visor and the droop nose. Removing the last would allow for an increase in payload.** Courtesy NASA

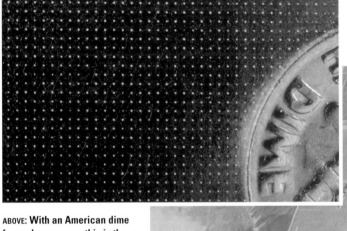

ABOVE: **With an American dime for scale purposes, this is the laminar-flow wing panel and its micropores as installed on the F-16XL test aircraft.** Courtesy NASA

RIGHT: **NASA F-16XL, 848, in flight with the micropore laminar-flow control panel installed on the leading edge of the port wing. Although the trials were successful no commercial applications have yet appeared.** Courtesy NASA

Captured landing at the Zhukovsky Development Centre near Moscow is the Tu-144LL flying laboratory under contract to NASA and interested US aircraft manufacturers. Courtesy NASA

regime, was being investigated, some effort was also being made in researching the possibility of a Hypersonic National Aero Space Plane. A similar project (known as HOTOL) was also being investigated by British Aerospace in co-operation with Rolls-Royce. This unique machine was intended to fly on the edge of space. Development began in 1982 and the project was reasonably well advanced, with a detailed engine design and mock-up, by the time the British government stopped its funding in the mid-1980s. HOTOL would have taken off horizontally, with a transition to pure rocket propulsion in the Mach 5.0–6.0 speed range, followed by an ascent into orbit. A moderate re-entry profile decreased the thermal loading constraints before HOTOL returned via a glide approach to a landing on normal undercarriage units on a conventional runway.

European Redivivus

Although the USA was pushing ahead with a high-profile development programme, the Europeans were forging ahead with similar ideas, albeit at a lower level. In March 1989 the two original Concorde partners met in Toulouse on the twentieth anniversary of the type's first flight to discuss a possible collaborative project for a second-generation European SST. Its initial costing was estimated at $10 million, with service entry in the early years of the next century. While these discussions were

being undertaken, the potential partners were investigating their own projects. Aérospatiale were engaged upon the Avion de Transport Supersonique Futur (ATSF), which was intended to cruise between Mach 2 and 2.5. Running parallel to this programme was the Avion á Grande Vitesse, a hypersonic transport intended to operate between Mach 4 and 5. British Aerospace were investigating their own machine, known as the Advanced Supersonic Transport. Both companies took their projects to the negotiating table in May 1990, from which emerged a joint declaration concerning the second-generation aircraft. This agreement was extended in April 1994 when Deutsche Aerospace joined the partnership. The three partners declared their collaborative venture to be the European Supersonic Research Programme. The outline sketch of the aircraft to replace Concorde was a Mach 2-capable aircraft which could carry 250 passengers, seated in three classes, over 6,210 miles (10,000km). At this point the public relation people stepped in to declare optimistically that the potential market for such an aircraft was between 500 and 1,000 units.

All this talk of European collaboration seemed to worry the Americans, since they invited the Europeans to a conference in New York in May 1990. At this were representatives from Boeing, McDonnell Douglas, Aérospatiale, British Aerospace and Deutsche Aerospace. The outcome was the formation of a joint study group to create an international, next-generation SST, by

now named the Supersonic Commercial Transport. The first inklings of its work were unveiled during the September 1990 SBAC show at Farnborough, when an announcement was made concerning the formation of two specialist working groups: the first would concern itself with the business practices needed for a collaborative project and the second would concentrate on technical and marketing aspects.

During 1991 the Italian manufacturer Alenia Aeronautica, the Society of Japanese Aerospace Companies and the Tupolev Design Bureau joined the consortium. Three years later, at a European conference, delegates from five of the companies presented an overview in which American, European and other technologies might be co-ordinated in a predevelopment phase, to be followed by a full-scale development programme to last through the 1990s.

While much of this looked promising on paper, the real progress was being made by NASA and its partners, who were actually spending money to push the technology for the HSCT project. Leading the industry side were Boeing and McDonnell Douglas, who were operating under a $400 million NASA contract on the HSR Phase 2 technologies. Honeywell were dealing with the avionics and flight-deck development. It was estimated that the final cost to NASA would reach $2 billion, with industry's contributions possibly reaching $4 billion. The upshot of this expenditure was that the development of an actual aircraft was pencilled in to begin in 1995, with the first deliveries to be made in 2001. To speed some of the technologies already available, NASA hired a Tupolev Tu-144D airliner as a flying test bed. By August 1997 the NASA scientific teams were reporting that the critical, high-risk technologies were coming close to fruition and therefore that the HSR programme should be progressed to its conclusion. In mid September 1998 a refocusing of the HSR programme was undertaken by NASA and its partners, in that they would concentrate upon supersonic research instead of pushing on with technologies that would lead to a prototype aircraft. The change was brought about by the realization that the original technological development path would not bring to a culmination a viable aircraft for deployment by 2010. There followed the complete cessation of the whole programme by the end of that year. This had, in part, been caused by the decision of Boeing (now the owner of McDonnell Douglas) to abandon

RIGHT: **Awaiting its next research trip is the Tu-144LL, RA-77114. Hard by the port nose are the entrance stairs leading to the flight deck.** Courtesy NASA

BELOW: **With the local equivalent of an aircraft tractor hooked to the nose leg, the Tu-144LL is moved towards the hangar for further maintenance. Although the visor was likened to a greenhouse, it faired into the nose extremely well.** Courtesy NASA

LEFT: **Parked on the ramp is the Tu-144LL dedicated to the HSR research programme. As the hydraulic systems have lost their pressure, the elevons are fully drooped hard against the range stops.** Courtesy NASA

BELOW: **Captured just after lift-off, the crew of the Tu-144LL are already retracting the canard wings into their fairings behind the cockpit. Once set into cruise mode, the afterburners are shut down and not used again, since the Tu-144 was capable of exceeding the speed of sound without them.** Courtesy NASA

BOTTOM: **Although the Tu-144 did not share the success of Concorde, it did look elegant in the sky.** Courtesy NASA

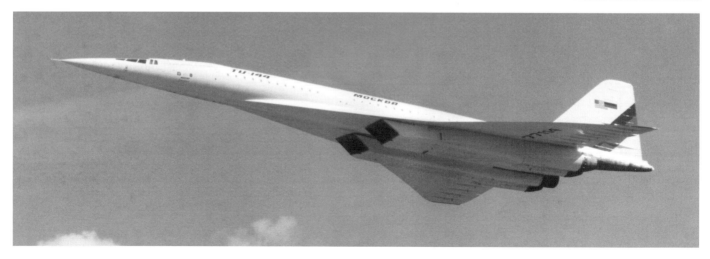

The Assessment of NASA's High Speed Research Program

In 1997 a meeting was held to thrash out a report on American supersonic commercial aircraft. There were two bodies present: the Committee on High Speed Research and the Aeronautics and Space Engineering Board, forming the Commission on Engineering and Technical Systems, which was to report to the National Research Council. The Committee on High Speed Research drew its members from numerous organizations including the USAF, General Electric, Belcan Engineering, Stanford University, Boeing, Northrop Grumman, American Airlines and the United Technologies Research Center. The Aeronautics and Space Engineering Board also had a diverse membership, once again Boeing, Lockheed and the USAF were prominent.

The assessment began with a description of the NASA High Speed Research (HSR) Program and defined it as a focused technology development programme intended to lead to the commercial development of a high speed civil transport. The HSR Program was not intended actually to design or test a commercial aircraft; this was the responsibility of the aviation industry. The HSCT was seen as a second-generation aircraft with a better performance than either Concorde or the Tupolev Tu-144.

Phase 1 of the programme was completed in 1995 and concentrated on environmental issues, including noise and engine emissions. Phase 2, to be completed by 2002 (but cancelled in 1999), was intended to investigate propulsion, airframe materials, structures, flight-deck systems, aerodynamic performance and systems integration. The HSR Program was confirmed as a well-managed operation on target to complete its goals.

The concluding paragraph stated that, following on from the completed Phase 2, the technology and information gleaned from it would enable American industry to build a second-generation prototype for test flying in 2006. However, one proviso was that the industry alone would not be able to fund such an aircraft and therefore that government support in depth would be required.

The Commission concentrated mainly on Phase 2 and its potential, and thus the next step, the Technology Maturation Phase, would need to be furthered. This would involve defining a manufacturing base, productivity demonstrations and the ground testing of full-scale components and systems. This phase should also cover the development of the engines and should include a pair of full-scale demonstration engines.

The difficulty of building a second-generation SST was already understood since the X-33 programme and its management had already demonstrated that it was feasible. On a more parochial level, the HSCT was seen as good for America and its economy and that it would give the aviation industry a much-needed technological boost, leading to spin-offs for the consumer market. Other areas that came in for praise included the dynamics of the integrated aircraft, the propulsion, flight-deck systems, supersonic laminar flow control and manufacturing technology and durability testing.

the project in order to cut operating costs. The departure of Boeing led to the disintegration of the study group in January 1999. A final pronouncement by Daniel Goldin of NASA stated that, 'The High Speed Research Program and the Advanced Technology programs are now discontinued for the foreseeable future.'

Japanese Interest

Although the USA, Britain and Russia have currently shelved their supersonic transport development programmes, the baton had been picked up by the Society of Japanese Aerospace Companies in 1995. This had been made possible by the Society's involvement with the study group, whose information formed the basis of their research. This programme, under the guidance of the National Aeronautics Laboratory of Japan, had three primary aims:

i. To acquire and establish advanced aircraft integration technology by developing scaled supersonic experimental aircraft and conducting flight experiments.
ii. To use computational fluid dynamics (CFD) and flight verification in the design of aircraft body shape.
iii. To increase the sophistication of composite-material technology and other next-generation supersonic technologies.

The result would be an aircraft capable of cruising at Mach 2.2, with a range of 6,340 miles (10,200km) with a passenger complement of 300. The intended span of this SST would be 142ft (43.3m), with a fuselage of 310ft (95m). This would result in a wing with an area of 9,200sq ft (855sq m), which in turn would support a maximum load of 399 tons (407 tonnes), of which 243 (248) were allocated to fuel. To flight-test this design and conduct research on related technology, two types of scaled supersonic experimental airplane, consisting of two non-powered and two jet-powered experimental aircraft, were built.

On 14 July 2002 a powered model of the Japanese SST was launched from the Woomera Test Centre in Australia. The National Experimental Supersonic Transport, NEXST1, project is at the leading edge of a push by Japan's National Aerospace Laboratory, NAL, to create a new generation of supersonic commercial airliners. The test launch, originally scheduled for a few days earlier, had been postponed

because of adverse wind conditions and rescheduled for 14 July, when it was briefly delayed again. The test model was to be launched to an altitude of 12.5 miles (20km) over South Australia on the back of a rocket booster. It would then have been put through a series of manoeuvres, during which telemetry measurements would be taken as it returned to earth at nearly twice the speed of sound. However, the scale model, 36ft (11m) long, and fitted with over 900 sensors was launched correctly but then went out of control and crashed in flames; the cause was determined to be a software failure. The project, which involved Mitsubishi Heavy Industries and the Nissan Motor Corporation, had cost $80 million. Japanese researchers had also spent five years and an estimated $350 million in redeveloping Woomera for the launch as part of the NEXST1 programme. NAL planned four more test flights at Woomera for 2003.

Radical Technologies

Helping to push the development of the next-generation SST were rapid advances in materials that were not only light but also exhibited great strength and resistance to high temperatures. Improvements in the accuracy of computational flight dynamics also aided development. Computers contributed extensively to improved flight control systems since their speed had increased dramatically from the period of Concorde. Powerplants also underwent radical changes, with the variable cycle engine being the preferred type. The arrival of these new technologies spurred on both Boeing and McDonnell Douglas to greater efforts, although the PR departments seized on the information to project these new technologies as long-range, high-altitude aircraft capable of flying across the Pacific in a few hours. The first of these new transports was estimated to be ready for commercial service in 2010.

The designs put forth by both organizations were remarkably similar in layout, the main difference between them being the flight envelope each was trying to fulfil. Boeing proposed an aircraft capable of travelling at Mach 2.4, while McDonnell Douglas pitched their design to reach no more than Mach 1.6. This design had the benefit of being slightly smaller and lighter, which would lead to a reduction in

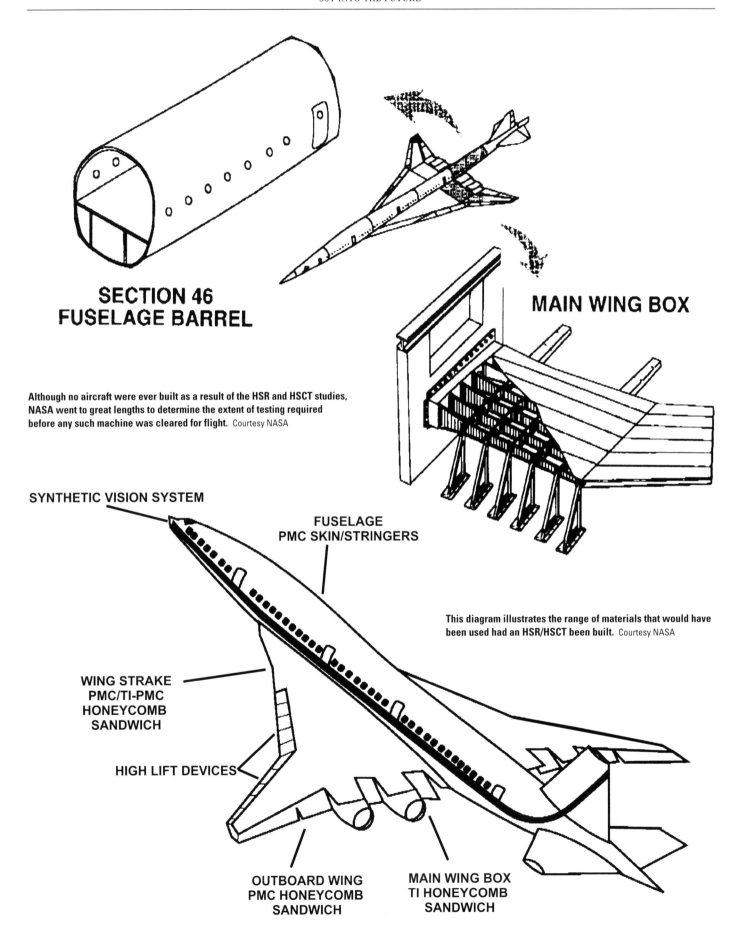

**SECTION 46
FUSELAGE BARREL**

MAIN WING BOX

Although no aircraft were ever built as a result of the HSR and HSCT studies, NASA went to great lengths to determine the extent of testing required before any such machine was cleared for flight. Courtesy NASA

SYNTHETIC VISION SYSTEM

FUSELAGE
PMC SKIN/STRINGERS

This diagram illustrates the range of materials that would have been used had an HSR/HSCT been built. Courtesy NASA

WING STRAKE
PMC/TI-PMC
HONEYCOMB
SANDWICH

HIGH LIFT DEVICES

OUTBOARD WING
PMC HONEYCOMB
SANDWICH

MAIN WING BOX
TI HONEYCOMB
SANDWICH

production and design costs. The construction of either aircraft would require the development of more exotic metals, the currently available range of alloys being thought unsuitable in this instance. The materials then available that were seen as usable in any new aircraft included titanium, elevated-temperature aluminium and high-temperature polymer composites, examples of which were already under close study and in some cases already being flight tested. Although optimistic forecasts had been given for service entry dates of an American SST, some caution was being sounded concerning the deployment of such new materials without proper development and testing.

In spite of these reservations, the basic airframe layout for each version of the SST had already been defined through extensive computer modelling which enabled the designers to alter details as required and then test them without spending scarce development money on solid models every time for wind-tunnel testing, as had been the case in the past. The wings destined for both aircraft consisted of four

sections whose outer panels were intended to be of high aspect ratio with a relatively gentle sweep angle. The construction of the outer wing sections was intended to be of the multi-rib type, sheathed in a honeycomb skin manufactured from high polymeric composites (HPC). The outer panels would be attached to the main spar and its attendant sub-spars, for it was here that the main load-bearing strength of each design was concentrated. Attached to the main wing section would be the engines, main undercarriage units and the trailing edge of the mid-wing panels. To emphasize the strength and heat-protection requirements of this major component it was sheathed in a four-layer titanium skin. Mounted on the forward face of the main spar was the mid-wing panel whose primary purpose was to act as a housing for the main undercarriage units. These would be constructed in a similar manner to the outer wing panels, also being encased in a skin of HPC. To the front of the mid-wing section was the wing strake assembly, to be of a lighter construction than the other wing sections. This was of a highly swept

nature and was to be cantilevered out from the fuselage, although it would incorporate a transverse wing carry-through box section to impart reasonable strength and rigidity. An imaginative element in this multi-part wing involved the use of expansion joints between each section to allow the stresses generated by thermal build-up to be safely dispersed, a vital need given the dissimilar metals used in its construction, with their differing expansion rates. By contrast to the wing, the fuselage was to be built as one structure with the nose radome and tail-cone being the only separate items. The primary load-bearing members in this area determined that it would consist of individual frames, to which would be attached Z-section stringers to give strength and shape; as before, the covering skin would be HPC bonded to both frames and stringers.

With the airframe manufacturers making progress, the engine builders began to give their part of the project serious consideration in conjunction with NASA, who were advancing the idea of a new engine concept under the title of the

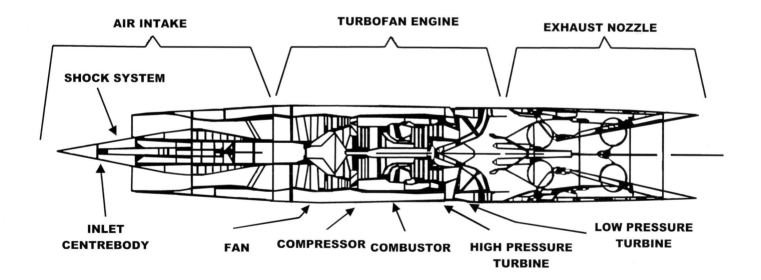

The original engine requirements postulated by NASA were based around a podded turbofan engine, the airflow of which would be controlled by the movable centre-body at the front of the powerplant, as in the B-58 Hustler bomber. Courtesy NASA

to confirm that the organization was not actually developing an SST but was leaving it to industry. The statement presented in January 1975 confirm that the supersonic research programme was not specifically directed to the design and development of an SST but limited to the identification of any major problems and the development of the technologies necessary for their solution. Further oversight was exercised by Congress in April 1978 when the Office of Technology Assessment was tasked with investigating the potential benefits of a second-generation SST and the funding associated with the SCR programme. Two years later the OTA informed a Congressional committee that the programme was delivering value for money; however, they commented that, unless the funding were increased, there would be a reduction in future technological benefits. In support of the OTA findings, NASA commissioned further research into aircraft designs capable of operating at Mach 2.2, 2.4 and 2.5 from McDonnell Douglas, Boeing and Lockheed, respectively.

While the airframe manufacturers were still in the process of sketching out their designs for the SST, rapid advances in technology were leading Boeing and Lockheed to revise their studies to incorporate those seen as important in supersonic flight. One of the most significant of these was fly-by-wire and the associated AFCS computers needed to control aircraft behaviour; similarly, advances in the field of aerodynamics were also relevant in second-generation SST design, especially in the application of high-lift devices. Thus both disciplines would be incorporated into the second-generation designs with alacrity. Further input came from Boeing who had flight-tested some developments on their B.757 test bed. But the most important advance was laminar flow control which was seen as essential for smooth, low-level, low-speed handling.

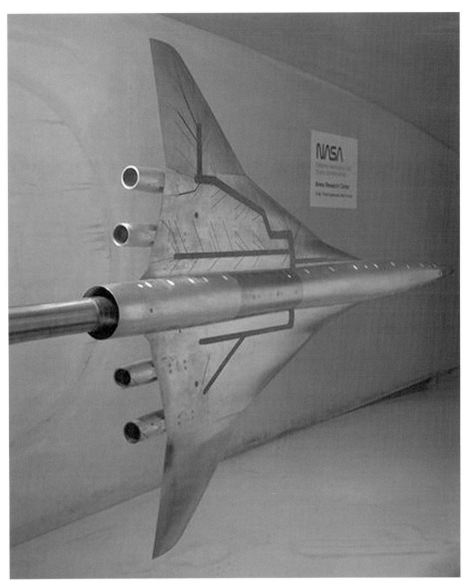

To test specific aircraft behaviour, the designers and scientists have sections of it manufactured separately for wind-tunnel use. In this view the model has no rear fuselage since the trials are concerned more with the interactions between the wing, the engines and the fuselage. Courtesy NASA

Flying Test Beds

Having developed the theories and some of the technology it was time to put them to the test. Given that no supersonic transports were available in the USA and that all the Air France and British Airways Concordes were fully occupied, NASA turned its attention further afield to find a flying test bed. Before the Concorde option was dropped, Alan Greenwood from British Aerospace had proposed in February 1980 to NASA

Variable Cycle Engine Development Program. Their starting assumptions were based on the available power, fuel efficiency and the two main constituents of pollution: noise and particulate matter. The major players were General Electric and Pratt & Whitney. The General Electric engine was based on the variable cycle principle, which offered good power output but would require further development to reduce the noise generated. Pratt & Whitney had settled on the turbine bypass engine, which used a convergent–divergent nozzle coupled to a chute suppressor

that would, it was hoped, control the noise output. As both types of engine had good points it was decided that a combined engine known as the mixed flow turbofan should be developed by both companies.

It should be noted that NASA were not in the business of designing or supporting any particular design for a second-generation SST. Their purpose was to foster the advance of the several technologies in conjunction with the primary manufacturers. When the programme had been running for four years James Fletcher, a NASA administrator, was called before Congress

and its assistant administrator Dr A.M. Lovelace that a Concorde would be ideal for the SCR programme. A joint technical team from NASA and BAe investigated one of the airframes at Filton in October. By March 1981 a wholly positive report was delivered. This was based on the fact that Concorde had been in commercial service for five years and thus a high level of understanding on the operating of a supersonic aircraft was available. The report specified the six goals that Concorde would be used for: advanced flight procedures for noise abatement, the assessment of handling qualities, the analysis of intake aerodynamic surge loads, wake vortices measurement, the measurement of airframe skin friction and engine nacelle drag, and the measurement of airframe noise due to supersonic speeds. The test-flying programme would be based in Britain, with engineering and computer simulation support from British Aerospace. NASA had $500,000 to fund the whole exercise; however in March 1982 the entire SCR programme was be put on hold as the Reagan administration had decided to reduce the technology development budget. Fortunately this decision was eventually reversed by the mid 1990s, although by that time the chance of using a Concorde had gone and therefore another aircraft type would be required. This was the Tupolev Tu-144D airframe, of which a few remained airworthy, having been grounded by Aeroflot

as uneconomic to operate. Since they were readily available, the most servicable was reclaimed by Tupolev for overhaul and upgrading. The backers of this venture would be NASA, the primary American airframe and engine manufacturers and, to a certain extent, the Russian manufacturers, who hoped to gain further insight into advanced SST flight behaviour. Designated the Tu-144LL, the aircraft undertook a sequence of successful test flights. Given the political uncertainty that always surrounded the American SST, it came as no surprise that the programme was suspended due to lack of further funding. A subsidiary reason was the absorption of McDonnell Douglas by Boeing Aircraft in 1998, which reduced the element of competition favoured by American politicians. The public pronouncements gave the reasons as a perceived change in the projected sales figures, plus the technical risks in pursuing such a programme. At this point NASA also placed the High Speed Research Program on a lower priority; the whole project was finally abandoned in early 1999.

Hope Springs Eternal?

Although it would appear that the quest for a successor to Concorde has for the time being been abandoned by the major manufacturers and associated government

bodies, some smaller organizations are still pursuing this most elusive of goals. In the USA Reno Aeronautical are concentrating on something smaller in the shape of a Mach 1.5-capable, twin-engined business jet. Also in America Gulfstream, the well-known business jet manufacturer, working in conjunction with the Russian aircraft manufacturer Sukhoi OKB, undertook joint design studies for a four-engined business cum small airliner design – later cancelled due to differences between the partners regarding design concepts. Meanwhile in Europe, both Airbus Industrie and British Aerospace continued low-level development both individually and jointly, although neither would commit to any form of production since no government funding was forthcoming.

Given all these half-started, half-finished programmes, will the Aérospatiale/BAC Concorde end by being the only one of its kind ever to be built? For all the trials and tribulations that beset Concorde since the day the idea was conceived, the aircraft eventually proved to be a winner. Let us hope that any successor is as good.

A fitting end is a view of a Concorde prototype. It was, and still is, the only successful supersonic transport – not bad for an aircraft deemed to be a white elephant. BBA Collection

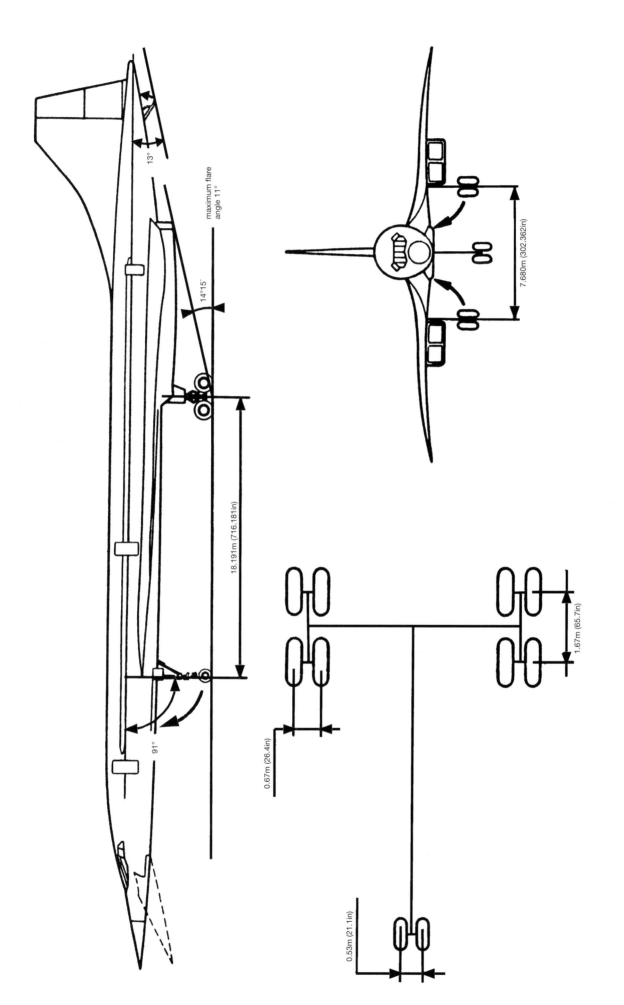

13°

maximum flare angle 11°

14°15´

18.191m (716.181in)

91°

7.680m (302.362in)

1.67m (65.7in)

0.67m (26.4in)

0.53m (21.1in)

This diagram illustrates the primary dimensions of the production Concorde. BBA Collection

Concorde Data

Engines
Rolls-Royce/SNECMA Olympus 593
reheat thrust: 38,050lb (16,925kN), at sea level
specific fuel consumption at 53,000ft Mach 2: 1.19lb/
lb thrust/hr (1.19 kg/kg thrust/hr)

Wings
span: 83ft 10.4in (25.56m)
area: 3,856sq ft (358.25sq m)
root chord: 90ft 9in (27.66m)

Elevons
area: 172.2sq ft (16sq m)

Fuselage
length overall: 202ft 3.6in (61.66m)
external height: 130.7in (3.32m)
pressure cabin length: 129ft (39.32m)
maximum internal height: 77in (1.96m)
maximum external width: 113.4in (2.88m)
maximum internal width: 103.4in (2.63m)

Fin
height: 37ft 1in (11.32m)
area: 365sq ft (33.91sq m)
root chord: 34ft 8.7in (10.58m)

Rudder
area: 112sq ft (10.41sq m)

Range of Movement
yaw: ±30 degrees
pitch inner elevons: 15 degrees up/17 down
pitch outer elevons: 15 degrees up/17 down
roll inner elevon: 14 degrees up/14 down
roll outer elevons: 20 degrees up/20 down
maximum range – inner elevon: 19 degrees up/19 down
　　　　　　　　　outer elevons: 23.5 degrees up/23.5 down

Landing gear
main – wheel base: 59ft 8in (18.19m)
　　　track: 25ft 4in (7.68m)
　　　tyre: 47 × 15.75; pressure: 187psi (12.9bar)
　　　steering range: ±60 degrees
NZG tyres: 43.3 × 15.74; pressure: 230psi (16bar)
nose – tyre: 31 × 10.75; pressure: 174psi (12bar)
tail unit – tyre: 3.20 × 120; pressure: 294psi (20bar)

Fuel system
tank 1: 9,361lb (4,255kg)
tank 2: 10,207lb (4,640kg)
tank 3: 10,207lb (4,640kg)
tank 4: 9,361lb (4,255kg)
tank 5: 16,072lb (7,305kg)
tank 5A: 4,963lb (2,256kg)
tank 6: 25,889lb (11,678kg)
tank 7: 16,525lb (7,511kg)
tank 7A: 4,963lb (2,256kg)
tank 8: 28,645lb (13,020kg)
tank 9: 24,747lb (11,248kg)
tank 10: 26,618lb (12,099kg)
tank 11: 23,218lb (10,554kg)
unusable: 1,021lb (464kg)
total: 211,797lb (96,271kg)

Electrical system
main: 60kVA 200/115V, 400Hz
emergency: 26V, 1,800Hz
batteries: 24V

Hydraulic system
fluid type: Oronite M2V
capacity: 74.8gal (340ltr)
pressure: 4,000psi (275bar)

Pressurization
normal differential: 10.7±0.1psi (738±7mbar)
temperature range: 15–30°C

Weights
maximum take-off weight: 389,000lb (176,445kg)
maximum taxi weight: 404,000lb (183,251kg)
maximum landing weight: 245,000lb (111,130kg)
maximum permissible weights – taxiing: 411,136lb (186,880kg)
　　　　　　　　　　　　　　take-off: 407,154lb (185,070kg)
　　　　　　　　　　　　　　landing: 244,486lb (111,130kg)
　　　　　　　　　　　　　　zero fuel: 202,576lb (92,080kg)

Baggage holds
combined total: 697cu ft (20.03cu m)
forward lower: 227cu ft (6.71cu m)
upper hold: 470cu ft (13.32cu m)

Concorde Incidents

Date	Operator	Registration	Location	Remarks
20.6.75	AF	N/K	Caracas	wheel damaged after hitting runway beacon light
7.6.76	AF	N/K	mid Atlantic	engine problem
15.12.76	AF	F-BVFB	Paris	No.2 tyre burst
22.7.77	AF	F-BVFA	Washington	Nos 1 and 2 tyres burst due to foreign object damage
5.10.77	AF	N/K	mid Atlantic	engine problem
28.11.77	AF	N/K	Dakar	tail/engine damage due to misjudged landing
1.12.77	AF	N/K	mid Atlantic	engine problem
10.12.77	AF	N/K	New York	engine shut-down before landing
19.12.77	AF	N/K	N/K	No.4 tyre deflated; tread separated
2.8.78	BA	G-BOAD	N/K	No.2 tyre burst; hydraulic leak/deflector damage
10.12.78	AF	F-BVFA	N/K	No.7 tyre burst
12.12.78	AF	F-BVFA	N/K	No.1 tyre burst
29.12.78	BA	G-BOAC	New York	engine shut-down after take-off; secondary air door unserviceable
4.2.79	AF	F-BVFC	Washington	No.2 tyre burst
15.3.79	AF	F-BVFC	Dakar	Nos 5 and 6 tyres burst; wheels, brakes and No.1 engine replaced
2.6.79	AF	F-BVFC	New York	No.6 tyre tread failed, causing damage to wing and hydraulics and undercarriage
14.6.79	AF	F-BVFC	Washington	Nos 2, 5 and 6 tyres burst on take-off, causing damage to undercarriage control circuits/fuel and hydraulic systems; aircraft returned to Dulles for emergency landing
21.7.79	AF	F-BVFD	Washington	tyre failure caused damage to No.2 engine compressor
23.9.79	AF	F-BVFD	Dakar	tread loss, No.3 tyre/wheel and No.3 engine replaced
6.10.79	BA	G-BOAA	Heathrow	No.4 tyre failed causing damage to Nos 7 and 8 wheels and Nos 3 and 4 engines
31.10.79	AF	F-BVFD	N/K	tread loss to No.7 wheel
5.11.79	AF	F-BVFD	Washington	aircraft hit two deer on landing, causing damage to right main gear
21.12.79	BA	G-BOAB	Heathrow	tyres burst on Nos 5, 6, 7 and 8 wheels
5.2.80	BA	G-BOAD	Heathrow	No.8 tyre burst causing damage to deflector/ brakes and hydraulic system
16.7.80	AF	F-BVFC	N/K	No.3 tyre burst
16.9.80	BA	G-BOAF	Washington	No.8 tyre burst on touchdown, damaging engine and airframe
19.2.81	AF	F-BTSD	Washington	Nos 1 and 2 tyres replaced after foreign object damage; aircraft diverted to New York

Date	Operator	Registration	Location	Remarks
13.7.81	AF	F-BVFF	Paris	tyre No.5 failed, causing damage to No.2 engine
9.8.81	BA	G-BOAG	New York	Nos 1 and 2 tyres burst, causing damage to No.2 engine and adjacent fuel tank
20.9.81	BA	G-BOAD	New York	No.6 tyre burst, causing damage to No.2 engine and brake servo valve
14.12.81	BA	G-BOAD	New York	Undercarriage failed to retract after take-off due to unbalanced gear truck
26.12.81	BA	G-BOAE	New York	No.2 tyre deflated
30.4.82	BA	G-BOAF	Heathrow	No.4 tyre deflated
3.6.82	AF	F-BVFB	Paris	No.4 tyre failure
9.5.83	AF	F-BVFB	New York	Nos 1 and 2 tyres deflated
29.4.84	BA	G-BOAE	Heathrow	No.8 tyre deflated
11.7.84	BA	G-BOAD	Heathrow	No.1 tyre burst; brake and deflector damaged
14.8.84	BA	G-BOAA	Heathrow	No.4 tyre burst; deflector damaged
20.2.85	AF	F-BVFF	New York	No.8 tyre burst; damage to undercarriage
27.2.85	BA	G-BOAE	New York	Nos 4 and 8 tyres lost tread on landing
14.11.85	BA	G-BOAE	Heathrow	No.7 tyre burst, causing brake fire
15.11.85	BA	G-BOAB	Heathrow	No.5 tyre burst, causing damage to main-gear door which in turn punctured No.5 fuel tank; Nos 1and 2 engines needed to be replaced after foreign object damage
18.5.86	AF	F-BVFB	Paris	No.5 tyre burst
11.8.87	BA	G-BOAC	New York	Nos 1, 2, 4, 5, 6 and 8 tyres burst due to braking problems locking brakes on; damage caused to No.3 engine, deflectors and undercarriage doors
10.9.87	AF	F-BTSD	New York	No.8 tyre deflated due to foreign object damage.
29.1.88	BA	G-BOAF	Heathrow	tyre hub failure, causing damage to No.7 fuel tank
9.3.88	BA	G-BOAC	Heathrow	No.1 tyre burst, damaging hydraulic pipelines
10.4.88	AF	F-BTSD	New York	No.7 tyre burst after tread failed, due to foreign object damage
18.6.88	BA	N/K	Heathrow	undercarriage failed to retract; aircraft returned to Heathrow
19.7.88	BA	G-BOAG	New York	hydraulic system failure, requiring return to base; aircraft veered off runway due to inoperative brakes
13.2.89	AF	N/K	Paris	outer window panel cracked after take-off; aircraft returned to base
12.4.89	BA	G-BOAF	Tasman Sea	failure of upper rudder section; aircraft continued on to Sydney
14.8.90	AF	F-BVFA	Paris	No.5 tyre burst due to foreign object damage on runway
4.1.91	BA	G-BOAE	mid Atlantic	upper rudder section failed; aircraft continued to New York
13.2.92	BA	G-BOAG	Heathrow	No.7 tyre tread separated; deflector damaged
21.3.92	BA	G-BOAB	Atlantic	upper rudder separated from aircraft in flight; No.2 engine shut down due to vibration
27.3.92	AF	F-BTSC	New York	No.1 tyre burst due to foreign object damage
4.9.92	AF	F-BVFF	New York	No.4 tyre burst due to foreign object damage
16.1.93	AF	F-BVFF	Paris	Nos 7 and 8 tyres lost tread, causing damage to deflector, undercarriage, No.3 engine and wing root

Date	Operator	Registration	Location	Remarks
15.7.93	BA	G-BOAF	Heathrow	No.4 tyre burst, causing damage to braking system, No.3 engine and No.8 fuel tank
28.7.93	AF	F-BVFC	New York	loss of tread on No.2 tyre
26.5.94	BA	G-BOAG	New York	No.2 engine shut down; high oil pressure; No.2 engine shut down on approach as a precaution
21.7.95	BA	G-BOAB	Heathrow	No.2 tyre burst, causing damage to hydraulic system
4.3.96	BA	G-BOAF	Atlantic	No.1 engine shut down due to fuel pressure warnings
18.9.96	BA	G-BOAB	Heathrow	blue hydraulic system total loss; aircraft returned to base
7.2.97	BA	G-BOAE	N/K	Nos 3 and 4 engines shut down due to surging and low oil pressure, respectively
8.3.97	BA	G-BOAB	N/K	No.2 engine experienced thrust reverser problems
27.5.97	BA	G-BOAE	N/K	No.2 engine shut down due to problems with thrust reverser
3.1.98	BA	N/K	Heathrow	fuel emergency declared after missed approach
25.5.98	BA	G-BOAC	New York	No.2 elevon lost section of surface; aircraft returned to base
22.7.98	AF	F-BVFF	Paris	No.8 tyre burst
28.8.98	BA	G-BOAE	New York	No.3 tyre deflated due to foreign object damage
8.10.98	BA	G-BOAC	Atlantic	partial separation of rudder; aircraft landed at New York
11.4.99	AF	F-BVFB	New York	nose gear failed to retract; aircraft returned to JFK
6.6.99	BA	G-BOAE	Heathrow	aircraft experienced hydraulic system problems on approach
22.1.00	AF	F-BVFF	New York	No.4 tyre burst
29.1.00	BA	G-B	Heathrow	aircraft suffered engine failure on approach
17.3.00	BA	G-BOAA	Shannon	No.3 engine shut down and landing made at Shannon
13.6.00	BA	G-BOAF	Heathrow	No.6 tyre burst
14.7.00	BA	G-BOAB	Heathrow	No.6 tyre failed due to foreign object damage; deflector damaged
25.7.00	AF	F-BTSC	Paris	aircraft crashed soon after take-off; all on board killed
15.3.02	BA	N/K	Heathrow	engine problems on take-off; flight abandoned
4.02	BA	N/K	New York	in transit engine surged; aircraft landed at JFK
7.02	BA	N/K	Heathrow	engine problem required aircraft to return to base
30.10.02	BA	N/K	Heathrow	cracks discovered in outer window panel
3.11.02	BA	N/K	Heathrow	engine surge required return to base
6.11.02	AF	N/K	New York	engine failure; aircraft continued to Paris
27.11.02	BA	N/K	Heathrow	partial rudder failure prompted return to base
19.2.03	AF	N/K	New York	No.3 engine shut down; aircraft diverted
27.2.03	AF	N/K	New York	partial rudder failure caused return to JFK

Concorde and Tu-144 Fleet Details

Concorde Fleets

C/N	Registration	Series	Operator	First Flight	Status
01	F-WTSS	–	Sud Aviation Aérospatiale	2.03.69	after test flying was retired to Paris Le Bourget 19.10.73 for display in the Musée de l'Air; hours: 812
02	G-BSST	–	BAC/BAE Systems	9.04.69	to MinTech 06.05.69, to MoS 19.02.71, arrived at RNAS Yeovilton 26.07.76 for preservation in Fleet Air Arm Museum; hours: 836
101	G-AXDN	–	BAC/BAE Systems	17.12.71	to MinTech 16.04.68; to MoS 19.02.71, to Imperial War Museum, Duxford for preservation, 20.08.75; hours: 633
102	F-WTSA	–	Sud Aviation Aérospatiale	10.01.73	to Paris, Orly for display 26.05.76 hours: 642
201	F-WTSB	100	Aérospatiale	6.12.73	withdrawn from use, on display at Aérospatiale, Toulouse; hours: 754
202	G-BBDG	100	BAC/BAE Systems	13.02.74	registered 7.08.73; for spare parts use at Filton, 12.81; owned by British Airways; For Brooklands Museum 2004? hours: 803
203	F-WTSC F-BTSC	100/ 101	Aérospatiale Air France	31.01.75	reregistered 28.05.75 crashed 25.07.00 hours: 11,989
204	G-BOAC G-N81NC N81NC G-BOAC	102	BAC BA Braniff BA	27.02.75	registered 5.01.74 delivered 13.02.76 joint register 5.01.79 returned to BA 11.08.80 returned to service after modification 11.07.02; preserved Manchester 31.10.03 hours 22,259
205	F-BVFA N94FA F-BVFA	101	Air France Braniff Air France	27.10.75	delivered 19.12.75 joint register 12.01.79 returned 1.06.80 returned to service 02.02; to Smithsonian 12.06.03; hours: 17,824
206	G-BOAA G-N94AA N94AA G-BOAA	102	BAC BA Braniff BA	5.11.75	registered 3.03.74 delivered 14.01.76 joint register 12.01.79 returned 28.07.80; in store Heathrow to East Fortune, Scotland 2004 hours: 22,786
207	F-BVFB N94FB F-BVFB	101	Air France Braniff Air France	6.03.76	delivered 8.04.76 joint register 12.01.79 returned 1.06.80

C/N	Registration	Series	Operator	First Flight	Status
207 *cont.*					returned to service 24.08.01 to Sinsheim Auto und Technik Museum, Germany 23.06.03 hours: 14,771
208	G-BOAB G-N94AB N94AB G-BOAB	102	BAC BA Braniff BA	18.05.76	registered 3.03.74 delivered 30.09.76 joint register 12.01.79 returned 17.09.80; aircraft in store at Heathrow; for display Heathrow 2004; hours: 22,296
209	F-BVFC N94FC F-BVFC	101	Air France Braniff Air France	9.07.76	delivered 3.08.76 joint register 12.01.79 returned 1.06.80 returned to service 10.01 retired to Airbus factory for display hours: 14,332
210	G-BOAD G-BOAD G-N94AD G-BOAD	102	BAC BA Braniff BA	25.08.76	registered 9.05.75 delivered 6.12.76 joint register 5.01.79 returned 19.06.80; returned to service 28.09.01; preserved New York 10.11.03; hours: 23,394
211	F-BVFD N94FD F-BVFD	101	Air France Braniff Air France	10.02.77	delivered 26.03.77 joint register 12.01.79 returned 1.06.80 damaged in heavy landing 27.05.82 reduced to spares 18.12.94 hours: 5,821
212	G-BOAE G-BOAE G-N94AE G-BOAE	102	BAC BA Braniff BA	17.03.77	registered 9.05.75 delivered 20.7.77 joint register 5.01.79 returned 1.07.80; returned to service 28.09.01; preserved Bahamas 17.11.03; hours: 23,372
213	F-WJAM F-BTSD N94SD F-BTSD	101	Aérospatiale Air France Braniff Air France	26.06.78	registered 06.78 reregistered 4.09.78 joint register 12.01.79 returned 12.03.79 returned to service 15.10.01; hours: 12,974
214	G-BKFW G-BOAG	102	BAE Systems BA	21.04.78	registered 2.01.78 delivered 6.02.80 reregistered 9.02.81 returned to service 19.10.01; preserved Seattle 5.12.03; hours: 16,232
215	F-WJAN F-BVFF	101	Aérospatiale Air France	26.12.78	registered 12.78 reregistered 23.10.80 not modified hours: 12,420
216	G-BFKX G-BOAF N94AF G-BOAF	102	BAE Systems BA Braniff BA	20.04.78	registered 27.01.78 delivered 9.06.79 joint register 14.12.79 returned 12.06.80 returned to service 17.07.01; preserved Filton 26.11.03; hours: 18,255

Tu-144 Fleet

Registration	Model	First Flight	Status
68001	Tu-144	31.12.68	prototype aircraft scrapped
68002	Tu-144	–	static test airframe
77101	Tu-144S	1.06.71	preproduction aircraft scrapped
77102	Tu-144S	20.03.72	first production aircraft; crashed 6.06.73 Paris Air Show
77103	Tu-144S	13.12.73	history unknown
77104	Tu-144S	14.06.74	history unknown
77105	Tu-144S	30.11.74	modified to Tu-144D development aircraft; last noted in scrapyard near Zhukovsky Airport 1993
77106	Tu-144S	4.03.75	Aeroflot, used for cargo flights; currently on display Monino Museum
77107	Tu-144S	20.08.75	on display at Kazan Aviation Production complex
77108	Tu-144S	12.12.75	in store at Samara-Ouchebny Research Institute
77109	Tu-144S	29.04.76	Aeroflot used for passenger flights, remains stored at Voronezh Aircraft factory
–	Tu-144S	–	static test airframe
77110	Tu-144S	14.02.77	Aeroflot used for passenger flights; on display at Museum of Civil Aviation, Ulyanovsk
77111	Tu-144D	27.04.78	crashed 23.05.78; remains scrapped
77112	Tu-144D		was on display at Tupolev OKB, Zhukovsky, sold to Sinsheim Museum, Germany
77113	Tu-144D	–	was on display at Tupolev OKB; aircraft now dismantled and stored
77114	Tu-144D	–	converted to Tu-144LL for NASA use, then to store at Tupolev OKB; reported for sale 05.01
77115	Tu-144D	–	on display at Tupolev OKB, Zhukovsky
77116	Tu-144D	–	in store in uncompleted state; construction ceased 1984

Bibliography

Blackall, T.E., *Concorde: The Story, The Facts, The Figures* (Foulis, 1969)

Calvert, Brian, *Flying Concorde* (Airlife, 2002)

Endres, Günter, *Aerospatiale/British Aerospace Concorde* (Crowood/Airlife, 2001)

Knight, G., *Concorde: The Inside Story* (Weidenfeld & Nicolson, 1976)

Owen, G., *Concorde and the Americans: International Politics of the Supersonic Transport* (Smithsonian Institute Press, 1997)

Trubshaw, Brian, *Concorde – The Inside Story* (Sutton Publications, 2000)

Concorde also features in numerous magazines; additionally there is a wealth of material publicly available at the Public Record Office, Kew for those who like the political in-fighting associated with such projects.

Finally, I recommend www.concordesst.com for the latest news about the aircraft.

Index